ÉMIGRÉ NEW YORK

ÉMIGRÉ NEW YORK

French Intellectuals in Wartime Manhattan, 1940–1944

Jeffrey Mehlman

The Johns Hopkins University Press
BALTIMORE AND LONDON

1002706400

© 2000 The Johns Hopkins University Press
All rights reserved. Published 2000
Printed in the United States of America on acid-free paper
9 8 7 6 5 4 3 2 1

The Johns Hopkins University Press
2715 North Charles Street
Baltimore, Maryland 21218-4363
www.press.jhu.edu

A catalog record for this book is available from the British Library.

Library of Congress Cataloging-in-Publication Data
Mehlman, Jeffrey.
    Émigré, New York : French intellectuals in wartime Manhattan,
1940–1944 / Jeffrey Mehlman.
        p.   cm.
    Includes bibliographical references and index.
    ISBN 0-8018-6286-8 (alk. paper)
    1. France—Exiles.   2. Intellectuals—Homes and haunts—New
York (State)—New York.   3. Intellectuals—France—History—20th
century.   4. World War, 1939–1945—Refugees.   5. New York
(N.Y.)—Intellectual life—20th century.   I. Title.
DC33.7 .M44 2000
940.53′089′4107471 21—dc21   99-044901

T

Frontispiece: Hours before capsizing, the Normandie burns in its
midtown berth on the Hudson River (February 9, 1942). From
Frank Bayard, A Picture History of the Normandie. New York:
Dover, 1987.

For Alicia, *émigrée*

CONTENTS

ÉMIGRÉ NEW YORK

Introduction

One is impressed, first of all, by the oddly juxtaposed eminence of those in attendance. Wartime New York was the city where French Symbolism, in the person of Maurice Maeterlinck, came to live out its last productive years; where French surrealism, in the person of André Breton, came to survive; and where French structuralism, in the person of Claude Lévi-Strauss, came to be born.[1] As such, in those brief years the city was curiously traversed by three of the four cultural vanguards bequeathed to the world by France over the last century. And when, during the final months of the war, French existentialism, in the person of Jean-Paul Sartre, came through—just long enough for him to dash off a few vindictive articles and claim he did not have the heart to let the Americans know he might not be the exemplary *résistant* they took him to be—even the fourth vanguard, poised to sweep the West, managed to put in a cameo appearance.[2]

They were émigrés fleeing France's most sadly ambitious exercise in counterrevolution—whence the paradox and inherent fascination of the figure they cut. For the émigré—in flight from the French Revolution—was as hoary (and suspect) a fixture of the French cultural imagination as might be encountered. New York, that is, might occasionally look like Paris-on-the-Hudson, a countermetropolis to

1. Born in Belgium, Maeterlinck had long since settled in France and was intimately associated with a quintessential French masterwork, Claude Debussy's *Pelléas et Mélisande*, based on Maeterlinck's play of 1892.
2. See Jean-Paul Sartre, "La France vue d'Amérique" and "Victoire du gaullisme," *Le Figaro*, January 24–25, 1945. A vigorous response to Sartre was published by Geneviève de Tabouis, a founding editor of *Pour la victoire*, in that weekly, February 3, 1945.

what the *Partisan Review* called Paris-am-Seine.[3] But there are ways in which the more illuminating tag might well be Koblenz-on-the-Hudson, after that center of French emigration in the German Rhineland to which French aristocrats repaired in the last decade of the eighteenth century.[4] Nothing, to paraphrase Georges Sorel, so resembled an antirepublican émigré as a republican émigré.[5]

Note the terms of the comparison. The émigrés of 1940, uncertain about the future, were, after all, the privileged notables of what must have seemed an *ancien régime:* the Third Republic. As *Fortune* magazine put it at the time, "The pilgrims of the seventeenth century came here to make their fortune; the *émigrés* of 1940 have come here to protect theirs."[6] An intellectual needed a sponsor (frequently the Rockefeller Foundation) prepared to pay cash and to make the case for that intellectual that only he (or, more rarely, she) could perform the task for which immigration was being allowed. It was, in brief, an aristocracy of sorts that went to New York during the war. *Emigrés de luxe* was Maurice Dekobra's aptly titled novel of the period we shall be evoking.[7]

Many of the New York French, moreover, especially at the beginning, considered themselves victims of what the émigré philosopher Jacques Maritain, in an open letter to Antoine de Saint-Exupéry, called an odious "revolution": Vichy's "national revolution." For the most part, these aristocrats or notables of talent arrived with no intention of staying. In this, they were quite different from the German intellectuals, mostly Jews, who felt they had nothing to return to. The French, encouraged by Archibald MacLeish to "retain their Frenchness," may, in fact, have been America's first multiculturalists.[8] Henri Torrès,

3. Jean Malaquais, "Paris-am-Seine," translated by Dwight MacDonald, *Partisan Review* (May–June 1943): 220–23. On the image of Paris-on-the-Hudson, see the wartime series "New York est-il français?" by Jacques Surmagne, former director of France Presse, in *Pour la victoire,* May 2, 9, 16, 23, and 30, and June 13, 1942.

4. See Guy Fritsch-Estrangin, *New York entre de Gaulle et Pétain: Les Français aux Etats-Unis de 1940 à 1946* (Paris: La Table Ronde, 1969), 82: "But exactly like their predecessors in Koblenz, the émigrés of 1940 showed that they had learned nothing and forgotten nothing."

5. On the earlier emigration, see above all Fernand Baldensperger, *Le mouvement des idées dans l'émigration française (1789–1815)* (Paris: Plon-Nourrit, 1924).

6. Quoted in Fritsch-Estrangin, *New York entre de Gaulle et Pétain,* 23.

7. Maurice Dekobra, *Emigrés de luxe* (New York: Brentano's, 1941).

8. See Archibald MacLeish, "French Culture in America," *Pour la victoire,* Octo-

comfortably ensconced in the Waldorf-Astoria, said that because of his Portuguese Jewish blood he belonged to the oldest aristocracy in the world and that he would be damned if he would assimilate.[9] Lévi-Strauss reported that the going joke in the French community was that American women did not dress; they disguised themselves. Under the circumstances, it became crucial to retain one's French identity.[10]

The émigré group, in addition, was for the most part eager to draw its host country into a war of liberation, or restoration. In the 1940s as in the 1790s, "bellicism," as the novelist Jules Romains put it, was the *péché mignon,* or characteristic offense, of political exiles.[11] Finally, reference should be made to exile support for the British blockade of France in Koblenz-on-the-Hudson—what some have seen as the counter-Terror of mass starvation. The issue was a thorny one: to send food to occupied France was arguably to fuel the Nazi war effort. But to contribute to the mass starvation or severe malnutrition of France, it was countered, was ultimately to further the demographic ends of Hitler's war. It is a debate I shall have occasion to address later in the volume, but for the moment I adduce it to flesh out the extent to which the new émigrés of 1940 shared the circumstances of their ideological opposites, the original émigrés of the French Revolution. Boris Mirkine-Guétzévitch, a prominent legal scholar and sometime dean at the Ecole Libre's university in exile, might be inspired to found a neo-Jacobin Society for the History of the French Revolution in late 1942.[12] Nonetheless, in the 1940s as in the 1790s, we find "aristocrats," the privileged subjects or citizens of an *ancien régime,* in sudden flight from a catastrophic "revolution," attempting to draw their host country into a campaign of restoration (and even a blockade of France) so they might return to the life of eminence they had left behind in France.

One episode speaks to the imagination so emblematically of the

ber 31, 1942, and "America's Duty to French Culture," *Saturday Review of Literature,* November 14, 1942, 5–6.

9. Fritsch-Estrangin, *New York entre de Gaulle et Pétain,* 133.

10. Claude Lévi-Strauss, "New York post- et préfiguratif," in *Le regard éloigné* (Paris: Plon, 1983), 354.

11. Jules Romains, speech delivered in Mexico City, 1942; quoted in Fritsch-Estrangin, *New York entre de Gaulle et Pétain,* 25.

12. Colin Nettlebeck, *Forever French: Exile in the United States, 1939–1945* (Oxford: Berg, 1991), 102.

4   parallel just sketched that I have elaborated it as the conclusion of this volume. Shortly after Pearl Harbor, the United States seized and "occupied" the *Normandie,* France's "floating cathedral," in New York harbor and set about converting it into a troop carrier to be named the USS *Lafayette.* The disaster that ensued offers as enduring—and as gigantic—an image as the subject has bequeathed to us. That the disaster should have occurred under the sign of Lafayette, hero of the democratic future, cannot but have impressed the émigrés of 1940 and driven home a parallel they had every reason, given the grim results, to want to hold at bay.

There was a second vast irony or paradox shaping—or topologically twisting—the space within which the émigrés pursued their existence in wartime New York. The host country to which they repaired was not only the world's principal hope in the battle against Hitler, but a country far more interested in maintaining relations with the "collaborationist" regime of Marshal Philippe Pétain than in entertaining the political pretensions of the leader of the anti-Hitlerian resistance, Charles de Gaulle. The subject is vast and complex, and is discussed at greater length in the chapter on Alexis Leger (the diplomat and informal advisor to Franklin Roosevelt better known by the name under which he won the Nobel Prize for literature in 1960, Saint-John Perse). Several of the more flamboyant instances of the contradictions to which American policy exposed the anti-Hitlerian French are nonetheless worth recalling at the outset.

On Christmas Day 1941, simultaneous with the Allied disaster at Wake Island, with the Axis advancing on all fronts, the Allies scored a rare (though admittedly minor) success. Commanded by Admiral Emile Muselier, the Free French succeeded in invading and liberating the tiny islands of Saint-Pierre and Miquelon off the Canadian coast.[13] A plebiscite was immediately held and revealed 98 percent support for the Gaullists. The American press was delighted. The *Times* invoked "the best tradition of Alexandre Dumas" and the *Christian Science Monitor* Cyrano de Bergerac.[14] The State Department, on the other hand, eager to maintain relations with Vichy, reacted by denouncing

13. On this entire episode, see Raoul Aglion, "The Day de Gaulle Invaded America," in *Roosevelt and de Gaulle: Allies in Conflict* (New York: Free Press, 1988), 57–71, as well as Fritsch-Estrangin, *New York entre de Gaulle et Pétain,* 56–59.

14. Aglion, *Roosevelt and de Gaulle,* 65.

what Secretary of State Cordell Hull referred to as the "so-called Free French" and invoking a new convention to the Monroe Doctrine, the Havana Act of 1940, as part of its assurance to Vichy's ambassador to Washington, G. Henry-Haye, that it would do what it could to return the islands to the status quo ante.[15]

The reaction of the American press was devastating. References to the statement by the "so-called Secretary of State" and the "so-called State Department" abounded. Walter Lippmann called the incident a "diplomatic Pearl Harbor" (self-inflicted by the United States).[16] I. F. Stone, in the *Nation*, thought Hull's intervention demonstrated a "stupidity" that merited his removal from office.[17] Eventually, in the face of de Gaulle's intransigence and the near unanimity of the American press, an arrangement was hammered out whereby the Free French were allowed to remain. It was a tactical victory for de Gaulle, but one that earned him the enmity of a humiliated Cordell Hull and the State Department.

After Christmas 1941 and Saint-Pierre and Miquelon came Christmas 1942 and the Darlan affair. Following the Allied invasion of North Africa (from which de Gaulle was pointedly excluded), the United States was desperate to find someone to head the French fleet in Algeria. Eisenhower turned to Admiral François Darlan, heir apparent to Pétain at Vichy, who was given control of the French navy, which he continued to command, in the name of Pétain, under the supervision of the United States. Darlan had been a key player in persuading the French not to resist the invading Americans.[18] Eisenhower claimed in his memoirs that Darlan and Darlan alone was able to pull off that feat.[19] Nonetheless, he had been a principal French interlocutor with Hitler only months earlier.[20] The appointment of Darlan was the first

15. For Cordell Hull's justification of American policy toward Vichy, see Hull, *Memoirs* (New York: Macmillan, 1948), 2:1192–93. Principal points included the "steady flow of information from France" it permitted, Churchill's tacit support, and the logistical aid it ensured during the preparation of the Allied invasion of North Africa.

16. Aglion, *Roosevelt and de Gaulle*, 66.

17. I. F. Stone, "Aid and Comfort to the Enemy," *Nation*, January 3, 1942, 6.

18. See G. Henry-Haye, *La grande éclipse franco-américaine* (Paris: Plon, 1972), 155: "With Darlan, France and America rediscovered each other."

19. Dwight Eisenhower, *Crusade in Europe* (Garden City, N.Y.: Doubleday, 1948), 109–10.

20. According to Marc Ferro, *Pétain* (Paris: Fayard, 1987), 313, Darlan, following

6 major United States decision regarding areas of France under its control, and it stunned the world. Varian Fry, the legendary hero of the evacuation of intellectuals from wartime Marseille, was not alone in voicing dismay at the sight of Darlan, "who was undoubtedly the second most hated man in France (Laval being the first), climbing on the American bandwagon, followed by the whole lot of Vichy officials who only a few days before had been directing the resistance to American occupation."[21]

Roosevelt defended the Darlan agreement with what he called the famous "Bulgarian or Serbian or Romanian . . . or Orthodox Church proverb" according to which it was "permissible in times of grave danger to accompany the devil to the far side of the bridge." He was also heard to say that "a saint, in order to safely ford a stream, can perch on the devil's shoulders." The Vichy regime was nonplussed by Darlan's decision to work for Roosevelt, and one Vichy wag was quoted to the effect that these were "sad times indeed when one could not even trust one's own traitors any more."[22]

The "undecidability" of Darlan—prized interlocutor with Hitler, and key Eisenhower appointee—sets the mind reeling. As though that very self-division were too much to be entertained, history itself drew the conundrum to a close with a bullet on Christmas Eve 1942. Darlan was assassinated by a young royalist, who was himself executed before the full story of the assassination could be investigated.[23] The case of the "turncoat" Darlan nonetheless remains particularly haunting. It offers a point of articulation not only between "collaborationist" and anti-Hitlerian France, but between "collaborationist" France and the United States. The French had a term for the particular mode of duplicity that was the medium within which reversals such as Darlan's took place: *double jeu.* In some respects, wartime France had become a

his meeting with Hitler at Berchtesgaden on May 11, 1941, had shown himself to be "more collaborationist than Laval."

21. Varian Fry, "Giraud and the Future of France," *New Republic,* January 11, 1943, 44.

22. Aglion, *Roosevelt and de Gaulle,* 146.

23. Darlan's son Alain, who suffered from polio, and the admiral's widow spent time in 1943 at the spa at Warm Springs, Georgia, where they stayed as the personal guests of President Roosevelt. See Fritsch-Estrangin, *New York entre de Gaulle et Pétain,* 87.

nationwide school of just such duplicity. Whence, for instance, Claude Roy, in his postwar memoir *Moi je:*

Decipherers of ruses were in the majority, Frenchmen wily by birth, "not born yesterday," refusing to take at face value the words of any speech, or for genuine marble the catastrophic boulder of the occupation. . . . A vast *double jeu* wove its web over the planet in the minds of many: Roosevelt was feigning; he was in cahoots with Churchill, who was in cahoots with de Gaulle, who was in cahoots with Pétain, who knew that Stalin was taking in Hitler, who knew that Mussolini was secretly throwing banana peels in his way. Thirty million Talleyrands, Richelieus, chess players taking themselves for diplomats of genius offered café-table assessments of offstage complicities in the wings of history.[24]

In a world whose texture seemed woven of strategic duplicity, the short-lived Darlan episode is perhaps the extreme case. It figures the Pétainist posture according to which the nation's honor would be vindicated by the supreme hypocrisy of a double betrayal: pretending to collaborate with Hitler in order better—in the putative long run—to defeat him.

It was against the backdrop of just such generalized duplicity that the New York émigré weekly *Pour la victoire* ran a political cartoon on January 20, 1945. A two-headed, four-legged Pétain, ensconced on a couch in front of a two-necked bottle of *vin rouge*, offers Pierre Laval an explanation for French policy during the war: "Mais si je jouais double jeu quand je faisais croire que je jouais double jeu!" [And what if I was being duplicitous when I led them to believe I was being duplicitous!]. Amid a generalized duplication or cancellation of identity, it is suggested that if things are indeed what they are, it is only because of a twofold betrayal affecting reality at its core. In claiming that he was in fact lying when he claimed to be lying, lying, that is, *about* the lie he claimed to be telling, the Pétain of the cartoon posits a principle of identity or truth: he did indeed mean what he said. But by then the double betrayal had succeeded in unsettling the texture of reality itself.

As such, the cartoon deserves to figure as part of a select anthology of literary-theoretical exempla: Freud's classic joke about Jew I berat-

24. Claude Roy, *Moi je* (Paris: Gallimard, 1969), 349–50.

FIG. 1. From *Pour la victoire*, January 20, 1945. Pétain "explains everything" to Laval: "And what if I was being duplicitous when I led them to believe I was being duplicitous!"

ing his colleague for claiming he (Jew II) was taking a train to Cracow so that he (Jew I) would believe he was going to Lemberg, whereas he (Jew I) happened to know that Jew II *was* in fact going to Cracow. Or Walter Benjamin's tale of the bootleggers who had the nerve to fill flasks ostentatiously labeled "Iced Tea" with . . . iced tea.[25] In each case a thing is identical to itself only because the betrayal or deception at its core has been undone by a second case of betrayal. And in the instance of the Pétain cartoon in New York, the entire phantasmagoria harks back to the quintessential case of *double jeu* or undecidability: the truncated Darlan episode, linking the fates of United States and Pétainist policy in 1942 Algeria.

It is a configuration worthy of the headiest excesses of deconstruction. And when one considers that Jacques Derrida—for whom every text seems busy betraying itself—spent his formative years in wartime Algeria, the link seems all the more intriguing. To say as much,

25. See Jeffrey Mehlman, *Walter Benjamin for Children: An Essay on His Radio Years* (Chicago: University of Chicago Press, 1993), 7–11.

though, is less to pose a genealogy (which would in any event be quite speculative) than to confess that my interest in émigré New York is part and parcel of my efforts as a literary critic over the last quarter century. *Émigré New York* is less a survey than a personal essay. One reason I have not written a survey of the period is that an excellent one already exists. Anyone interested in an informative panorama of the French colony in wartime America—its newspapers and journals, leading personalities and institutions—would do well to consult Colin Nettlebeck's *Forever French,* a book I have profited from in these pages.[26] The present volume is rather a record of my thoughts about the individuals and circumstances I have found most intriguing. As such, it is, to an extent, a speculative memoir. I was born to non-French-speaking American parents in wartime New York. Researching the book, I regularly came across personalities and sites I recalled with some nostalgia. As a New Yorker growing up right after the war and swept away by the charms and promises of French culture, I am, I suppose, very much the child of my subject. My first book, *A Structural Study of Autobiography,* ended, more or less as this one does, with a (very different) chapter on Lévi-Strauss.[27] Although it was well received, and regarded in some quarters as a pioneering initiation of American academia into structuralism, the most intriguing response, in retrospect, was surely Lionel Abel's in *Encounter.* Abel, who had been a close associate of Breton's in wartime New York, wrote against four "structuralist" critics, as the journal called them—Harold Bloom, Paul de Man, Jonathan Culler, and me—whose apparent prominence at the time he chose to contest. In my case, the observation I never quite forgot related to what the critic took to be my contentious tone. "I see in him a version of the early André Breton, who would pick a fight with you, as Giacometti once told me, if you intimated you could bear to look at a Chardin."[28]

26. See as well Fritsch-Estrangin, *New York entre de Gaulle et Pétain;* Aglion, *Roosevelt and de Gaulle;* and Henry-Haye, *La grande éclipse franco-américaine.* From differing perspectives, all these volumes focus centrally on the French in wartime America. In addition, an important colloquium, "The French in New York during World War II," was held at Columbia University in April 1992. My thanks to Antoine Compagnon for providing me with tapes of the proceedings of that gathering.

27. Jeffrey Mehlman, *A Structural Study of Autobiography: Proust, Leiris, Sartre, Lévi-Strauss* (Ithaca: Cornell University Press, 1974).

28. Lionel Abel, "It Isn't True and It Doesn't Rhyme: Our New Criticism," *Encoun-*

10   At the time the curious mix of Lévi-Strauss, whose champion I took myself to be, and the surrealist Breton seemed so wide of the mark as not to retain my attention. But in the course of writing the present work I came to realize that not only were the two together in the New York of my birth, but they could be heard "in dialogue" on the airwaves of the Voice of America broadcast from downtown New York.[29] Who knows, I was tempted to think, what inadvertent flick of the radio dial, what fluke of radio transmission, during what prenatal stage of my existence may have issued in the Breton-like champion of Lévi-Straussian structuralism lamented more than thirty years later in the pages of *Encounter*? It was no doubt in response to just such fanciful queries that the present volume was written.[30]

---

ter (July 1978): 57; on Abel's dealings with the surrealists during the war, see his *Intellectual Follies* (New York: Norton, 1984), 88–115.

29. Claude Lévi-Strauss and Didier Eribon, *De près et de loin* (Paris: Odile Jacob, 1990), 50.

30. A Lévi-Straussian childhood? In 1943, in the *Gazette des Beaux Arts*, the anthropologist mused: "There is in New York a magical place where childhood dreams have contrived to convene" (175). Thus begins a stunningly Baudelairean evocation of the vast hall of the American Museum of Natural History devoted to the Indian tribes of the Pacific Northwest. Walter Benjamin's dream (in "Zentralpark") of meditating Baudelaire's mix of the urban, the exotic, and the tantalizingly outmoded while strolling in Central Park was not crushed, it would appear, but displaced—across the street. See Claude Lévi-Strauss, *La voie des masques* (Paris: Plon, 1979), 9, for the original French, which I have translated, and Walter Benjamin, "Zentralpark," in *Gesammelte Schriften,* edited by Rolf Tiedemann and Hermann Schweppenhäuser (Frankfurt: Suhrkamp, 1980), 1:655–90.

ONE

Dress Rehearsal

They were the oddest of political couples, Pétain and Laval: deeply distrustful of each other, each plotting to rid himself of the other, but condemned by circumstance to spend the darkest years of French history, the Nazi occupation, in barely interrupted tandem. On the fall day in question, they approached the city separately. Laval, fresh from an apparently successful trip to Berlin, proud of the expanded grounds for "collaboration" he had hammered out with his German hosts, arrived on October 22. Two weeks in advance, the local newspaper of record had reported that the reception planned for him would "equal anything the city had seen in diplomatic, military, and civic formality."[1] Pétain, the hero of Verdun, would arrive two days later.

The last day of Laval's journey had been beset by storms, so he was no doubt relieved to arrive. As the *Ile de France* approached the harbor, the skyline came into view. Josette Laval, the premier's nineteen-year-old daughter, dressed in a shade of blue called lapis, her costume "at least six months ahead of New York," agreed with her father that it was *formidable*. The *Ile de France* was left in quarantine, and Laval and his party were taken to the Battery aboard the city tug *Macom*. A fleet of army, navy, and police airplanes escorted the *Macom* up the bay. As the tugboat passed Governors Island, the French premier received a nineteen-gun salute from the army post at Fort Jay.

The poet Paul Claudel, ambassador to the United States, was there

1. *New York Times*, October 10, 1931. All elements and quotations reported below regarding this "dress rehearsal" have been culled from the *New York Times* for October and November 1931, unless otherwise noted.

to receive him, as was a special welcoming committee formed by Mayor Jimmy Walker and headed by Albert H. Wiggin, chairman of the governing board of the Chase Manhattan Bank. Secretary of State Henry Stimson joined the party.

Laval arrived in the early morning, which was the reason given for the absence of ticker tape on the parade up Broadway to City Hall. At one point a single roll of ticker tape, dropped from a window, fell threateningly close to the premier's car. Secret Service members descended on the "missile," but were quickly reassured. The arrival was nonetheless singularly auspicious. Stéphane Lauzanne, editor in chief of *Le Matin,* wrote in the *Times* on October 23 that Laval's arrival was striking above all because the itinerary followed by the premier, "penetrating into a gulf banked by two terrific walls of iron and stone," was exactly that followed by Marshal Ferdinand Foch ten years earlier in celebration of the visit of the triumphant French generalissimo of World War I.

Foch's old colleague and rival, Marshal Pétain, meanwhile, was gradually making his way north to New York from Yorktown, Virginia, where he had gone aboard the cruiser *Duquesne,* accompanied by General Adalbert de Chambrun, a descendant of Lafayette, to represent France officially at the sesquicentennial celebration of the Battle of Yorktown, the "little battle big with fate," as the *Times* put it on October 16, that had marked the birth of the nation. General John Pershing, joined by General Douglas MacArthur, showed up at the Hotel Chamberlin pier in Old Point Comfort to meet his comrade in arms as he stepped ashore. Pétain would eventually be given the ticker-tape parade up Broadway that Laval had missed. Like Laval, he would receive New York City's gold medal at City Hall. He would dedicate two plaques to French soldiers of the Great War who had left from New York, one plaque at Pier 57 and the other on Riverside Drive adjacent to the statue of Joan of Arc.

Honors abounded in America for the hero of Verdun, yet he seemed strangely ill at ease during his American trip. On October 22, the day of Laval's triumphant procession up Broadway, Pétain, already in Washington, was to receive an honorary doctorate from St. John's College in Annapolis. He sent word he would not be able to make the trip, dispatched Rear Admiral Descottes-Genon to receive the honor in his stead, then, "apparently changing his mind," according to the next day's *Times*, arrived amid a blast of sirens, interrupting the ceremony so he might receive the doctorate in person. He sped off back to Washington in his car within fifteen minutes of his arrival. Years later, during the war, Pétain would claim to have been following a temporizing policy of *double jeu:* (feigned) collaboration, the subtlest ruse of resistance. For anyone in Annapolis that October 22, the simultaneous entertainment of mutually exclusive alternatives—to go, not to go—would have seemed more a flaw of character than a refinement of policy.

But even before leaving Toulon for America, Pétain had given a bizarre display of ambivalence. On the eve of a journey intended to honor him at every stop, Pétain waxed indignant. At a press conference on October 14, reported in the *Times* the following day, the marshal identified the "duty" that drove him to America: "I want to ask the meaning of the flood of anti-French propaganda coursing virtually unchecked through a considerable part of the American press. What sinister power lurks behind this? Who is responsible for the ungenerous hints that France is a sort of vindictive wild beast wanting to sink its claws into the weaker peoples of Europe?" Pétain, it would appear, was in a state of rage against the country claiming to honor him: "The American people are consciously being incited against France and we feel the thing has gone far enough." It would appear that it was less the legacy of Lafayette than the "monstrous lies" through which American popular opinion—and journalism—dishonored France that he was eager to discuss. Here too one detects an anticipation of the marshal of the war years. A rage impotent in the face of the dishonoring of France by a foreign power seemed constrained to conceal itself and get on with the tawdry business of official pageantry.

Laval, meanwhile, did not miss a beat. He was unruffled when Hector Fuller, the official announcer of distinguished visitors to City Hall, mistakenly introduced him to all assembled as "His Excellency, the Prime Minister of France, M. Paul Claudel." He did not react when Mayor Jimmy Walker, in an encomium on the cosmopolitan tolerance of New York, observed in passing, "There are no discriminations and no distinctions in this city, because the fifty thousand Frenchmen are as welcome and as happy as the million Germans or more." Laval responded graciously to Mayor Walker's words of welcome. The *Times*

14

was grateful that neutral France, in Laval's opening sentence, had at last adjudicated the dispute between London and New York as to which was the largest city in the world—and done so in New York's favor. Just as Pétain, in Yorktown, was commemorating the defeat of Britain, Laval in New York was consecrating a second British "defeat."

The premier's principal display of public rhetoric occurred in Washington later in his trip, and related to his exchanges at dinner with the cantankerous chairman of the Senate Committee on Foreign Affairs, Senator William Borah of Idaho.[2] The isolationist senator had given a news conference at which, to the embarrassment of many, he held forth cavalierly on the need to revise the Versailles Treaty and reduce German reparations payments. A former secretary of state, Bainbridge Colby, reacted sharply: "It was very blithe—a sort of Borahesque stunt. But it is not to be taken seriously. It did not even reach the plane of flaming indiscretion." A front-page article in the *Times* of October 25 was devoted to French anxiety over the senator's statements. The Germans, on the other hand, were delighted by Borah's comments, which "ripped the mask off France's face," according to a headline in the nationalist newspaper *Reichsbote*. The Poles referred to Borah as a "German agent." And Laval? The *Times* wondered what the French premier would have to say about the "redoubtable Senator from Idaho." The answer was not long in coming: "Earlier in the day it was learned that the Premier had changed his impression of the whole affair. The essentials of the Borah statement were translated to him, and before noon, he let it be known that, far from regarding it as a bitter attack on France (an unfortunate construction placed upon the matter by numerous French newspaper men), it actually registered a complete advance toward the French point of view on two vital points, disarmament and reparations."

While the French press grew anxious and the Germans applauded, that is, Laval attempted to show that the apparent insult to France was only apparently so. Here we may already glimpse the advocate of collaboration at work in America in 1931. Whereas Pétain reacted to apparent insults to France with a silent rage betrayed only by the

---

2. Laval's interpreter in his exchanges with Borah was G. Henry-Haye. See Henry-Haye, *La grande éclipse franco-américaine*, 58.

awkwardness of his performance (disrupting with his untimely arrival the ceremony awarding him an honorary doctorate), Laval, ever the conciliator, attempted to demonstrate that things were the opposite of what they appeared to be (the insult to France was in fact a rallying to France's best interests).

It was as a conciliator, a man who invariably managed to "find a way to comprehend and compromise," that Laval was presented in utterly winning terms to the American people. "He is sparing with gestures and he does not relish flowery oratory," the *Times* reported on October 23. "His virtues are those which have made France strong and prosperous—the power of practical application, devotion to duty, an unsparing realism." He seemed more amiable than the distant, somewhat marmoreal Pétain. The "dark gleaming eyes," "black drooping mustache," and "sober expression" of this man of "strong peasant stock" were frequently tempered by "playful outbreaks of humor." Not only did he confess a weakness for American cigarettes, but "a typically Rooseveltian grin" was perceived as "one of his pleasing mannerisms."

On that October 22, it was Claudel, the poet-ambassador, who intuited that the joint presence of Pétain and Laval, two eminent Frenchmen whose first meeting was slated for a state dinner in Washington that night, might be rife with historical significance. In the aldermanic chamber of New York's City Hall, Claudel, introducing Laval to Mayor Walker, was eloquent:

Yesterday we witnessed again the magnificent pageant in honor of the delegates and the descendants of Rochambeau, de Lafayette, de Grasse, that France has sent to these shores, and a reminiscence was evoked by me of the days when our two countries were united in a common accord on the way to victory and on the way to democratic liberty. Today, at a no less solemn hour for the future of the civilization of the world, France and America again and together realize that a new moment has arrived for them to face earnestly their responsibilities, and to study the possibilities of an entente that is very necessary on account of their many common interests, and consecrated by all the glory of their sacrifices.

Yorktown and New York, Pétain and Laval: the historic link was forged in the poet's peroration. But rarely has poetry gotten things so precisely wrong. The notion that the Pétain-Laval nexus might become a key link in the historic chain through which the Enlightenment legacy of democratic freedom could be sustained through the middle of the twentieth century would receive the cruelest of refutations a mere nine years later.

Pétain and Laval, men of (a shared) destiny, had not yet met. After the ceremony at City Hall, the premier was escorted to Pennsylvania Station, where he boarded the business car of George Le Bouteillier, vice president of the Pennsylvania Railroad, which left for Washington at eleven o'clock. Of the state dinner at the White House that night, Richard Oulahan reported on the front page of the *Times* the next day that it was "in honor of the foreign emissaries to the Yorktown sesquicentennial celebration." On an inner page, the "stag" event was characterized as "one of the largest State dinners given at the White House in recent years," but something of a corrective to Oulahan's article was offered: "Eighty-five men were present at what originally was designed as a tribute to the French and German delegations at the Yorktown Sesquicentennial celebration but finally was turned into the nation's high honor to Premier Laval." Laval, that is, had at the last moment eclipsed Pétain. At the horseshoe table, which was decorated with pink roses, pink snapdragons, pink cosmos, and "sprengerie," a table bereft of "the gay conversation of women," pride of place was accorded to Laval, who sat to the right of President Herbert Hoover. Pétain was seated somewhat down the line, to the left of Vice President Charles Curtis. It was on that evening—one of relative humiliation for the already brooding Pétain—that the two men met for the first time.

From Washington, the marshal left for New York, where he was received with military honors at Pennsylvania Station by General Pershing on October 24. He stayed as Pershing's guest at the Waldorf-Astoria while Laval conferred with Hoover in Washington. At a ceremonial dinner at the Waldorf that night, Pétain would brood about the "evil-minded propaganda" threatening Franco-American friendship in words translated by General Count de Chambrun, a lineal descendant of Lafayette and brother-in-law of the late Nicholas Longworth. René de Chambrun, a relative of Pétain's Yorktown aide, would eventually marry Josette Laval, who had just been obliged to turn down the invitation of Reine Claudel, Paul Claudel's daughter, to the Princeton-Navy football game and join the Hoovers and her father instead in the making of a "talking movie" on the steps of the White House. But as a relative of Nicholas Longworth, Chambrun, and thus

Laval, would also be related by marriage to Franklin Roosevelt, then governor of New York, who responded to a toast to the State of New York at the Waldorf that night with an informal excursus on the French discoverers of Lakes Champlain and George. Pétain's ticker-tape parade and the honors at City Hall were reserved for October 26. The night before, Laval was back in New York; he dined with the marshal and his party at the Waldorf. A final reception for Laval was slated to be held on October 26 aboard the *Duquesne* by Pétain, just hours before the premier's return home on the *Ile de France*. (Unpredictable to the end, Pétain, whose departure from Newport was reported in the *Times* on October 29, would secretly make his way back to New York, and leave for France aboard the *Lafayette* on November 5.)

Journalists and, later, historians would debate the concrete results of this first official American journey of a French prime minister. The trip no doubt played a role in *Time* magazine's choice of Laval as its "Man of the Year" for 1931. Yet in a world reeling from the Great Depression, there would be no easy resolution of currency, reparations, or war debt issues. "Concrete result of the White House negotiation," *Time* reported on January 4, 1932, "was almost nil." In retrospect one is inclined to view the principal achievement of the trip in terms of the pregnancy of this first crisscrossing of paths on American soil of the two protagonists of collaborationist France.

Their next joint diplomatic mission took place nine years later to the day, and would live in infamy. On October 22, 1940, Laval met secretly with Hitler in Montoire to work out the details of his imminent meeting with Pétain. Two days later Pétain would be bundled up personally by Laval and trundled off to Montoire for his own encounter with the *Führer*. Laval, in his shrewdness, had sensed an opportunity to turn things around. Pétain, quietly enraged, would never forgive Laval this humiliation: to be virtually "abducted" from Vichy like a girl from her convent.[3] The marshal would wrest a revenge of sorts on December 13 by placing his minister and heir apparent under house arrest.

But the unexpected reversal on Laval's part was already there in his

3. Henri Amouroux, *Les beaux jours des collabos* (Paris: Laffont, 1978), 70.

18 surprise reaction to Chairman Borah, the alleged "German agent" in the Senate, in Washington in 1931. And the mute rage was already there in Pétain's press conference about "monstrous lies" just prior to his departure for Yorktown. Even the fear of usurpation was present in the changed seating plan for the memorable White House dinner of October 22, 1931.

On October 24, 1940, arriving once again two days after Laval, Pétain, plainly disoriented, made his way into the station at Montoire. Hitler came to greet him and murmured words in German Pétain did not understand. The Frenchman parried what he assumed to be words of politesse with a gesture of acknowledgment.[4] There was a hand-shake and a barrage of photographs: in the eyes and imagination of the world, French collaboration with the Nazis had begun.

4. Concerning Montoire, see Christian Delage and Vincent Guigeno, "Montoire, une mémoire en représentations," communication to the Rutgers Colloquium on French Film during the Occupation, fall 1997.

The *New Yorker* Pétain and the 1870 Paradigm

It was a difficult task to convey to an American readership during the years of the Second World War something of the sheer charisma of Marshal Pétain, who had assumed power in France, giving "his person" to the nation, after the defeat of June 1940, in his eighty-fourth year. How indeed might one conjure up the power of the "almost excessively handsome face,"[1] in René Gillouin's phrase, of the hero of Verdun? Years after the war, Emmanuel Berl, the marshal's spokesman in the first months of the new regime—and a Jew—admitted that the sheer prestige of the man was such in 1940 that, despite hindsight, Berl was not sure he would have been able to turn down that assignment from the marshal if it were offered to him again. Plainly, a mere photograph could not transmit charisma of this magnitude. Janet Flanner's solution, in the *New Yorker,* was to appeal to the temporal majesty of the marshal's unique circumstance: he was, she told her readers, the "only Frenchman who ever survived a hundred and seven French governments, and then founded one of his own, the hundred and eighth."[2] To speak of Pétain was somehow to invoke French history at its most incommensurate.

Yet Flanner, the *New Yorker*'s legendary commentator on matters French—under the pen name Genêt—believed she had found a prece-

---

1. René Gillouin, *J'étais l'ami du maréchal Pétain* (Paris: Plon, 1966), 69.
2. Janet Flanner, *Pétain: The Old Man of France* (New York: Simon and Schuster, 1944), 1.

dent for Pétain. Her articles in the magazine allude teasingly to Ulysses S. Grant, another distinguished military officer who turned out to be less than successful as head of state; it was not the United States president, however, but his contemporary, Marshal Achille Bazaine, whose career Pétain's seemed to repeat. Bazaine was the French marshal who surrendered his starving troops, 179,000 in number, under siege in the fortress of Metz, to the victorious Prussians in the fall of 1870. Here is Flanner on the disastrous final years of the career of the soldier who had been viceroy of Mexico during that country's curious "Second Empire" and was widely referred to as "notre glorieux Bazaine": the marshal "was so scandalized on hearing, toward the end of the war in 1870, that, upon the fall of the Empire, a French republic had been founded, that he refused to proclaim it to his troops, whom he whisked out of battle and into walled safety in the fortress of Metz, where he set up a little dictatorship aimed at saving France from herself and restoring post-war order, with the help of the perennial order-loving, salvationist Germany" (8). Thus runs Flanner's principal historical conceit in the articles she would eventually publish as a volume in 1944 under the title *Pétain: The Old Man of France*.

Pétain and Bazaine would be grandly symmetrical figures flanking the history of the Third Republic. As defeat at the hands of the Germans ushered in the republic, so a comparable defeat would usher it out. Metz, the fortress surrendered without resistance, would be Bazaine's anticipation of Vichy: a petty autocracy bent on achieving the salvation of France in spite of itself under German tutelage. Small wonder, then, that in June 1940, according to Flanner, patriotic French democrats had taken to calling Pétain "Bazaine the Second." Indeed, when we are informed that after the war, Bazaine was tried for treason as a defeatist and anti-Republican and sentenced to life imprisonment, Flanner's article of 1944, considerably before the Pétain trial, seems positively prescient.

Not the least remarkable aspect of the conceit, so devastating in its apparent precision and prescience, is that it has not survived. One would, for instance, search in vain for the name Bazaine in the index of Marc Ferro's exhaustive study *Pétain*. Might it be that the mix of precision and prescience was merely apparent? The question is further complicated by the circumstance that a book quoted in passing by Flanner, which was published in New York in 1943, before Flanner's

New Yorker series even appeared—Philip Guedalla's historical study *The Two Marshals*—already had begun providing an answer. Guedalla's intriguing contention was that Bazaine and Pétain were in curious ways historical opposites. Amid catastrophic defeat by the Germans and grave suspicions of premature capitulation, he contended, there nevertheless appeared to be a crucial difference: whereas Bazaine was made a scapegoat for the 1870 defeat, Pétain, in the ascendant, conspired to make France itself the scapegoat in 1940.[3]

To refer to Bazaine as a scapegoat, to be sure, is to affirm some measure of exoneration.[4] And Guedalla does indeed attempt a partial rehabilitation of the first of his two marshals. The principal mitigating factors are the imminent starvation of the soldiers garrisoned at Metz, the hopelessness of France's military situation once Sedan, under Marshal Marie MacMahon's command, had fallen, and the "mounting mood of hysteria" sweeping the demoralized troops once news of the fall of the empire had been proclaimed. Metz, that is, was anything but the proto-Vichy spa town that the *New Yorker* articles, eliminating all reference to starvation, had evoked. Bazaine had been chosen late in the day to head the last army of the empire with a specific thought to his eventual usefulness as a scapegoat, a role he could be made to play only if one failed to take into account, as Guedalla put it, the "cards dealt by Napoleon III to Bazaine" (148, 158).

But the Guedalla argument went further than a mere critique of the scapegoating of Bazaine. Was there not an element of heroism in Bazaine's having held out as long as he did? Guedalla: "The war was lost when Germany defeated the armies of the Empire in August and September 1870. But their defeat was not followed by ignoble surrender, since the war went on. For when the Second Empire was struck down, the Third Republic stepped into the breach and angry Frenchmen, symbolized by a stern-featured young woman in a Phrygian cap, fought in the ruins. Their effort, which was without effect upon the military situation, saved the soul of France; and that could not have happened unless Bazaine had kept the Army of the Rhine in being"

---

3. Philip Guedalla, *The Two Marshals* (New York: Reynal and Hitchcock, 1943), 327.

4. Note, however, the intriguing category of the "guilty scapegoat," floated by Jean Daniel, editor of *Le nouvel observateur,* with considerable pertinence during the Papon trial in 1998.

(172). Bazaine, that is, whose strategic thought had always championed the defensive virtues of firepower, provided the material conditions for the pursuit of the spiritually vital business of resistance. He functioned as something of a shield, enabling defeated France to brandish the sword of whatever resistance it could muster in 1870. Small wonder that Guedalla should take particular pleasure in the subsequent discrediting of virtually all the witnesses for the prosecution at Bazaine's court-martial within a few years of their testimony (207).

If Pétain in 1940 was indeed "Bazaine the Second," as Flanner would have it, the case for exculpation was being successfully clinched with regard to the prototype even before the ink drawing the damning implications of the genealogy in the *New Yorker* could dry. It was as though Bazaine's shield had passed intact into the hands of Pétain, destined to enact its ultimate defense in the trial for treason that, in the case of Pétain, was in a still unforeseeable future. For Guedalla, however, Pétain, as we have seen, was less a repetition of Bazaine than his opposite: there was a crucial difference between serving as scapegoat in the midst of defeat and presiding over the scapegoating of France in the wake of a comparable defeat. Here is Guedalla on the fundamental opposition between his "two marshals": Pétain's "capitulation had already consummated a surrender far beyond the basest imputations of Bazaine's accusers. For Bazaine had been condemned for the surrender of a fortress before its starving garrison had been required to do all that (in the judgment of the court) was demanded by honour and duty. But Pétain's surrender demobilised whole armies in Syria and North Africa before they had been called upon to fire a single shot and disarmed an undefeated navy" (322). Whereby the author, having come close to exonerating Bazaine, rallies in 1942 to a version of the Gaullist position in order to condemn Pétain.

Guedalla's argument, then, is quite different from that of Flanner. His powerful defense of Bazaine, prominently reviewed in the New York press during the war, proposes a *continuity* between the two marshals' careers, as *Time* noted, which is anything but a repetition. Metaphor, as Roman Jakobson used to imply, is the opposite of metonymy. Flanner, however, opts for metaphor: Pétain, in her extended conceit, as "Bazaine the Second." Curiously, to the extent that Guedalla regards Pétain at Vichy as the return of a historical figure, it is of a third marshal, Bazaine's rival and persecutor, MacMahon. Marshal MacMahon was the man more responsible than any other for the French defeat in the Franco-Prussian War, the commander whose strategic blunder at Sedan sealed the fate of Metz. It was MacMahon who suffered the crucial defeat of the war in 1870 and the same Mac-Mahon who rose to the presidency of the Third Republic in a time of national penitence. Whence Guedalla's speculation: "Europe had already seen the Caesarism of defeat in Germany; and as Pétain followed suit, the young hopefuls of French Fascism (most of whom had started life as Communists) waited to play Hitler to his Hindenburg. But he had watched a better precedent in France, when the wounds of 1870 were healed by another Marshal and men sang songs in honour of '*Notre Bayard couvert de gloire, Notre chef, illustre vaincu.*' Was Mac Mahon in his mind, when Pétain came to power?" (325). As a new moral order settled over France in the wake of defeat at the hands of the Germans, the ghost of MacMahon, the marshal who presided over the persecution of Bazaine, was in the ascendant.

The debate in New York, in sum, was to a considerable extent over just how the debacle of 1940 meshed with that of 1870. Was Pétain the return of the dishonorable Bazaine, as one might read in the *New Yorker,* or was he the return of the partially exonerated Bazaine's tormentor, MacMahon, as Guedalla would have it? And how might each argument have contaminated the other? In retrospect, the debate, in its innocence of the genocide then under way in Europe, seems hard to credit. It is difficult enough, after all, for the current generation to entertain efforts to relativize Hitler's atrocities by comparison to those committed by Stalin, but the notion that Hitler's war should find its crucial point of comparison in Bismarck's seventy years earlier seems faintly ludicrous. Yet 1870 was indeed the central precedent for imagining the horrors of World War II among the French and French-minded in New York during the war. It is a model, we shall see, whose interpretive yields as a guide to the imaginative world of émigré New York we have only begun to tap.

For Flanner the "great exception" to the parallel between 1870 and 1940 lay in the extent of French resistance. Instead of fleeing the German advance, Parisians in 1870 hunkered down to endure a five-month siege in which the rich "ate elephants from the zoo and the

24

poor ate rats from the gutter."[5] Blind to the starvation at Metz, Flanner waxes picturesque regarding the circumstances of hunger in the capital. Even as she draws a clear distinction between the worlds of Bazaine and Pétain with regard to resistance, she sketches a possibility that has, in fact (or in myth), provided a principal lineament of one interpretation of the French experience of World War II: "Yet the war had not been finished in 1870, even when the Empire fell. The fight had been carried on into 1871 against Bismarck, shocked at such Gallic frivolity, by the bobtail Gambetta army, backed by the proletariat of Paris, soon to establish the Commune, one of whose vulgar principles was that it should refuse to admit that the Germans had won. It was to prevent anything so *populo* and chaotic as a second Commune that Pétain, sixty-nine years later, advised immediate capitulation to the Nazis." Flanner's tone here is one of amusement, a luxury afforded by the distance separating New York from the fighting, but before long it appears that Pétain, in her eyes, might have been right to fear a second Commune, because the first stands accused of far more than lapses of taste. Lasting a mere ten weeks, styling itself the First Workers' Republic, the Commune is evoked as a "sidewalk revolution" that, having "cost the lives of twenty thousand workers alone, was, day for day, bloodier than the Reign of Terror" (9). Here Flanner remarkably attributes to the Commune the death toll exacted principally by those who crushed it.

Another curious feature of her argument consists in positing that a second revolutionary Commune might have been in the offing in 1940 when the Hitler-Stalin pact was still in force. It is almost as though she were as eager as Pétain to shut down the possibility of a second Commune before it could be examined. Had not Guedalla, in his history of the seventy years from Metz to Vichy, spent no more than a single phrase on the "ten weeks' dementia of the Commune"?[6] Plainly there was something bordering on the unspeakable in the Commune as it was evoked in wartime New York.

But the paradigm of Gambetta followed by the Commune had been launched and would prove effective. Here is Gambetta, minister of the interior in the new Government of National Defense, after the

5. Flanner, *Pétain*, 8.
6. Guedalla, *Two Marshals*, 204.

fall of Metz (as quoted by Guedalla): "Metz has capitulated!!! The
general [Bazaine] on whom France counted, even after the Mexican
expedition, has just deprived the nation in its peril of more than a
hundred thousand defenders. Bazaine has committed treason" (199).
It would be difficult to read those words in wartime New York without
thinking of them as an anticipation of de Gaulle's celebrated call to
resistance of June 18, 1940. Boris Mirkine-Guétzévitch, a leading émigré scholar at the Ecole Libre, would publish Gambetta's words in the
weekly *Pour la victoire* and applaud the Germans for removing his
statue from Paris in 1940, for at least they understood what it meant.
He derided the French who in 1870 told Gambetta that without his
resistance the Prussians would have offered far better terms, and asked
"Where have we heard the same words? Yes, such is the agonizing fate
of France that it befell us to hear those very words in Bordeaux in June
1940."[7] If the 1870 paradigm, in sum, was in force in the wake of the
defeat of 1940 (as Flanner and Guedalla, in different ways, suggested),
it could meaningfully be expanded to de Gaulle's status as a latter-day
Gambetta.

But within weeks after the flamboyant Gambetta resigned from the
National Assembly (rather than agree to Bismarck's terms), the Commune had erupted. Might de Gaulle be a forerunner of a second Paris
Commune? Support for the proposition was supplied to August Heckscher by Alexis Leger (Saint-John Perse) in an interview conducted on
behalf of the Office of Strategic Services. Reporting confidentially on
March 18, 1943, Heckscher summarized the anti-Gaullist Leger's position: "De Gaulle, from the international point of view needing Russian recognition to use against Britain and America, and from the
domestic point of view needing the Communists to give him control
of the underground, had linked himself irretrievably with Russia and
was fundamentally at odds with the Anglo-Saxon countries. Russia,
M. Leger continued, is opposed to collective security and will use
de Gaulle to check any advances in this line."[8] And a year later, in
March 1944, a confidential in-house memorandum to the director of
the Office of Strategic Services entitled "France in the United States"

7. Boris Mirkine-Guétzévitch, "Histoire républicaine: Léon Gambetta," *Pour la victoire*, April 11, 1942.
8. August Heckscher, OSS Interoffice Memo FR-557, "Interview with Alexis Leger," March 18, 1943, 3.

made it clear that it was Leger's view that the rapid increase of Communists in France from eighty-five thousand to fifteen million was largely the result of de Gaulle's efforts.[9] Indeed, according to the memorandum the "de Gaullist and strongly pro-Russian" newspaper *France-Amérique* persisted in citing "American bombings of French cities in unfavorable conjunction with . . . Soviet victories" (7). Thus de Gaulle, widely viewed as a man of the right, as "authoritarian" a partisan of democratic freedom as Mirkine-Guétzévitch took Gambetta to be, was no less than Gambetta a stalking-horse for a left-wing uprising. There was every reason to doubt, as Leger made clear, that de Gaulle would be able to control the passions he was unleashing.

In wartime America, the tripartite configuration of Bazaine–Gambetta–the Commune, in sum, was compellingly superimposable on that of Pétain–de Gaulle–the Communists. It is a circumstance that goes a long way toward explaining the ambivalence with which de Gaulle himself is viewed in Flanner's wartime series in the *New Yorker*.

The leader of "la France combattante" makes his principal appearance, in Flanner's *Pétain*, under the surprising heading of "comic relief." The history of his relations with the hero of Verdun allowed for one of those delectable ironies that the *New Yorker,* safely distant from the fray, could not forgo. De Gaulle, we are not quite reminded, had for years been Pétain's principal protégé, and the record of the extraordinary affection the two had for each other survives in print in the form of a series of "de Gaulle–Pétain eulogies" that the supporters of each man were loath to "touch with a ten-foot pole." In a preface to de Gaulle's first book, the marshal had opined that "the day will come when a grateful France will call upon him." In de Gaulle's second book, *Le fil de l'épée*, the compliment was returned in a preface by the protégé: "This essay, Maréchal Pétain, can be dedicated only to you, as nothing shows better than your own glory the benefits which action derives from enlightened thinking." The series comes to a climax in de Gaulle's 1938 opus, *La France et son armée*, where the future Free French leader goes all out for Pétain. As Flanner noted, de Gaulle, in that volume, wrote: "A chief appeared [in the last year]. . . . Upon the day when we had to choose between ruin and reason, Pétain was

---

9. OSS Interoffice Memo 12FR-756, "France in the United States: French Thought and Activity Here as Affected by Recent Developments," March 9, 1944, 6.

promoted. In him harmony is so complete as to seem a decree of nature."[10]

The *New Yorker*, we now know, got only half the story, and a fraction of the irony. *La France et son armée* had originally been composed by de Gaulle as an assignment from his superior officer Pétain. The marshal, eager for election to the French Academy, had essentially commissioned his deputy, working in the office Pétain had given him, to compose a work of military philosophy in high literary style that might appear under Pétain's own name and secure his entrance. The manuscript, whose first title was *Le soldat*, was a source of tension between the two men from the outset. In a letter to an associate whom Pétain had asked to revise the manuscript, de Gaulle bridled at his protector's inability "to acknowledge the difference between a book and a military staff report." He then wrote to Pétain, "consenting" that Pétain appear as sole author, but insisting, "Monsieur le Maréchal," "that you admit openly, in a preface or foreword, the fact of our collaboration."[11]

When Pétain's election came on June 20, 1929, without such publication, de Gaulle's ghostwritten manuscript was consigned to a desk drawer. Eventually the ghostwriter, not a man to expend his prose to such futile ends, requested permission, in November 1937, to retrieve his manuscript and publish it with Editions Plon under his own name. Permission was denied. In a letter of August 18, 1938, with the Munich crisis approaching, de Gaulle wrote Pétain that at age forty-eight, he no longer had the kind of anonymity that would allow him to ascribe to others whatever talent he might possess as a writer and historian. He would, however, be happy to acknowledge the marshal's role in a preface. In ten years, then, an inversion had been effected. In 1928, de Gaulle insisted that Pétain acknowledge his role in a preface; in 1938, he was willing to acknowledge Pétain's role in a preface.

The quarrel continued. A stormy confrontation occurred in Pétain's apartment on the Square Latour-Maubourg on Sunday, August 28, 1938. The most dramatic retelling of the encounter (by Guillain de Benouville, relying on information from de Gaulle) has Pétain re-

10. Flanner, *Pétain*, 26.

11. My sources for de Gaulle's vexed identification with Pétain are R. Tournoux, *Pétain et de Gaulle* (Paris: Plon, 1964), and H. Guillemin, *Le général clair-obscur* (Paris: Seuil, 1984).

questing the last two chapters of the manuscript for his perusal, de Gaulle refusing, then Pétain ordering him to lay the manuscript on the table. De Gaulle responded: "You have no orders to give me in this domain." Finally, an agreement was reached: de Gaulle would publish a dedication to Pétain, to be written by the marshal himself. When de Gaulle tampered with Pétain's wording of the dedication, all hell broke loose. Pétain, when called to power in 1940, was still—or already—in a rage against de Gaulle, to which he gave vent on June 6, twelve days before the unexpected appeal to resistance of June 18. Such is the *New Yorker* story buried in the *New Yorker* story, the sequence behind the sop to Pétain quoted by Flanner from *La France et son armée,* the eminently literary quarrel subtending the most notorious French political and military enmity of the war.

There were traces, nonetheless, of the mix of identification and acrimony in Flanner's Pétain portrait. The comment, for instance, that *Le fil de l'épée* "oddly enough" contained "a psychological recipe for what a modern dictator must be like," aside from the ambiguity between the normative and the probabilistic senses of *must,* might leave the reader in doubt as to whether it was an understanding of Pétain or a Gaullist political program that was at issue. The notion that de Gaulle had developed a psychological blueprint for a modern dictator had been a theme of journalism in French New York and would culminate in the philosopher Louis Rougier's article "La psychologie de la dictature" in *Pour la victoire* on March 11, 1944. Plato may have given us his Hiero II of Syracuse, Rougier tells us, and Machiavelli his Cesare Borgia. We may be indebted to Benjamin Constant for his remarkable portrait of Napoleon, and to Curzio Malaparte for his versions of Lenin, Mussolini, and Hitler. "But no book has conducted a more acute analysis of the psychology of the dictator than the author, who was quite obscure at the time, of a little book published by Berger-Levrault in 1932, under a rather enigmatic title, *Le fil de l'épée.*"[12]

To associate de Gaulle with dictatorship was not at all incompatible with the 1870 paradigm. In his piece on Gambetta, Mirkine-Guétzévitch quoted Joseph Reinach, according to whom, for all Gambetta's com-

---

12. Louis Rougier, "La psychologie de la dictature," reprinted in *La défaite des vainqueurs* (Brussels: La Diffusion du Livre, 1947), 93.

mitment to freedom, the tribune of 1870 wanted "an extremely strong authority." And if Gambetta brought the dreaded Commune in his wake, and de Gaulle (pace Leger) might well bring the Communists, a totalitarian de Gaulle in no way clashed with the imaginative possibilities abroad in wartime New York. But de Gaulle, it would appear, might also be a man of the right, a Pétain with none of the Teutonic baggage that had become the crushing burden of the rapidly aging marshal. Thus Flanner: "It was during the first summer of France's defeat that there sprang up throughout both the Unoccupied and Occupied Zones the widespread, worshipful cult of the Marshal which was known as *la mystique autour de Pétain*. It was slightly offset by the rarer but more martial emotion in France for General de Gaulle."[13] True, Flanner does not conceal that de Gaulle was condemned to death by Vichy as a traitor, but the suggestion that Pétain and de Gaulle were beneficiaries of twin mystiques brings us back to the identification behind the "de Gaulle–Pétain eulogies." Indeed, to posit that de Gaulle's was "the more martial" variant toys with the shield/sword conceit that would be trumpeted by Pétain at war's end, and whose prototype one observes in Guedalla's defense of Bazaine.

De Gaulle—Mirkine-Guétzévitch's latter-day Gambetta, Leger's stalking-horse for the Communists, Flanner's alter ego to Pétain—remained something of a cipher in wartime New York. In retrospect, one of Flanner's more suggestive remarks concerns his legendarily prescient support for a mechanized army. General Maxime Weygand, we are told, had concluded, not unreasonably, that an army of mechanics might well be "a regular hotbed of Communism" (34). Pétain, whose admirers said, after his observational trip to France's eastern border in 1929, that the Maginot line should more properly be called the Pétain line, ultimately came down on the same side of the issue as Weygand. So we return to de Gaulle–Gambetta, forerunner of leftist mayhem, sowing the seeds of insubordination in the army.

That observation brings us to World War I, an extended episode whose absence from the discussion until now is all the more surprising in that the precedent that brought Pétain to power in the first place in 1940 was presumably his historic victory in that war. For in 1940 it appeared to Flanner that the great victory of Pétain's career was not

<hr>

13. Flanner, *Pétain*, 41.

Verdun but his restoration of morale in the face of widespread troop mutinies in 1917. For Guedalla, Pétain's handling of the mutinies—in which, according to Flanner, "over twenty thousand soldiers deserted and by which more than half of the French army was contaminated" (21)—was one of the great remaining secrets of modern history.[14] The immediate precipitating events were "cocky" General Robert Nivelle's devastating April offensive at Chemin des Dames (in which there were 120,000 new French casualties) and the Bolshevik Revolution in March. The most astonishing image of the episode is that of French soldiers bursting out, with apparent spontaneity, in a loud "open chorus" of *baaaa-baaaa,* like so many sheep being led off to slaughter. It was amid these symptoms of general disintegration, with leaflets reading "Peace and the Russian Revolution" making their way through the ranks, that Pétain intervened and through a combination of "clemency, personality, and reforms" managed to restore order. Flanner: "He toured the lines, listened to grievances, made few promises and kept them all; improved food, lodging, leave, and pay; gave fresh straw for billet mattresses and the Croix de Guerre to the obscure heroes whose comrades said they deserved them."[15] By the time the wave of mutinies had died down, Pétain had condemned only twenty-six men to death, but he insisted that the government forbid any Frenchman whatever to attend the International Socialist Congress, which was about to be held in Stockholm.

Thus it was that 1917, no less than 1871, offered Pétain its prototype of threatening leftist insurrection. The difference was that 1917's was pacifist and 1871's prototype, the Commune, was "bellicist." De Gaulle, that is, may have been a latter-day Gambetta (pace Mirkine-Guétzévitch) preparing the ground for a new Russian-inspired Commune (as Leger more or less told the Office of Strategic Services). But it is hard to imagine that the situation of the "mutineer" in London was not still further complicated in Pétain's mind by recollection of what was in many ways the high point of his career, the handling of the pacifist mutinies of 1917.

As for Verdun, "le boulevard moral de la France," in the marshal's memorable phrase, the historic victory that inspired François Mitter-

14. Guedalla, *Two Marshals,* 274.
15. Flanner, *Pétain,* 22.

rand to lay a wreath year after year on Pétain's grave, it was, by 1943, totally absorbed into the 1870–1940 paradigm. Pétain, it was said, had been too young for the first battle of Sedan (1870) and too old for the second (1940), but there emerged, above all in New York, a belief that had matters been solely in his hands, he would have turned Verdun itself into a catastrophic French defeat. Flanner took pleasure in ending her second article on Pétain with Weygand's wry aside at the ceremony in Metz that awarded him his marshal's baton: "To think that we brought him there on the kicks we gave to his backside" (27).

Flanner's Pétain at Verdun is an anthology of memorable quips about the marshal's legendary pessimism. Georges Clemenceau observed that "everything Pétain says is full of good sense—much too much sense. He wants a grain of madness in him" (24). The prime minister admitted he was depressed when he heard Pétain, pointing to the British Commandant Douglas Haig, mutter: "There is one who will be forced to capitulate in the open field within a fortnight, and we'll be very lucky if we don't have to do likewise" (23). It was for such comments that the title "Generalissimo of the Allied Forces" fell to Foch rather than Pétain.

Allies found Pétain a difficult colleague. Flanner quotes Foch, who, in his memoirs, recalls the American General Bliss, frustrated by Pétain's timidities, challenging the Frenchman: "We have come over here to get ourselves killed. . . . What are you waiting for?" Pétain's first exercise in what would later be known as the politics of *attentisme* came during World War I with the timid directive "Il faut attendre les Américains" [Wait for the Americans]. And as in the Second World War, so in the First, he appears still to have been waiting after the Americans showed up. As for the British, Flanner records a showdown between Lloyd George, who referred to the Frenchman as "a good soldier . . . cautious to the point of timidity," and Pétain. Pétain: "I suppose you think I can't fight." Lloyd George: "No, General, but I am certain that for some reason or other you won't fight" (25). The shadow of Bazaine lay heavy over even liberated Metz.

Contemporary historiography accords New York pride of place in the genesis of the anti-Pétainist counterlegend of Verdun. In 1941, the émigré playwright Henry Bernstein wrote two long articles in the *New York Herald Tribune* in which he underscored his conviction that the marshal "was not the savior of Verdun, as is generally thought. Verdun was saved despite the Marshal Pétain," who "during the battle of the Somme in March 1918 wanted to abandon the British just as he did in 1940 and was prepared to ask for an armistice and a shameful peace." He quotes in support Field Marshal Bernard Law Montgomery, who confessed that the whole course of recent French politics made perfect sense once one recalled Pétain's readiness to withdraw his troops toward Paris in March 1918, leaving the British to face the Germans on their own.[16]

Flanner does her best to present both sides of the Verdun legend, but the reader inevitably emerges more impressed with the novelty of the counterversion. By the closing years of the war, Verdun itself had been reinscribed in the context of the two catastrophes at Sedan; the paradigm of 1870 had decisively eclipsed that of 1916 for understanding the case of Pétain.

There was no *New Yorker* letter from Paris during the war. A. J. Liebling was following the American troops, accumulating the observations that would end up in *The Road Back to Paris.*[17] Flanner's reference to the "pro-Pétain French comfortably exiled here in the United States" makes it clear that the "salty cosmopolitan Hoosier," as she is described in a blurb for the Pétain volume, had stayed in New York.[18] As she was, of course, obliged to: no American journalists were allowed to file from Hitler's Paris. For which reason we shall make do, in apparent digression from our charting of the 1870 paradigm, with the only "Paris Letter" coming our way from wartime Paris, the "Lettre à un Américain" published by Alfred Fabre-Luce in the first issue of Drieu la Rochelle's newly collaborationist *Nouvelle Revue Française.*[19] Fabre-Luce, whom Raymond Aron would call the "most intelligent of the collaborationists," offers a distressingly charming evocation of Paris in the first winter of its defeat.[20] The recurrent motif of his missive to an American friend is: spare us your pity; we are in the

16. See Marc Ferro, "New York 1941: Portrait d'un défaitiste," in *Pétain*, 680–83.

17. A. J. Liebling, *The Road Back to Paris* (New York: Random House, 1997).

18. Flanner, *Pétain*, 21.

19. Alfred Fabre-Luce, "Lettre à un Américain," *La Nouvelle Revue Française*, December 1, 1940, 64.

20. Concerning Fabre-Luce, see Pierre Hebey, *La Nouvelle Revue Française des années sombres* (Paris: Gallimard, 1992), 304–17. Raymond Aron discusses Fabre-Luce in "Au service de l'ennemi, II," *La France libre* (March 1943).

process of discovering unimagined—or thoroughly forgotten—wonders. Do not allow yourself to be unduly influenced by those who have deserted the city and who will soon be as heavy a burden for you in America as they have been for us these many years. As for the wonders, there is first of all a marvelous silence, a silence of the sort one can enjoy in New York only from a sixtieth story, and whose effect has been to reveal to us to what an extent the city's treasures had been, as it were, "effaced" by the ambient noise. Then there is the new verdancy of the city: "In July we breathed in for the first time the fragrance of linden; in October there were many trees, depolluted of gasoline, still green."[21] All in all, Fabre-Luce on occupied Paris in its first winter is a bit like Paul Valéry on the *gênes exquises,* the "exquisite constraints" of French classical theater. France is always at her best, we are told, in "periods of restriction." As for political freedom, it had never been more than a theological figment in the alcohol-ridden France of the Third Republic. In Paris become Sparta perhaps it will now take on some reality. So no pity, dear Americans, is called for. As we forge a new "race," mindful of the burden our European castoffs will soon be for you, we are almost inclined to return your expressions of heartfelt sympathy in kind.

Fabre-Luce, however, had more serious matters to deal with than writing charmingly threatening "Paris Letters" to imaginary Americans. And it is here that our apparent digression from the 1870 paradigm reveals itself to have been merely apparent. For Fabre-Luce took it upon himself to prepare an anthology of cultural references that might prove particularly illuminating or enriching in the new cultural climate ushered in by blitzkrieg. His *Anthologie de la nouvelle Europe* was published by Plon in 1942 and is a strikingly revealing achievement. Fabre-Luce, who was anything but a fanatic, felt some obligation to include the author of *Mein Kampf* in his new manual of philosophy. But it was a potentially embarrassing gambit, and there is perhaps no aspect of Fabre-Luce's volume more interesting than his tactic in accommodating or mitigating that embarrassment, for it consisted in prefacing his principal Hitler selections—on "biological politics"—with a long passage from Ernest Renan's *Dialogues philosophiques.* According to the philosopher's spokesman Théociste,

21. Fabre-Luce, "Lettre à un Américain," 68.

"The government of the world by reason, if it is to take place, seems . . . well suited to the genius of Germany, which has little concern for the equality or even the dignity of individuals, and whose aim is above all augmenting the intellectual strengths of the species."[22] For Fabre-Luce, Hitler's principal accomplishment had been to undertake to realize—eugenically and politically—Renan's sublime dream. It is, in sum, as though nothing could better prepare the reader for the new dispensation at its most inadmissible than a proper reading of the very French lessons drawn by the great Renan in the wake of the Franco-Prussian War. Whereby the 1870 paradigm attains an intellectual dignity whose legacy, we shall see, continues into the present.

Renan's principal statement on the events of 1870–1871, *La réforme intellectuelle et morale de la France,* was published in 1871. Given that the fall of the Third Republic and the traumatic emergence of the Vichy regime has so often been interpreted as the *reverse* of the fall of the (presumably autocratic) Second Empire and emergence of the (presumably democratic) Third Republic, the major surprise afforded by Renan's essay is that it presents the crisis of 1870 in terms that may be read far less as a reversal than as an anticipation of 1940. The catastrophic war, we are told, was the product of the democratic principles running amok in the liberalized Second Empire: "All this stemmed from universal suffrage, since the emperor, who was the source of every initiative, and the *Corps législatif,* the only counterweight to the emperor's initiatives, issued from it. The miserable government was indeed the result of democracy."[23] And the war given us by the democratized empire was nothing less than an act of treason: "There is not an example of such utter betrayal (*trahison*) of a state by its sovereign, assuming the word betrayal to designate the act of an elected official who substitutes his own will for that of the electorate. Is this to say that the country is not responsible for what transpired? Alas! we can not maintain as much. The country stands guilty of having given itself a minimally enlightened government and above all a wretched Chamber, which, with a frivolity that defies the imagination, voted on the strength of a minister's word the most sinister of wars" (22). Thus

22. Alfred Fabre-Luce, *Anthologie de la nouvelle Europe* (Paris: Plon, 1942), 82.
23. Ernest Renan, *La réforme intellectuelle et morale de la France* (Brussels: Editions Complexe, 1990), 46.

when Renan speaks in *La réforme* of France "enervated by democracy," he is speaking about the Second Empire (2). But what of the regime that succeeded the corrupt Second Empire, the nascent Third Republic? For Renan, we shall see, it is not a democracy but the amorphous interim regime in which one is at liberty, in the wake of defeat at the hands of the Germans, to assess just what a protracted error French history since the French Revolution has been. It is, that is, the perfect context in which to rediscover the signal virtues of the *ancien régime*. Moreover, there is a necessary link between that political project and the fact of German victory and occupation. For the France of the *ancien régime* was at its inception a "Germanic construct, built by a Germanic military aristocracy out of Gallo-Roman materials." Indeed, the Revolution was nothing but the culmination of a long process of de-Teutonization: "The centuries-old labor of France has consisted in eradicating from its breast all the elements left by the Germanic invasion, until the Revolution, which was the final convulsion of that effort" (24). On one level a German occupation of France was a logical impossibility, because France in its deepest recesses remained a Germanic realm. On another there could be no better medium within which to work the "intellectual and moral reform of France"—with the nation reeling under the effects of Germanic superiority—than the suicidally inclined conservative Third Republic.

Renan's France of 1870–1871, in sum, was a nation caught up in the transition not from autocracy (Second Empire) to democracy (Third Republic), but rather from corrupt and terminally mediocre democracy (the liberalized empire) to a rediscovery of the specific excellences of the *ancien régime* under violent Germanic tutelage. The medium of the transition, moreover, was defeat by Germany in a war whose declaration, by the French, was tantamount to an act of treason. As such, that very defeat deserves to be "blessed and considered the beginning of a regeneration" (111). It will be observed just how precise an anticipation of Vichy's position Renan's analysis of 1870 contains. A corrupt, warmongering democracy declares war on Germany and is roundly defeated by a superior adversary; in the wake of the loss, the nation exploits the "divine surprise" of that defeat and ensuing German occupation to erect a (Maurrassian) regime, inspired by old-regime values, and work toward the regeneration of the nation.

36   Renan's crisis of 1870 was simultaneously geopolitical and philosophical. The nineteenth century, he claims, offered two ideal types of society between which France was called on to choose. The first was the "American type" and was predictably lacking in "distinction" and "nobility" (112). The second Renan calls "the amplified and corrected version of the *ancien régime*," and Prussia is posited as its "best model" (113). Ultimately, the opposition between America and Prussia is between two conceptions of political legitimacy: "One of the features of the Germanic race has always been to combine the idea of conquest and the idea of security (*garantie*); in other words, to give precedence to the brute material fact of property stemming from conquest over all considerations relating to the rights of man and all abstract theories of a social contract" (128). Thus Germany is to America as right through conquest is to right through contract. And paradoxically, for France to opt for the Prussian model was to side with what was most deeply French—or Frankish.

    Vichy, it would appear, had as many—though opposite—reasons to be enthralled with the 1870 paradigm as did Janet Flanner in the *New Yorker*.

    For Renan in 1870, racial considerations would weigh more heavily than market realities in a newly reactionary Europe: "Questions of rivalry among races and nations seem destined to prevail over questions of salary and well-being for a long time to come" (83). With the racial component added to the rest, the 1870 paradigm attained near perfect congruity with the ideological configuration dominant in Vichy France. Curiously, the entire configuration would make a final and shockingly resplendent return in 1997 with the posthumous publication of Michel Foucault's highly polished university course of 1976, "Il faut défendre la société." Foucault's aim is to demonstrate that no discursive tradition has a greater pedigree in the struggle against all forms of statism than the polemical tradition of race war. On January 28, 1976, he suggested that his audience might think he was engaging in a paean (*éloge*) to "racist discourse." "And you would not, in fact, be wrong, with the exception that what I intended to praise is not quite racist discourse, but the discourse of race war."[24]

---

24. Michel Foucault, *Il faut défendre la société* (Paris: Gallimard, Seuil, 1997), 57.

Foucault's course was a commentary not on Renan, however, but on the eighteenth-century reactionary noble Boulainvilliers, whom Foucault would promote to a certain intellectual centrality in the modern era. The Franks, according to Boulainvilliers, were Germanic warrior aristocrats who made short shrift of the Gallo-Roman mercenary opposition but who, in the long run, would lose the power and freedoms they had justifiably seized through the ruses of a usurpatory king (who was originally one of them) in complicity with the Latinized dregs of Gallo-Roman society now congregated in the towns. What gives the Frankish aristocracy its intellectual interest is its need to fight on two fronts: to invoke Germanic freedoms in its dealings with the king, and the rights of conquest in its dealings with the Third Estate. Mimicked by the Third Estate, the discourse of freedom against the king would turn into the rhetoric of the French Revolution. But that development, with its favoring of (social) contract over conquest and its irreducibly juridical bias, was the result of a degraded and partial reading of a configuration that, in its totality, would issue in a new pathos "that would mark right-wing thought in France with its splendor." *Frank,* Foucault reminds us, was commonly regarded as related not to freedom, but to *ferox,* "ferocious" (132).

Like Renan, then, Foucault's Boulainvilliers affirms conquest against contract, and Germany, land of the legendary "barbarian," against America, land of the "noble savage." Like Renan, Foucault (via Boulainvilliers) engages in a sustained critique of the political culture flowing from the French Revolution, the juridically minded charade of 1789. What would be needed, Foucault's Boulainvilliers tells us, is a reinstating or reactivating in its "originary rectitude" of the inaugural phase of Germanic invasion, conquest, and occupation. And because what Foucault is proposing is a manner of Sorelian myth, it matters little whether Boulainvilliers's argument is true. Indeed, "it is even totally false!" What counts is that "we"—by which, I take it, Foucault in particular is being designated—"think within its grid of intelligibility" (144–45). It is a grid, I would submit, that passes crucially through Renan's vision of 1870 and the French experience of World War II before completing the trajectory from Boulainvilliers to Foucault.

Renan, it will be recalled, termed the irresponsible war declared by an increasingly "democratic" Second Empire an act of "treason." Once that ominous word had been uttered, Renan immediately went on to amplify the reasons such a war could not but be catastrophic. Principal among these were the "extraordinary awakening of material appetites among workers and peasants," for it was clear to the old master that the "socialism of the workers was diametrically opposed to the military spirit."[25] Combine the two motifs—socialist hedonism turned reckless in the international realm and the declaration of a war whose outcome would be so predictably catastrophic as to render the declaration in itself treasonous—and one has the basis for an important episode of the Vichy years that is tellingly discussed in Flanner's series on Pétain: the Riom trials of the winter of 1942.

It was the "hilarity" of the trials held in Riom, a "harsh, handsome Auvergnat town of black stone fountains and façades cut from the local volcanic rock," that attracted Flanner to Vichy's attempt to pin guilt for starting World War II on Léon Blum, prime minister of the Popular Front government, his successor Edouard Daladier, and Generalissimo Maurice Gamelin. Having undermined France's defenses, the argument would go, Blum and company plunged France into war while it was still treacherously underprepared.[26]

The main vulnerability of the prosecution's case lay in Pétain himself having been in 1934 a notoriously ineffective minister of defense who had cut the war budget by a third. Indeed, as late as 1939, Pétain had written an extended laudatory preface to his friend General Narcisse Chauvineau's polemical book against tanks, which had the quaint title *Une invasion est-elle encore possible?*[27] Under such circumstances, the scene was set for turning the tables on the prosecution, which is more or less what happened. The anti-Semitic cartoonist Ralph Soupault published a caricature of Blum as prosecutor addressing an unseen defendant with the words "Accusé Pétain, levez-vous!" It was Daladier rather than Blum who served as the principal polemicist against the men of the new regime. But Flanner savors every ironic reversal as though the trial were, in effect, the Molièresque "farce" she took it to be. From the reading by Blum's lawyer in open court of Vichy's secret instructions governing press coverage of the trial to the

25. Renan, *La réforme*, 23.
26. Flanner, *Pétain*, 49.
27. Narcisse Chauvineau, *Une invasion est-elle encore possible?* (Paris: Editions Berger-Levrault, 1939).

aptly named presiding judge, Caous, which many chose to hear as *chaos,* the trial is milked for all the buffoonery it will yield, until it is left to the Nazis, in dismay, to close down the proceedings. The *Völkischer Beobachter,* the Nazi Party paper, observed in an editorial that the trial was demonstrating the guilt of the men of Vichy, precisely the opposite of its stated purpose. The *Frankfürter Zeitung* judged Riom a "stupid farce," and Hitler, as though confronted by an exercise in the theater of the absurd, opted, in disbelief, to close the whole show down (51).

For all its brio, however, Flanner's evocation of Riom is revealing less for the episodes it narrates than for the larger context in which it places them. For Flanner's Riom, a bravura bit of comedy, is paired with a second exercise in high humor, Pétain's attempted firing of Laval on December 13, 1940. In her words, "In the two-and-a-half-year drama of Unoccupied France before the Nazis came in and lowered the curtain on November 11, 1942, the Marshal's two most spirited performances were against Pierre Laval, and against a handful of imprisoned statesmen left over from the Third Republic whom and which Pétain put on trial at the court of Riom. Both Laval and Riom were tragic issues in France, yet at moments they afforded the French the only real laughter of their defeat" (45). The details of the action of December 13, if not their ultimate intention, are well known: to mark the centenary of the transfer of Napoleon's ashes to the Invalides, Hitler had exceptionally allowed the ashes of Napoleon's son, the "Aiglon," to be brought from Vienna. A torchlight procession at midnight would mark the occasion, and Laval insisted that it was out of the question that Pétain not attend. Pétain, still smarting from the manner in which Laval had bundled him off to Montoire in October to meet Hitler, vowed that he would not go. A cabinet meeting was held; all ministers were asked routinely to submit their resignations, but only Laval's and that of one other minister were accepted. At that point, on cue, Laval was placed under house arrest in his château at Chateldon. Vichy, as Henri Amouroux put it, had famously won a battle, but was in no position to win the war. The German ambassador, Otto Abetz, arrived at Vichy's center of government, the Hôtel du Parc, and, gun in hand, secured Laval's liberation. His reinstatement in the government would await the German occupation of the whole of France in late 1942.

It is an inherently fascinating episode, raising all sorts of issues regarding Pétain's motivation. Was it revenge for the humiliating rush to Montoire of October 1940? Was it an impulsive move on the part of a man who was capable of confiding to an American journalist in early 1941 that Laval, an unprepossessing individual whom *Time* took pleasure in characterizing as "swart as a Greek," filled him with physical revulsion?[28] Was it the only form of anti-German resistance Pétain thought he could afford?

Flanner complicates her account by claiming that Pétain's house arrest of Laval was meant to intercept a Laval-engineered house arrest of Pétain should he ever make the trip north to the Occupied Zone for the "December 15th mummery" at the Invalides. The Laval episode was as much a turning of the tables, in Flanner's telling, as the Riom episode with which it is symmetrically paired. And just as Riom was a "farce," the initial intrigue culminating in the coup of December 13 was, in Flanner's words, "as comic, and as implausible, as that of any Berlin *opéra-bouffe*."[29] The net effect of pitting the two farcical episodes against each other is to designate Pétain as the more or less empty stage on which forces greater than he battle it out. After all, if he was as opposed to Laval as he was to Blum, which is plainly the implication of Flanner's essay, he—and Vichy—represented an admittedly ineffective middle of the road. Or is it merely the constraint of *New Yorker* journalism to provide amusement for the sophisticate that has the three principal adversaries of Pétain in Flanner's essay—from the "comic relief" provided by de Gaulle to the "hilarity" of Blum at Riom to the "opéra bouffe" of the conflict with Laval—all emerge as figures out of farce performing on the increasingly empty stage or blank (and thus, by implication, innocent) page of Pétain's mind?

That blankness is a subject of speculation in the *New Yorker* essays. Pétain at age eighty-four, we are told, was a man of "phenomenal health," but who nonetheless required a drug—was it benzedrine? ephedrine?—from his trusted Action Française physician, Dr. Bernard Ménétrel, to get through his morning (47).[30] The day would regularly begin with his blue eyes "sapphire-clear," his features merely middle-

---

28. *Time,* January 4, 1942, 46.
29. Flanner, *Pétain,* 45.
30. For more on Dr. Ménétrel, see Ferro, *Pétain,* 605–8.

aged in their "neatness." "For an hour after he has left his doctor, he is a match for anyone, even Laval."[31] Then the "swift and startling" decline: "By afternoon, the Marshal has turned into an old man." Before your eyes, he becomes an "empty shell."

Is the "emptiness" of that shell not akin to the empty stage on which de Gaulle, Laval, Blum, and Daladier are consigned to their farcical roles? And is not Pétain's apparent aestheticism in Flanner's retelling, the failure to sustain his every political initiative, not a form of implied innocence? The suggestion may be sustained by consideration of the circumstance in which Flanner leaves her subject. On November 18, 1943, Pétain was scheduled to deliver a speech, which the Germans suppressed. The key passage, according to Flanner, depending on Swiss sources, was to be the following: "We, Marshal of France, Chief of State, decree . . . that if we die before having been able to attain ratification by the Nation of [our] new Constitution . . . the power mentioned in the [Third Republic's] Constitutional Law of 1875 will return to the Senate and Chamber"(52). After Laval and Darlan, Flanner writes, Pétain's final dauphin or heir apparent was to be Marianne, the "battered figurehead of the Third Republic." But if such were the case, Vichy would indeed have been a mirage of sorts, a mere hiatus in time between different phases of the Third Republic.

Flanner, we now know, was right about the projected speech in November 1943 and its censorship. The plan, then, was to prepare a government that Washington might find it possible to deal with. The sine qua non for such a government would be the removal of Laval, a task that was placed in the hands of a Pétain henchman, Admiral Charles Platon.[32] The plan was to effect under Platon's devious guidance both a return to parliamentarianism and the ouster of Laval. But if the elaborately ineffectual politics of deferment and theoretical neutrality known as Pétain's *attentisme* were to culminate, under Platonic tutelage, in a regime or regimen of representation, then the entire configuration—*attentisme* or *différance*—would be pregnant with intellectual futurity indeed. The marshal's speech, however, was suppressed; the Vichy interim was not allowed to self-efface before the majesty of Parliament restored; Platon was executed by the Resistance.

31. Flanner, *Pétain*, 48.
32. Concerning Platon, see Ferro, *Pétain*, 489–93.

42   The world would have to wait for the reading of a very different "Platon" for deconstruction to be born.

Of the war at its most horrendous, the genocide of the Jews, we learn next to nothing from the *New Yorker* articles. Vichy's anti-Semitic policies, in fact, are represented by a single misleading reference: "Having eliminated labor unions, Vichy set up, like a cruel ersatz, a Jewish union, the Union Générale des Juifs de France, which every Jew had to join."[33] The reference occurs, then, in the context of a discussion of Vichy's labor policies. But it is based on the plainly erroneous supposition that *union* in French might in any way be translatable as *union* in English. Not the slightest suggestion that the Union Générale des Juifs de France was a French *Judenrat* charged, among other things, with facilitating the transport of Jews to the death camps in the east. Caught between the "opéra-bouffe" of Pétain's relations with Laval, the "farce" of Riom, and the "comic relief" provided by de Gaulle's violently interrupted identification with Pétain, Flanner's Vichy had little room for the most tragic episode of the war years.

Might a stronger reference to the apparently compelling paradigm of 1870 have improved chances for coming to terms with the grisly horror of Auschwitz? Renan, the exemplary commentator on the lessons to be drawn from the events of 1870, could, of course, be depended on for a vigorous display of theoretical anti-Semitism. From the first chapter of his *Histoire générale des langues sémitiques:* "The Semitic race may be identified almost entirely by its negative characteristics: it has neither mythology nor epic nor science nor philosophy nor fiction nor plastic arts nor civic life; in everything, an absence of complexity and nuance, solely a sense of unity."[34] But it is a long way from such judgments to the particular grisliness of the camps.

Consider rather, on the way to an answer, the classic of Resistance prose in France, a book whose positive portrait of a German officer was to provoke considerable polemical response in the French community of New York: Vercors's *Le silence de la mer.* That novella famously recounts the protracted nonencounter between a German officer, Werner von Ebrennac, and two French citizens, an aging country

33. Flanner, *Pétain*, 46.
34. Quoted in Zeev Sternhell, *La droite révolutionnaire: Les origines françaises du fascisme* (Paris: Seuil, 1978), 163.

gentleman and his niece, in whose house he is stationed during the Second World War. The officer, a polished and devoted Francophile who sounds at times as though he were modeled on Ernst Jünger, speaks eloquently of the joys of a future Franco-German union at the heart of Europe. On every occasion, he is received with a dignified and principled silence on the part of his hosts. Eventually, he learns from a superior officer that official German protestations of respect for France (and thus, unintentionally, his own nightly monologues as well) were a sham, so many lures intended to entice the French into "selling their soul for a plate of lentils."[35] The virtually psychoanalytic silence of the two French characters, as violent a departure from the conventions of hospitality as may be imagined, has afforded the German officer time to discover the unsustainability of his own discourse. Shattered by his discovery, he takes off for the eastern front.

In *Qu'est-ce que la littérature?* Sartre comments on the universal hostility that greeted the book among the émigrés of New York and London.[36] His point is that this was a book so clearly intended for a French audience in 1941 (when the Germans were on their best behavior in the Occupied Zone and might appear quite seductive) that to read it anywhere and at any time else would necessarily be to betray it. Here, then, is World War II at its most sanitized. There are no death camps in sight. In the course of evoking the novella, Sartre makes a literary comparison: "This silence of two French citizens is without psychological plausibility; it is even faintly anachronistic: it reminds one of Maupassant's stubbornly taciturn patriotic peasants during another occupation."[37] Philippe Burrin, who has written well about the importance assumed by the imperative to avoid eye contact, a *grève du regard*, was also led to evoke Guy de Maupassant (*Boule de suif*) with reference to the Vercors text.[38]

But the Maupassant story that speaks—or sustains its muteness—most eloquently with regard to the subject at hand is rather "La Folle," a curious short story in the author's collection of 1883, *Contes de la*

35. Vercors, *Le silence de la mer* (Paris: Albin Michel, 1951), 56.
36. Jean-Paul Sartre, *Qu'est-ce que la littérature?* (Paris: Gallimard, 1948), 79. See the polemic of Ilya Ehrenbourg, "A propos du 'Silence de la mer,' " *Pour la victoire*, June 17, 1944. Ehrenbourg accuses Vercors of wanting to "pervert" the reader.
37. Sartre, *Qu'est-ce que la littérature?* 80.
38. Philippe Burrin, *La France à l'heure allemande* (Paris: Seuil, 1995), 207.

bécasse. Not that it is in any way anti-Semitic. Rather, the story hints at dimensions of cruelty and abjection that leave the reader with the admittedly anachronistic sense that the dignified encounter of *Le silence de la mer* might be the façade that first the story's German protagonist, commenting on his own discourse, and then Sartre, commenting on the reaction of the émigrés of New York and London, realized it turned out to be. "La Folle," five pages in length, looks back to an allegedly true episode of the Franco-Prussian War. Shortly before hostilities begin, a woman suffers a series of personal catastrophes: in a month's time, her father, husband, and newborn child all die. After six weeks of raving, she takes to her bed as a bizarre and almost catatonic calm takes hold of her. War comes; a German officer, considerably less polished than Vercors's exemplar, is garrisoned in the woman's house and informed of her exceptional situation, which he accepts. After a while, however, the Prussian commandant suspects that the Frenchwoman is merely feigning her illness in order to avoid contact with the enemy. He issues an ultimatum. When she fails to leave her bed, he has her carried on her mattress out the front door to an unknown destination. It is only the following spring, while hunting birds, that the narrator, obsessed by the madwoman's fate, understands what has happened to her. A woodcock (*bécasse*) he has shot is retrieved from the ground, where it is lying next to a human skull that must be hers. She had been left on her mattress in the woods with the thought that the cold would soon break her silent resistance. Because resistance was not what was at stake, she remained there in the snow, froze to death, was devoured by wolves. Birds made their nest in what remained of her mattress. The narrator is transfixed by the revelation.

The Maupassant tale, in sum, without the slightest reference to anti-Semitism, hints with masterly reserve at depths of abjection that make the restrained nondialogue of *Le silence de la mer* feel almost like a cover-up. That a tale out of the conflict of 1870 should bring the reader far closer to the horror of the Second World War than anything in Flanner's portrait of the France of Pétain is an indication that understanding lies less in a corrective of the anachronism—1870 for 1940—within which the war was being imagined in New York at the time, than in its exacerbation.

THREE

Endgame
Maeterlinck in Manhattan

Wartime New York, Lévi-Strauss observed, was one of the most temporally heterogeneous cities in the world. In the antique shops on Third Avenue, one could find artifacts of every conceivable historical era. Indeed, for the collector, New York had proved itself to be a step ahead of Paris: in promoting objects of the 1890s to the status of antiques, it anticipated a shift in taste that would not arrive in France until well after the war.

Maurice Maeterlinck, the Belgian Symbolist poet who had long since settled in France, managed to embody Lévi-Strauss's observation in the flesh. More than a half-century had passed between his memorable contribution to Jules Huret's *Enquête sur l'évolution littéraire* in 1891, one of the charter texts of French Symbolism, and the interview he gave the *New Yorker* in his two-room second-floor suite at the Plaza Hotel in the summer of 1943. Gide's character André Walter had been categorical: "In sum, Mallarmé in poetry, and Maeterlinck in drama."[1] Breton had identified Maeterlinck as one of the two Symbolists who would endure. For Artaud, he—and he alone—had introduced literature to the "polyvalent richness" of the unconscious.[2] During the war years, Maeterlinck was the doyen of the French literary community in New York, as close to an 1890s *literary* antique as one might hope

1. Quoted in W. D. Halls, *Maurice Maeterlinck: A Study of His Life and Thought* (Oxford: Clarendon Press, 1960), 86.
2. J.-M. Horemans, "Maeterlinck, Goffin, et les Etats-Unis," *Annales de la Fondation Maurice Maeterlinck* 15 (1969): 24.

to behold. In between, in the fifty-two years separating the Huret and the *New Yorker* interviews, there had been the stormy collaboration with Debussy on the great French opera of the new century, *Pelléas et Mélisande;* the *Peter Pan*–inspired *féerie L'oiseau bleu* that had prompted a "Blue Bird craze" throughout America in the 1910s; and the Nobel Prize for literature in 1911.[3] A rich career indeed appeared to be coming to a traumatic end under the *New York Times* headline: "Maeterlinck, Impoverished Exile, Arrives with Wife from France." The date was July 13, 1940.

The otherworldly Maeterlinck was an unlikely émigré to America. It must have been wrenching for him to move out of his Riviera home. Orlamonde, as he called it, was an unfinished casino designed and half-built by a White Russian architect on the Basse-Corniche leading from Villefranche to Nice—a Symbolist's version of Sunset Boulevard. The poet had paid three and a half million francs for the building in 1930 and moved in—to a life of reclusion—early the following year. Orlamonde was an extravagant structure, adorned with variegated marble and enjoying a view of the Bay of Nice. Yet in early 1939, as war approached, the poet, for safety's sake, had decided to settle in Portugal. It was an understandable move. Maeterlinck, like Pétain, was a great admirer of Oliveira Salazar, the Portuguese dictator. Pétain, we now know, kept a copy of the French edition of the Portuguese president's *Comment on relève un Etat* on his desk.[4] The poet, for his part, went the marshal one better: Maeterlinck had written the preface for the volume of Salazar's speeches published by Flammarion under the title *Une révolution dans la paix.* The poet was unremitting in his praise of Salazar's probity, intelligence, and disinterest. "His mind is a veritable laboratory in which utopian inspirations become pragmatic."[5] And the leader of Portuguese fascism returned the compliment. Maeterlinck was decorated by the Portuguese leader personally with the sash of Grand Officer of the Order of Santiago da Espada. In a letter of November 19, 1939, he informed a friend that his address

3. On the "Blue Bird craze" in America, see Robert Beachboard, *Le théâtre de Maeterlinck aux Etats-Unis* (Paris: Société d'Edition d'Enseignement Supérieur, 1951), 44.

4. Ferro, *Pétain*, 214.

5. Maurice Maeterlinck, preface to *Une révolution dans la paix* by Oliveira Salazar (Paris: Flammarion, 1937), ix.

for the remainder of the war would be Avenida Augusto de Aguiar, 165, Lisbon.

Why come to America? Speculation has followed two paths. The first suggests that Maeterlinck's radio denunciation of King Leopold III's surrender to the Nazis had soured the political and diplomatic atmosphere around him in Lisbon.[6] The second harked back to his openly anti-German play of World War I, *Le bourgmestre de Stilemonde*. Diminutive Portugal, after all, was the Belgium of the Iberian peninsula. It would be sufficient for Franco's Spain to enter the war on Hitler's side (which was a distinct possibility) for Portugal to fall as quickly and as unceremoniously as the poet's native land. Whence the improbable departure from Lisbon aboard the Greek liner *Nea Hellas*. Despite the headline in the *Times*, the Maeterlincks arrived with a "tiny French motor car," as the *New Yorker* referred to it, thirty-two pieces of luggage, two Pekingese lap dogs, and a pair of parakeets. Maeterlinck emerged from the ship in Hoboken with a copy of *Gone with the Wind* in his hand, and raised no objection when the customs officials confiscated his birds. "Perhaps it is for the best; bluebirds," he remarked, "are the symbol of happy times."[7] Was it the inveterate fatalism of the inventor of the Symbolist drama or the sheer industrial ugliness of the Jersey shoreline that muted his will to object?

America had first surfaced on Maeterlinck's horizon years earlier as an episode in the vexed history of Debussy's *Pelléas et Mélisande*. That great opera ended up pitting the poet against the composer in what at times reads as a farcical replay of the aesthetico-metaphysical polemic staged by Mallarmé between "la musique et les lettres." Maeterlinck, in the years since he had agreed to give his text to Debussy, had become the lover of the formidable singing actor Georgette Leblanc. Mallarmé had written a memorable page about "this strange and entrancing woman."[8] George Bernard Shaw was of the opinion that she had ruined Maeterlinck's *Monna Vanna* by insisting that he turn the play into a vehicle for her to enjoy a "Sarah Bernhardt success."[9] An

6. Horemans, "Maeterlinck, Goffin, et les Etats-Unis," 152.

7. Fritsch-Estrangin, *New York entre de Gaulle et Pétain*, 161.

8. Stéphane Mallarmé, "Sur Madame Georgette Leblanc," in *Oeuvres complètes* (Paris: Gallimard, 1945), 861.

9. Halls, *Maurice Maeterlinck*, 76.

enthralled Maeterlinck was of the opinion that the role of Mélisande, by joint agreement, would go to Leblanc. The poet was mortified to learn in a newspaper that the composer, who was unimpressed by her singing, and his director, Albert Carré, at the Opéra Comique, had awarded the role to Mary Garden. He threatened Debussy with a lawsuit, then a duel, and finally a caning with his walking stick. Frustrated on all fronts, he published a letter in *Le Figaro* on April 14, 1902, claiming that he had the impression of "being shut out of his own work" and wishing for its "prompt and resounding failure" (77). It was as though the prototypal Symbolist conflict between poet and composer, Mallarmé and Wagner, had worked its way into the new French *Tristan, Pelléas et Mélisande*.

America entered the *Pelléas* fray in 1911. The British impresario Henry Russell had arranged for Georgette Leblanc to sing the role of Mélisande in the Boston Grand Opera House. It was decided that something more than a straight performance of Debussy's score would be needed to make the production succeed, and thus Russell began floating the rumor that the great Maeterlinck himself might well have accompanied his mistress incognito aboard the *Olympic*, and that Russell had bet Maeterlinck that he would not be recognized by journalists were he to show up at the opera. The publicity worked— initially at least—like a charm; proceeds were high; a surrogate Maeterlinck was even engaged to put in a phantom appearance at the performance. But before long the Boston public tired of *Pelléas*, and the production was deemed a flop.

Finally, in 1920, Maeterlinck did make the trip to America. It was not an unqualified success. Difficulties with English marred his lecture tour. Misunderstandings abounded. When told in faltering French at an ostentatious dinner that his host was a "steel king," or *roi de steel*, he could only respond: "Mon Dieu, quel style!" (128). But perhaps the failure of that first American journey had deeper roots. The poet's arrival on Christmas Eve 1919 aboard the liner *Paris* was the occasion for the launching of a "Blue Bird Campaign for Happiness." Maeterlinck the fatalist, that is, was taken as the bard of a facile optimism. It was a reception curiously parallel to the welcome accorded Freud a few years earlier: the tragic dimension of each thinker would be smothered in a tawdry display of goodwill. Ego psychology, shall we say, was already a triumphalist effort to turn psychoanalysis into a

Blue Bird Campaign for Happiness. Small wonder that Maeterlinck at the time would comment that he "liked the Americans too much to be sincere in his remarks regarding them."[10]

The arrival of the Maeterlincks in 1940 had nary a trace of triumphalism; it was the occasion of a muting of his criticism of King Leopold's accommodation of the Nazis. "I wonder," he wrote shortly after his arrival, "what our King Albert the Great would have done had fate put him in the same position" (16). True, he went on to ask: "But would he have allowed fate to put him there? I shall soon be on the other side of the shadows midst which we live. He'll tell me." It is a query that some have taken as a retraction of the very recantation he appeared to be making.

The query also points to the specific oddity of Maeterlinck's circumstance. After years of semimystical speculation on the meaning of death—was it a mere awakening?—and preparation for that ultimate journey, he found himself at age seventy-eight forced to make a very different journey, to the optimistic wonderland of America. It was an irony that would play in the writings of Maeterlinck during these, his final productive years, and one to which we now shall turn.

Maeterlinck's first significant theatrical project in New York was a failed version of the story of Joan of Arc. The author would wax ironic on the reasons for the failure: a Broadway producer suggested to him that only making Joan the mistress of Charles VII would revive the dramatic appeal of the stilted legend (21). The story of Joan, though, was of distinctly topical interest. De Gaulle had chosen the cross of Lorraine as his emblem, and Henry Bernstein, the French dramatist spending the war years in New York, would write two stirring (though exaggerated) articles on Charles de Gaulle and Joan of Arc in the *Herald Tribune* in May 1943. On the occasion of the Fête de Jeanne d'Arc, the author concluded (and was joined in his conclusion by the editorialist of the newspaper) that if his "poor country [did] not die of privation, the time [would] come when she [would] celebrate the Fête de Charles de Gaulle." The theme was thus in the air, and, coming from the pen of an esteemed Nobel Prize winner, could not but enjoy considerable anticipatory goodwill.

The play, though, is wooden. It spends relatively little time on the

---

10. Horemans, "Maeterlinck, Goffin, et les Etats-Unis," 9.

inspiring tale of Joan triumphant and considerably more on the details of her trial for witchcraft, from whose proceedings Maeterlinck claims to quote passages verbatim. And even then the author fails to register his point forcefully. Nonetheless, *Jeanne d'Arc*, which would not be published until after the author's return to Orlamonde in 1947, is fascinating in its central failure. It is as though Maeterlinck in his New York period represented Symbolism on all fours, a movement plainly inadequate to the historical era through which the Belgian Nobel laureate found himself incongruously surviving. Longevity, it would appear, is the supreme ironist.

For all her receptivity to "voices," Jeanne seems less the centrally Maeterlinckian figure in this play than does the dauphin, Charles. For it is Charles who seems in the grips of that odd passivity that has the reader (or spectator) sensing that he or she is confronting something qualitatively new. We first meet Charles on his throne, but in a shabby state of semisomnolence. He is the object of barely contained jeers on the part of members of his court. Jeanne thinks he is feigning, testing her, but he disabuses her: "No, no, I was almost actually sleeping. . . . When I am moved, I fall asleep."[11] Here then is a Maeterlinckian king, less *agissant* than *agi*, a would-be sovereign in an aesthetic domain that had Maeterlinck thinking that his every play aspired to the status of marionette theater.

This would-be king is only twenty-six years old and enjoys a special bond with his servant from Lorraine. Yet the very lapse of his mind into blankness is oddly reminiscent of the daily ordeals of Pétain in France. The parallel grows scene by scene. Charles's is a discourse of atonement, yet his mind is perpetually on the brink of unraveling: "And then, I have no memory. . . . I must be sick. . . . I forget everything, even the evils done me. . . . Moreover, I am always of the opinion of the last man to speak to me" (19). "Like a weathervane [*une girouette*], you turn with every wind," as Laval famously told the marshal during the crisis of December 1940.[12] The parallel is further elaborated after the brief tableaux devoted to Jeanne's successive victories and the coronation (in the presence of "le jeune de Laval," among others) in Reims. The play's fifth tableau deals with the offer of peace made by the duke of Burgundy,

11. Maurice Maeterlinck, *Jeanne d'Arc* (Monaco: Editions du Rocher, 1948), 10.
12. Ferro, *Pétain*, 208.

Philippe le Bon. The Burgundians, it will be recalled, were the party of collaboration with the British occupiers within France. At a time when the "enemy still occupies more than half of France," Philippe le Bon calls, through Charles, for a general armistice.[13] The name is crucial, for the Vichy years, with their calls to replenish the French population, were years in which the name Philippe—after Pétain—had its widest statistical currency in French history, as many a university professor, casually reviewing class lists twenty years later, could not help noting. It was Philippe le Bon, then, duke of the collaborationist ranks of Burgundy, who now held sway over Charles, dictating the terms of a premature armistice. Moreover, consider the core of passivity within the new policy. Charles, become Charles-Philippe, proposes the prototypal case of Fabius Cunctator in the Punic Wars, whose "masterly inactivity" was ultimately responsible for the defeat of Hannibal. What exactly did Fabius do? "Il temporisait," Charles responds (45). And "temporizing" is defined by the king as "gaining time by doing nothing." In Vichy France, the name of that policy was *attentisme.*

Charles, then, under the sway of Philippe, is the exemplary Maeterlinckian figure in the play: almost sleepwalking his way through his role, a figure of latency itself. More than a half-century earlier, Maeterlinck had written his major poetic collection, *Serres chaudes.* From which:

> Ayez pitié de mon absence
> Au seuil de mes intentions!
> Mon âme est pâle d'impuissance
> Et de blanches inactions
> Mon âme aux oeuvres délaissées
>
> Mon âme pâle de sanglots
> Regarde en vain ses mains lassées
> Trembler à fleur de l'inéclos.[14]

The lines, from "Oraison," are a touchstone of sorts for the Maeterlinckian sensibility. The slide into blankness, the eschewing of the

---

13. Maeterlinck, *Jeanne d'Arc,* 47.

14. Maurice Maeterlinck, *Serres chaudes* (Paris: Gallimard, 1983), 33 [Have pity on my absence / At the threshold of my intentions! / My soul is pale with impotence / and blank inaction / My soul, its works abandoned, / My soul pale with sobs / considers in vain its tired hands / tremble with unfulfillment].

intentional, the muted celebration of the *inéclos*—all that *fails* to reach fruition—might well have been recited by Charles in his defense of "temporization" or *attentisme*. For which reason the scenes between Jeanne and Charles are the most successful in the play. But Charles, we have seen, became an *attentiste* under the influence of Philippe le Bon and his call for a premature armistice. And Philippe, tutor in *attentisme* and advocate of just such an armistice in a France more than half of whose territory was occupied, could in 1942 have evoked only Pétain.

Maeterlinck nonetheless guides his audience through the rest of the story. We find Jeanne imprisoned, abandoned by her king, escaping after dropping her sword from the prison window (a bit like Mélisande and her ring), then being recaptured and brought to trial for heresy. The trial (the ninth tableau) is the longest scene in the play and is accompanied by the following footnote: "The questions and answers below reproduce *verbatim et literatim* those of the trial that began on January 9, 1431, and ended with the execution of May 14."[15] The author goes on to admit that he has been obliged to condense four months of proceedings in which "the same dubious and imbecilic accusations were pitilessly rehashed." The most remarkable feature of Maeterlinck's version of the trial is the inclusion of an invisible supernatural voice erupting from on high and periodically interrupting the proceedings with results that seem alternately comic and threatening. It is a voice, we are told, that only the damned can hear. It condemns the judges, leading to a general suspicion that the courtroom has become haunted. One judge asks to be excused for reasons of health; the infamous Cauchon appears "ravaged"; a general air of panic settles over the courtroom as a decision is precipitously taken to restore some measure of truth to the proceedings by submitting Jeanne to torture. The general evolution of the trial, in which a manifestly unjust authority is reduced to infantile helplessness through supernatural means, is toward the farcical. After which, we are treated to the undramatic episodes of Jeanne's abjuration, in a state of confusion, at the abbey of Saint-Ouen; her unimpressive admission that the abjuration was merely a reaction to her fear of the stake; her relapse into a state of

15. Maeterlinck, *Jeanne d'Arc*, 77.

insubordination; and her burning at the stake before a febrile crowd shouting alternately "Saint!" and "Sorceress!"

The specificity of Maeterlinck's *Jeanne d'Arc*, which—for understandable reasons—has never been produced professionally, lies, on the one hand, in the somnambulant passivity of Charles, and on the other, in the evolution of Jeanne's trial toward farce. Charles is a mere twenty-six, but in his inveterate passivity and incomplete emergence from the realm of dreams he seems the most Maeterlinckian character in the play, far less the corrupt, overgrown child of, say, Jean Anouilh's *Alouette* than a final version of the aged, fatalistic King Arkël of *Pelléas et Mélisande.* Give him Arkël's old age, and combine it with (1) his *attentisme* or will to "temporize"; (2) his role as spokesman for Philippe le Bon's call for a premature armistice at a time when France had more than half its territory occupied; and (3) the time—December 1940—of the play's completion, and one is hard put not to detect the aura of Philippe Pétain (even in the detail of the early solidarity with Joan–de Gaulle) around him. The period had indeed been hard on Maeterlinck. World War II was no time to write a version of Joan of Arc centered on the metaphysical wisdom of Charles VII.

But it is the second feature of the failed play—the evolution of the trial toward supernatural farce—that proved rich with future developments for Maeterlinck. Shortly after completing *Jeanne d'Arc*, the playwright composed a drama, *Les trois justiciers,* whose principal conceit all but rewrites the structure of the central episode of his version of Joan of Arc. The play tells the tale of a corrupt judge, Salomon, eager to victimize a young woman, Tristanelle, in a legal proceeding in which the judge's iniquity is brought to life through the supernatural intervention of three allegorical figures—Ombre Rebelle, File-tout-nu, and Saute-au-Ciel—who are none other than agents of Salomon's own conscience. Salomon, then, is a version of Cauchon and the agents of the Inquisition; Tristanelle, his would-be victim, is Jeanne; and the three allegorical figures correspond to the "invisible voice" denouncing the architects of the trial against Jeanne.

Salomon has attempted to strip Tristanelle of her inheritance by rewriting—and forging—her mother's will, thus arranging to have her fortune "left" not to her daughter but to her daughter's guardian, Salomon himself. It is the kind of crime that landed Gianni Schicchi deep in Dante's hell (with Puccini, centuries later, pleading extenuating circumstances). Salomon's misdeed, however, is worse yet: he has retained the original will and wants now not merely to discredit it, but to prosecute Tristanelle for forgery. But he will be foiled in his plan. The crucial evidence, known to the allegorical figments of Salomon's conscience, concerns the watermark "inscrit dans la pâte même du papier"—worked into the very pulp of the paper on which the false will has been written. For whereas the date of that false will, leaving a fortune to Salomon, is June 5, 1932, slightly before the decease of Tristanelle's mother, the watermark of the paper on which it is written is 1935. The invisible File-tout-nu will intervene in the proceeding intended to establish the legitimacy of the false will to confound Salomon—and administer a series of slaps to the guilty. Panic settles over the courtroom; accusations of ventriloquism and demonic possession are lodged; when the trees around Salomon appear to be on the march and the play to be turning into what Maeterlinck once called a "Shakespitrerie," all flee, leaving Salomon "more miserable than Job."

Was it the lapsed Symbolist who dreamed up the conceit of the watermark in New York? It was Mallarmé, in his preface to *Un coup de dés,* who speculated on the importance assumed by the "intervention" of the paper in the poem on which it was written: "The paper intervenes each time an image, of itself, ceases or recedes."[16] Just so does the very pulp—or *pâte*—of the paper intervene to undo Salomon's nefarious plan. It is as though the tendential blankness of Charles's mind in Maeterlinck's version of Joan of Arc were present (or absent) here as the white "filigreed" paper invalidating the very will written on it. Twin touchstones of the Symbolist sensibility.

Maeterlinck, however, does not leave Salomon in his Job-like distress. In one of the more arbitrary developments in the play, he contrives to work Salomon's salvation. This occurs when Salomon is led in a dreamlike state to the river's edge. Although he does not know how to swim, when he hears the screams of a mother pleading for someone to save her drowning child, Salomon dives in and—with the crucial assistance of the allegorical figures—succeeds in rescuing the child. Such is the episode in which Salomon, for all his greed and dishonesty,

16. Mallarmé, *Oeuvres complètes,* 455.

works his salvation. Saute-au-ciel, one of the *trois justiciers,* has become a figure of saving grace.

It is an odd resolution to a conflict that began as a replication of the central episode of the Joan of Arc legend; it is as though Joan's "voices" had come to realize that their principal mission was to work the salvation of Joan's principal persecutor. How are we to understand it? The record presents us with three curious elements to guide us:

1. In the *New Yorker* story of July 1943 on Maeterlinck, we read of a new play he has written that "developed out of a traffic accident Mme Maeterlinck got into while driving [their] little French car. It was in collision with a Cadillac containing a banker's wife and it sustained abrasions which Mme Maeterlinck considered were not her fault. She took the matter to Magistrate's Court, as a step toward bringing suit for the damage, but the magistrate, whose name was Solomon, benevolently said, after hearing the case, 'Why don't you ladies just shake hands and forget about it?'" Mme Maeterlinck did so, but her husband, we are told, was "burned up" by the incident and turned it into a full-length play.[17] Thus the corrupt judge Salomon was originally a woefully indifferent American magistrate whose defects were deliberately blackened in Maeterlinck's tale of Tristanelle and her corrupt guardian. But why then work his salvation?

2. In a 1942 text of homage to America, published in *La voix de France,* a journal edited by his fellow Belgian Robert Goffin, Maeterlinck spun the following image for America's relation to Europe: "A skiff on which a woman, children, an old man, several who are wounded and one who is sick have taken refuge is swallowed up by the eddies of the river. A decent man sees the shipwreck from a bridge above. He doesn't know how to swim, but without hesitating plunges into the water to help those about to perish. He learns how to swim by saving them. That is what America is doing. More recently civilized than those she is snatching from death, she is saving thirty centuries of civilization."[18] The figure of the nonswimmer effecting his own salvation by saving a drowning innocent is thus simultaneously that of Salomon in *Les trois justiciers* and wartime America itself. Combine

17. "Sore at Solomon," *New Yorker,* July 24, 1943, 15.

18. Maurice Maeterlinck, in *La voix de France,* May 15, 1942; quoted in Horemans, "Maeterlinck, Goffin, et les Etats-Unis," 18.

the reference to the corrupt magistrate in the *New Yorker* and the image of the self-sacrificing lifesaver in *La voix de France,* and one has the image of an evolving affection for the country he had spent years holding at bay.

3. There is a third Solomon in Maeterlinck's wartime writing. In *L'autre monde ou le cadran stellaire,* the sixth volume of what he called his "Pascalian" series, the author inserts a short development titled "Le jugement de Salomon."[19] After rehearsing the famous anecdote from the Book of Kings (culminating in Solomon's announcement that he would cut a baby in two and divide it between two bickering mothers), Maeterlinck notes that additional parchment fragments relating to the episode had been found in the vicinity of Alexandria. The new material informs us that the women vying for the surviving child were mistress and servant. The mother of the dead child was the mistress, and after the ruse had revealed the true mother, Solomon nonetheless awarded the surviving child to the mistress because he would in any event be happier with her. "Whereupon," Maeterlinck continues, "he invited the two rivals to make up and shake hands. The slave did not dare disobey." But this was precisely Magistrate Solomon's counsel in the New York courtroom as relayed by the author to the *New Yorker.* The mistress in the revised version of the Bible was the driver of the Cadillac. As for the servant (Mme Maeterlinck), *L'autre monde* tells us, "barely had she touched the hand of the other woman than she let out a howl of grief and took flight, rushing up the steps of a stairway leading to a terrace, from which she threw herself into the void, crashing against the stones of a courtyard as bleached as a gravestone" (152). Now "Le jugement de Salomon" is coupled in the volume with another episode from the Old Testament (Genesis), "Les circoncis de Sichem," in which the sons of Jacob massacre an entire population as the males lie prostrate convalescing from circumcision. Maeterlinck waxes ironic on the mores of the saintly family of Jacob. Indeed, there are moments of *L'autre monde,* a book of Vedic enthusiasm, in which one feels the Jews alone are excluded from the broader spiritual community: "Our planet is beginning to vomit up certain peoples. It was about time" (54).

19. Maurice Maeterlinck, "Le jugement de Salomon," in *L'autre monde ou le cadran stellaire* (New York: Editions de la Maison Française, 1942), 150–52.

But if the Solomon of *L'autre monde*, in his corruption, is essentially Jewish and the Salomon of *Les trois justiciers*, in his, is tendentially American—if a certain anti-Americanism came to reinforce a certain anti-Semitism—it should not be forgotten that Maeterlinck's "Salomon" is preeminently en route to salvation. The final whiteness would be neither the blanking out of King Charles's mind (in *Jeanne d'Arc*) nor the watermarked paper "intervening" to vitiate the will inscribed on it, but the white radiance of paradise. For the poet, it appears, had decided to spend his New York years writing, in dramatic form, his own *Paradiso*. He called it *Le jugement dernier*.

The play's central conceit is the emergence of a number of families from their respective mausoleums as though they had just awakened from a long night's sleep. "To die is to awaken" [*Mourir, c'est se réveiller*], as Maeterlinck, offering the flip side of life-is-but-a-dream, put it in *L'autre monde* (213). Gradually it dawns on all assembled that they are not dead, but have returned to life; Judgment Day has come. As the resurrected mill about their tombs, taking stock of "Life as it returns," it is almost as though they were figures for the community of exiles, stunned, amid the killing, to realize that they are still alive. For Maeterlinck in particular, preparing his final journey, the irony that such a journey should be to the land that had organized a Blue Bird Campaign for Happiness for his last arrival must have loomed large.

It may even have played a role in shaping the plot of *Le jugement dernier*. For the eschatological vision offered by Maeterlinck is of an "other world" in which there are no losers: purgatory does not exist; hell is there, but empty; and finally, heaven is the only viable option. Dante must surely have been on the playwright's mind. His own Paolo and Francesca, Pelléas and Mélisande, make a cameo appearance. It is as though the "primal love" or will to perfect moral order that Dante had inscribed over the gates of his Inferno had attained such a pitch of metaphysical grace that Inferno itself—*sub speciaie aeternitatis*—had been emptied in the process. Everyone has done what he or she was "born to do" and thus need not fear damnation. Not Cain, not Judas, not Torquemada, not even, we are told, Hitler.

Or perhaps *Le jugement dernier* represents the triumph not of Dante, but of the Goethe who finally opted to *save* Faust—despite the bargain!—at the end of his poem. For Maeterlinck, in any event, heaven is our only option. With Pelléas and Mélisande, and then Hitler, out of the way, the play, in its third and final act, turns into something of a patriotic pageant. Among those seen streaming heavenward are those who have died for their country and mothers who have borne great losses during the war. Strains of *La Marseillaise* are heard. Maeterlinck had opted to exit with a kitsch *Paradiso*, in which all contestants in the game of life would be winners. The blindnesses of such a perspective are patent. When a child is being beaten because her father is a Jew, we are told we can anticipate a solution: on the day of the resurrection there will be no more—not anti-Semites, but—Jews! It is a perspective that may have intrigued the great Zola in his novelized version of the Dreyfus affair, *Vérité*, but to hear the cheery anticipation of a world without Jews in 1942 is as chilling a perspective as any in Maeterlinck.

As for the roots—or entelechy—of his eschatology in *Le jugement dernier,* they become clearest in the final stage direction in the play: "Clash of cymbals. The light at the gates goes out in a final flash. The curtain falls brutally. One sees floating on it the inscription over the entrance to the principal cemetery of Palm Beach: DEATH IS TOO UNIVERSAL NOT TO BE A BLESSING."[20] The world exists, then, in order to attain the luminous perfection of Palm Beach, Florida. With his no-fault eschatology, the poet of the Flemish north had finally come to the luminous end of the road. As though paradise—where one need not speak, wrote Maeterlinck, because all that is required is a beatific smile—perpetually hummed a chorus of "I'm O.K., You're O.K."

> Les sept filles d'Orlamonde,
> Quand la fée fut morte,
> Les sept filles d'Orlamonde,
> Ont cherché les portes.
>
> Ont allumé leur sept lampes,
> Ont ouvert les tours,
> Ont ouvert quatre cent salles,
> Sans trouver le jour.
> — MAETERLINCK, *Quinze chansons*

There was a final bit of business the American press in particular delighted in. If Caligula and even Hitler seemed condemned to heaven,

20. Maurice Maeterlinck, *Le jugement dernier,* unpaginated.

perhaps it might be time to put a posthumous end to the legendary spat with Debussy. On February 10, 1941, *Newsweek* ran an article under the headline: "A First for Maeterlinck: Poet Buries Old 'Pelléas' Feud to Hear Opera in English." The weekly recalled the circumstances of the disagreement over the casting of Georgette Leblanc in the role of Mélisande and noted that Maeterlinck had sworn never to attend a performance. "Maeterlinck's 'never' became 'hardly ever' in New York January 17, 1920, when he heard Mary Garden sing the first act at the old Hammerstein Opera House before clumping out in disgust. Last week the author of 'The Blue Bird' again broke his resolve: he attended the Philadelphia [Opera Company's] rendition, and, although, the opera was in a language he does not understand very well, this time he stayed to the end of the performance in the Academy of Music."[21] When asked for his impression at a reception after the performance, Count Maeterlinck remained grimly silent. The countess, however, explained: "Well, you see, he doesn't like music . . . he doesn't hear it."

An odd reconciliation, in many ways as tone-deaf as the larger reconciliation, Palm Beach of the soul, toward which Maeterlinck progressed, play by unplayable play, during his years in New York. Performances were few and far between. In the sketch *L'enfant qui ne voulait pas naître*, performed at Carnegie Hall in the summer of 1942, a mother fleeing the war could be heard encouraging an imaginary infant who would prefer not to be born into a world of such woe. For aficionados of Maeterlinck, the pessimism of old King Arkël, the Maeterlinckian motif of the *inéclos*, had made it to the age of the blitzkrieg. A legacy? When Symbolist listlessness descends to the level of farce, and the plays and sketches become truly laughable, one detects on the horizon perspectives about to be opened by Beckett alone.

The dramatist whom Octave Mirbeau had famously saluted in 1890 as "superior" to Shakespeare would hang on long enough to pick up an honorary doctorate at Rollins Park College in Palm Beach, and deliver a speech in English from which it was clear above all that Florida

21. W. D. Halls, *Maurice Maeterlinck*, 131, on the other hand, quotes a letter of praise from Maeterlinck to Mary Garden on the occasion of her performance in 1920: "I had sworn to myself never to see the lyric drama *Pelléas et Mélisande*. Yesterday I violated my vow and I am a happy man. For the first time I have entirely understood my own play, and because of you."

was for him a surrogate Orlamonde. When the war finally ended, health problems—double pneumonia, a broken arm—kept him in America another two years. Then, in August 1947, at age eighty-five, he sailed back to the Riviera and the last months of a life of seclusion by the sea.

FOUR

Denis de Rougemont
New York Gnostic

... but rest assured: we were no more absent from you than from ourselves. You were "occupied," we were in exile, and each of us in the inadmissible, in a state of profound dispossession, cast into question at
the worst moment, in the hour of least resistance. Our anguish was
to think: will we speak the same language on the day of our return to
France—to which France, and to which Europe? We were subject to
the erosion of exile, less brutal, to be sure, but more intimate than that
of occupation. A conqueror never occupies anything but the exterior,
but the foreigner infiltrates the very heart of being. How would one
resist him? He's a friend.

—DENIS DE ROUGEMONT, *Journal d'une époque*

There was a tendency, on the part of more than one émigré, to view
the momentous trip to New York as somehow fated, as though it were
some incalculably circuitous trip *home*. The Belgian poet Robert
Goffin, for example, Maeterlinck's closest associate in the city and the
force behind the reconstitution of the International PEN Club, spent
his years in the city under the spell of his discovery that the Latin on
the original seal of New Amsterdam read NOVA BELGICA.[1] A combination of dogged research and inspired speculation led him to the
conclusion that a significant portion of the Dutch who settled Man-

---

1. Robert Goffin, *Les Wallons fondateurs de New York* (Gilly: Institut Jules Destrée,
1970), 93.

hattan were in fact French-speaking Walloons in flight from persecution after a failed plot to assassinate the duke of Alba. So "French was
the original language of the families of New York," as W. E. Griffis, one
of Goffin's sources, claimed; Gowanus was the result of a calligrapher's
embellishment of the initial O in Owanus, Latin for the Belgian town
Ohain; and, most irresistibly—because most transparently, in this
midnight of Franco-Belgian aspiration—Peter Minuit, the legendary
purchaser of the island of Manhattan, was as Francophone as his
name, misspelled and mispronounced by generations of New York
schoolchildren, plainly implied (39, 47, 73).

Then there was the case of the irrepressible Gustave Cohen, eminent medievalist at the Sorbonne, dean of the School of Letters at New
York's newly founded Ecole Libre des Hautes Etudes, and staunch
Gaullist.[2] Was there not something vaguely familiar about Manhattan,
he wondered, as he first took in the city's skyscrapers? "Yes, it's the
impression of a cathedral, not one, since everything in this vast country is in scale with its greatness, *a Forest of Cathedrals* whose sheaves of
columns and twinned towers are evoked by its buildings—ever upward."[3] Whereby the author of *La grande clarté du moyen âge* begins a
Gothic riff on *Excelsior*.

For all its bustle, New York had something of the empty neutrality
of a mirror offering a reflection of intimate realities left behind in
Europe. Whence our third example, the first impression of the city
received by Denis de Rougemont, the Swiss intellectual, a longtime
resident of Paris, who will be the focus of this chapter. No, for all its
towering heights, Manhattan was not at all Gothic. There was something about the quality of the light filtering between the skyscrapers
into the canyons of downtown that was key. As he observed in a
journal entry of October 1940: "No one had told me . . . that New York
was an Alpine city. I sensed it on the first evening of October, when the
setting sun ignited the heights of the skyscrapers with that ethereal
orangelike color that one sees on the crests of the rocky walls while the
valleys fill up with cool shadow. And there I was at the bottom of a

2. On Gustave Cohen, see Henri Peyre's letter to Colin Nettlebeck, quoted in Nettlebeck, *Forever French*, 88: Cohen is said to be "full of ideas and plans, full of himself,
too, and often criticised here for personality reasons."
3. Gustave Cohen, *Lettres aux Américains* (Montreal: Editions de l'Arbre, 1942), 30.

gorge, in that street of blackened brick through which there passed a harsh and salubrious wind."[4]

In many ways, Denis de Rougemont was the most ubiquitous French-speaking intellectual of the wartime emigration. Less than two years earlier, on November 29, 1938, he had presented the enthralling chapter called "Love and War" of what would soon be *L'amour et l'Occident* to the Collège de Sociologie in Paris.[5] Publication of that volume, delayed to make allowance for Plon to bring out Charles de Gaulle's *La France et son armée*, did not come until the following year. It was a book to which Rougemont would return throughout his career, enriching successive editions of what Jean Starobinski called one of the "landmarks of the intellectual life of the century."[6] Rougemont, that is, arrived in New York on the crest of his major work, and his ubiquity in the émigré intellectual life of the city offers some measure of the energy he derived from riding that crest.

We find him, for instance, writing copy for the French section of the Office of War Information in May 1942. It was the words of Rougemont, read on the Voice of America and broadcast by the BBC, that informed France itself, once clearance arrived, of the Allied landing in North Africa on November 8, 1942.[7] Rougemont himself wondered what the effect on his prose would be of writing only French that he could readily imagine transposed into English. Already in 1943, he could be heard voicing a query that would not gain wider currency— once again under pressure of American English—for another forty years: "What would it be like to be a great writer in a dead language?" (534).

To be writing for the Voice of America meant, curiously enough, to have one's words parroted by André Breton and Claude Lévi-Strauss, to be in the extraordinary position of ventriloquizing the intellectual founders of surrealism and structuralism. And indeed one finds a sporadic record of both Breton and Lévi-Strauss in Rougemont's wartime

4. Denis de Rougemont, *Journal d'une époque, 1926–1946* (Paris: Gallimard, 1968), 451.

5. See Denis Hollier, *Le Collège de Sociologie, 1937–1939* (Paris: Gallimard, 1995), 403–47.

6. Jean Starobinski, "Un essai au long cours," *Cadmos* 44 (winter 1988–89): 27.

7. Rougemont, *Journal d'une époque*, 508.

diary. Breton: "Superbly *courtois*, patient as a lion intent on ignoring the bars of his cage. . . . He arrives to lend us his noble voice, embellished by the whistle of its slight hiss" (514). We find Breton eventually predicting the arrival of fascism in the United States within six months of an American victory (551). But perhaps the most notable touch is the use of the word *courtois* to characterize the surrealist "pope" on the part of a writer whose major work had just grounded so much of Western culture—putting the *oc* back in *Occident?*—in a proper assessment of *cortezia*, the southern tradition of courtly love and its ramifications throughout European history. As for Lévi-Strauss, he figures in Rougemont's journal above all for his wryness. After so many years of searching for money in Europe in order to bring ideas to fruition, Lévi-Strauss lamented that the American dilemma appeared to be precisely the inverse: searching for ideas in order to justify the expense (501).

Yet it would be an error to restrict Rougemont's engagement with surrealism and structuralism to the bizarre ventriloquism of the Voice of America. For the surrealists he wrote a stunning few pages—entitled "Angérone," after the goddess of silence—for *VVV*, the New York version of *Minotaure*. (The threefold V was intended to transmit a *voeu* or will to return to an inhabitable world, a victory over the "forces of regression and death," and, compounding that, a further victory or two over everything standing in the way of that greater "emancipation" the surrealists found so intoxicating.) "Angérone" is a text, we shall see, that resonates remarkably with the larger theoretical project that had been occupying Rougemont since those few feverish months in 1938 during which he wrote *L'amour et l'Occident*.

As for Rougemont's relation to structuralism, it takes us to the position he held before working for the Office of War Information, for it was at the same Ecole Libre des Hautes Etudes where Lévi-Strauss met Roman Jakobson and dreamed up the merger that would sweep the world under the label "French structuralism" that Rougemont delivered his lectures called "Les règles du jeu." Years later he would refer to the effort as "something of a first definition of structuralist thought *avant la lettre*" (736). A principal relic of the course survives as a grant application (presumably to the newly founded Bollingen Foundation) outlining his project. An effort is made in the outlined project to subordinate the ludic function to considerations of structure:

"It's regular." Wherein one recognizes a constraining structure, be it fragmentary, rudimentary, limited in its power (time and space), or englobing a complete set.

There is as well play [*jeu*], when there is structure.

A definition of the ludic function: *to play is to test the structures of the real.* (509)

A structuralist Rougemont? The evidence of the lectures remains too fragmentary to allow incontrovertible conclusions, but to anyone who has worked through Rougemont's construction of what may be called the homology between *cortezia* and the theological heresy of Catharism in a crucial "book" of *L'amour et l'Occident,* indeed to anyone who has taken seriously the author's admission in that work that his effort has been to construct "illustrative and illuminating analogies" rather than to confirm "any specific thesis," the protostructuralist impetus of Rougemont's masterwork of 1938—before the Jungian mantle descended on his work—will be clear.[8] In the interim, it may be recalled that Rougemont's sole Swiss associate at the Ecole was the psychoanalyst Raymond de Saussure. That Rougemont, in frequent contact with Ferdinand de Saussure's son, should be dreaming of himself as a structuralist *avant la lettre* even as Lévi-Strauss—how many doors away?—was preparing to launch what would officially be known as "French structuralism," is in any event a circumstance almost iconic in its suggestiveness.

Protostructuralist, sometime surrealist, lecturer at the Ecole Libre, writer for the Voice of America, Denis de Rougemont was all over wartime New York. In May 1941 he was saluted at Carnegie Hall when the emphatically Swiss oratorio *Nicolas de Flue,* on which he collaborated with Arthur Honegger, was performed with the Dessoff Choirs under the direction of Paul Boepple—before ever being heard in Switzerland.[9] In September 1942, we find him posing—on his belly, his legs raised up—for Saint-Exupéry's illustrations for *Le petit prince* in Bevin House, the palatial home on Long Island that he shared with the Saint-Exupérys (521). "Someday you'll be able to say, pointing to the drawing: 'It's me!'" as "Saint-Ex" joked. "Saint-Ex": Rougemont, who had sailed to America on September 12, 1940, aboard the SS *Exeter,* once

8. Denis de Rougemont, *L'amour et l'Occident* (Paris: Plon, 1972), 134.
9. Rougemont, *Journal d'une époque,* 521.

observed that all the ships leaving Europe for America at the time seemed to bear names beginning with *Ex: Exeter, Excalibur, Excambion* (446). Might it be because he was particularly alive to the danger of exile degenerating into sterile nostalgia, a world subordinated to the category *ex-,* that Rougemont's New York years proved so prolific?

Of all his New York projects, the most significant was the book he wrote under the title *La part du diable.* He would later recall Breton's envy of his ability to redeem the apparent *temps perdu* of an American exile through that volume. " 'It's rather strange,' Breton told me one day, 'yes, you know, we are wasting precious years here in America, but you at least will have done *that,* you will have redeemed your stay in America,' which was a great joy for me, the fact that that sentence had been uttered by him" (778). *La part du diable* was published in 1942 in Brentano's French series. When it appeared, Brentano's decided to devote a full window display to the book, an opportunity that inspired Marcel Duchamp, André Breton, and Kurt Seligmann to volunteer their services and execute a memorable surrealist window display on Fifth Avenue. Among Rougemont's admirers was Mary Mellon, who, with the intention of publishing Jung's complete works in English, founded (with her husband Paul Mellon) the Bollingen Foundation, named after the Swiss village where Jung lived. Gradually, it was decided to launch the Bollingen publishing venture with an expanded English version of what was called, in Haakon Chevalier's translation, *The Devil's Share.* A generous fellowship was awarded Rougemont so that he might revise the work—on the Mellon estate in Oak Hills, Virginia. When the book appeared in 1944, it was reviewed by Hannah Arendt (in the *Partisan Review*), Lionel Trilling (in the *Kenyon Review,* which had run an earlier review of the original New York French edition), and Reinhold Niebuhr (in the *Nation*). All felt the book important, though Arendt and Trilling, as we shall see, voiced considerable reservations. Here, then, was a work of grand ambition by a member of the Francophone exile community, a work on Satan that Breton read as a kind of redemption of that very exile. It is to its curious argument and its relation to Rougemont's masterwork, *L'amour et l'Occident,* published just three years earlier, that we now shall turn.

It was no doubt Gide who communicated the impact of *L'amour et l'Occident* most forcefully when he confided to Jean Delay that Rougemont's book had succeeded in explaining to him what a reading of

Freud had been unable to clarify. Rougemont's argument hinged on positing a forgotten "psychical revolution of the twelfth century" within whose parameters mental and emotional life in the West continued to function.[10] That revolution consisted in the cryptic survival—indeed, flourishing—of Catharism, a mystical Christian heresy in the south of France, long after it had been violently suppressed in the Albigensian Crusade. The heresy survived by way of its twin manifestation, *cortezia,* the love poetry of the troubadours and the literature of love that spread north in the courtly novel and from there came to dominate the literature of the West. Catharism, a mix of Platonism at its most "Oriental" and Manicheanism, was a mystical will to return to the "luminous indistinction" of divinity, a gnostic aspiration to leave behind the foul materiality of this world in an experience of mystical rapture (68). Rougemont's claim was that the troubadours, poets of erotic rapture, were at bottom the "poorly disciplined disciples" of the Cathars. Moreover, they lived at the same time and in the same territory (and on occasion in the same châteaux) as the heretics, and wrote something on the order of erotic allegories of Catharist theology. Finally, it was argued that we, their literary heirs, whether readers of novels (classically of adulterous passion) or viewers of cinema (romance), were unwittingly in the grip of a twelfth-century "spiritual heresy whose key we have lost" (153).

Tristan, the courtly myth of adulterous passion, with its odd investment in proliferating obstacles to fulfillment, was Rougemont's tutelary text, the tale in which the secular myth of self-annihilation in mystical union came close to perfection. Indeed, it was for the author as though the West had long been living with a Tristan complex whose surprising ramifications *L'amour et l'Occident* would undertake to chart. Thus Gide's comparison of Rougemont and Freud becomes clearer, though Rougemont's project was in fact a significant reversal of that of Freud. Whereas Freud was inclined to ground mystical propensities in sexuality, it was Rougemont's contention that modernity's obsession with sexual transgression was to be traced back to a forgotten mystical heresy. In this, the Swiss thinker no doubt had greater affinities with Gershom Scholem, who at the same time was grounding the Jewish Enlightenment in a very different mystical

10. Rougemont, *L'amour et l'Occident,* 120.

heresy, Sabbatianism, whose nature and persistence had long since lapsed into oblivion.[11]

Still, what binds Rougemont to the case of Freud is the oddly impassioned compulsion of his argument (against the delusions of passion). There was something uncanny about the status of the "Catharist hypothesis" in the author's mind. He claimed to know few hypotheses that were "more stimulating and more irritating to the mind": "for it seems equally difficult to reject it and to accept it, to demonstrate it and to renounce all belief in it."[12] Reading of the compelling attractiveness of the idea, unprovable but too entrancing to relinquish, one thinks of Freud's quite analogous statements about his attraction to the notion of a "death instinct" in *Beyond the Pleasure Principle.* Years later Rougemont would react to Henri Marrou's suggestion that the "Catharist hypothesis" ended up imposing itself on the reader of his book like an "obsessive temptation" by suggesting that such—beyond any criterion of falsifiability—was precisely his own experience, one that, as a reader, he had had with Ferdinand de Saussure's compulsive decoding of anagrams encrypted in Latin poetry (394).

Against the Catharist-troubadour cult of sublimation into divinity, a kind of dying upward, Rougemont would affirm the *descent* of the divine Word into flesh in the orthodox Christian doctrine of incarnation (69). Eros and its passion would be countered by Christian agape, content to love the other not in her assumption into divinity, but rather in her earthly humility. The Christian, we are told, "loves the other *as he is*—instead of loving the idea of love or its fatal and delectable *brûlure*" (70). Agape's symbol is the marriage of Christ and the Church—which becomes an emblem of marriage itself. But to affirm the nonconformity of fidelity in marriage in Kierkegaardian terms *by virtue of its very absurdity* is a strikingly weak conclusion. For the passion of Rougemont's work lies not with marriage but with . . . passion. More specifically, the intellectual charm of the work lies in

11. Sabbatianism flourished in the wake of the apostasy of the "false Messiah," Sabbatai Zevi, in the seventeenth century and after. Based on the proposition that at this stage of the redemptive process, Jews must enter transgressively into evil in order to defeat it from within, it issued in what Scholem called a full-blown antinomianism. See Gershom Scholem, "Redemption through Sin," in *The Messianic Idea in Judaism* (New York: Schocken, 1971).

12. Rougemont, *L'amour et l'Occident,* 88.

the will to effect a fusion, against all probability, between the "dark Cathars, whom their asceticism constrained to flee all contact with the other sex, and the luminous troubadours, mad with joy, it is said, singing of love, springtime, dawn, blossoming orchards, and the Lady" (88). Plainly agape, with its imperative to respect the otherness of the other, would be on the side of those traditional scholars who had little truck with Rougemont's ingenious conflation of the two. So Rougemont's impassioned polemic against inherently masochistic passion as it descends to us, in degraded form, from the Albigensian mystics of southern France is at significant cross-purposes with itself.

There is a second circumstance in Rougemont's work that runs suggestively counter to the principal polemical thrust of *L'amour et l'Occident*. Recall that the Catharist infusion into literature was effected decisively in the various versions of Tristan—from Gottfried von Strasbourg to Richard Wagner. Indeed, if passion, as Rougemont later suggested, resembles in its disabling effects nothing so much as an allergy *that one would find delectable,* his book would in some respects resemble the philosophico-literary equivalent of a potent antihistamine. Now in his *Journal d'une époque,* Rougemont recalls that at the time he was writing his treatise on love, specifically during the night of the June solstice of 1938, he went to see Wagner's *Tristan* at the Paris Opéra. "The taxi taking us there at dusk crosses the courtyard of the Louvre midst the sudden blaze of huge flames surging from the colonnade. At the Opéra, the sets are frightful, as usual, the German voices quite suitable, and Brangaine's cry from atop the dawn tower: '*Habet acht! Habet acht!—Schon weicht dem Tag—die Nacht!*' renews unfailingly the most submerging-exalting emotion I have ever received from an art."[13] The passage reads as a succumbing to an attack. Here too, then, we find Rougemont manifestly overwhelmed by the very myth he would dismantle.

Significantly, at the time he made his way through the flames (more accident than apocalypse), Rougemont was also working on a "long article on Hitlerism." It may well have turned into "Passion and the Origin of Hitlerism," one of the first texts he would publish in the United States after his arrival in 1940. That extended essay, which interpreted Nazism from the perspective of the categories of *L'amour*

13. Rougemont, *Journal d'une époque,* 366.

et l'Occident, appeared in the *Review of Politics* in 1941, and offers an intriguing transition to the major work of Rougemont's New York exile, *La part du diable.*

The essay's principal argument is that "Hitlerism" effected a massive displacement of individual passion to the collective entity of the nation, whose representatives were the party and the *Führer.*[14] Rougemont proceeds to a cursory reading of *Mein Kampf* and determines that Hitler has worked a surprisingly effective transformation of Western "passion" in the newly demoralized Europe of the post–World War I era. Through a technique of "collective hypnosis," he has keyed into the unconscious of the German masses, cathected their passions in the newly sublime entity of the nation, proliferated those obstacles—the ever expanding geographical borders of a Germany said to be stifling for want of Lebensraum—on which passion, since Tristan, had thrived, and finally invoked the ideal of transfiguration through death (in this case, the heroism of war) that had been the aim of passion since its Catharist origins in the twelfth century. It is a powerful mix, worked to demonic perfection by the "most gifted" of the West's *directeurs d'inconscient,* in the face of whom our liberal democratic leaders are understandably "in a position of psychological inferiority," indeed "helpless" (72, 80).

It is as though Rougemont could be so effective a reader of "Hitlerism" solely because Hitler, unlike the liberal leaders of democracy, had at some level intuited (and adapted) the central intuition of Rougemont's thesis on the overwhelming importance of self-destructive idealist passion in Western culture. Or rather: the leaders of democracy, to the extent that they were heirs of the French Revolution, were no more than outmoded predecessors in the very process that Hitler had brought to a pinnacle of sinister perfection. According to the section of *L'amour et l'Occident* that Rougemont had read to the Collège de Sociologie in November 1938, just after Munich, it was the French Revolution, culminating in the campaigns of Bonaparte, that had effected the first massive transposition of individual passion to the collective level.[15] The Battle of Valmy, which had according to Goethe

---

14. Denis de Rougemont, "Passion and the Origin of Hitlerism," *Review of Politics* 3, no. 1 (1941): 64.

15. Hollier, *Le Collège de Sociologie,* 432.

marked a decisive change in world history, represented a victory of collective passion over "exact science." Thus Hitler's accomplishment had been to revive the grand achievement of the French Revolution: effecting a massive transfer of libido from individuals to a collective object. In between had come the mass long-range killing of Verdun. War had become less a victory over the other than a will to annihilate the other, a process that effectively neutralized the collective passion of the nation in arms that had been the grand legacy of the French Revolution. For the prewar author of *L'amour et l'Occident,* this meant that the catastrophic tradition whose evolution Rougemont had so ingeniously tracked was alive and well, alas, above all in Germany. One senses as much when the author, so recently overwhelmed by Wagner's *Tristan,* asks: "What superhuman Wagner will be up to the task of orchestrating the grandiose catastrophe of passion gone totalitarian?" Or when Rougemont observes that the totalitarian state constitutes a "solution" of sorts: "It is the response of the twentieth century, born of war, to the permanent threat that passion and the death instinct hold suspended over every society" (445).

In the 1941 text in the *Review of Politics,* the time was no longer for speculating on the coming of a super-Wagner to orchestrate the new collective *Tristan.* But Rougemont persisted, in a minor key, in affirming a certain continuity between the culture spawned by the French Revolution and that born of the Nazi revolution. "Once again," we read, "bourgeois demoralization and totalitarian moralization move in the same direction."[16] The suggestion here is that the anything-goes of private mores in the democracies and the government-dictated eugenics or higher hygiene of the new totalitarian dispensation had each stripped private life of those possibilities of exaltation through transgression without which "passion" will wilt. The big difference was that Hitler, in conformity with the central insight of *L'amour et l'Occident,* had found a thriving collective outlet, however sinister, for that propensity, and the democracies had not. All of which may explain the rushed conclusion of "Passion and the Origin of Hitlerism." If the liberal democracies were infected in their seed with the same ill that had given rise to the malign flower of Nazism, help would have to come from elsewhere. "Therefore, I can only conclude this essay with

16. Rougemont, "Passion and the Origin of Hitlerism," 79.

an appeal to the Churches" (82). The essay, in which Catharism does not even appear (presumably for reasons of economy), nonetheless throws itself, in a closing gesture, a mere final sentence, at the foot of a church whose betrayal, in a twelfth-century heresy, marked the inception of the entire dialectic whose ramifications Rougemont had charted.

In a prewar review of *L'amour et l'Occident*, Sartre had suggested a profound affinity between Rougemont and his associate at the Collège de Sociologie, Roger Caillois.[17] Caillois had spent the war years in Buenos Aires, editing the Gaullist journal *Lettres Françaises*, and had in fact invited Rougemont to Argentina, a trip that was ultimately taken once funds were secured. In the last year of the war, Caillois published in Mexico a volume of essays titled *La communion des forts*. It was reviewed in a lengthy essay by Meyer Shapiro in the *Kenyon Review* under the title "French Reaction in Exile." Several affinities between the Caillois volume, as reviewed by the eminent New York critic, and Rougemont's own writing at the time are worth noting.

La communion des forts calls for intellectuals after the war to band together "as a communion of the strong to form a new society within the old and by force of their moral ideals [to] impose an authority on the chaotic unspiritual masses."[18] The model of the elite society would be either the Jesuits or the glamorous "secret brotherhood of noble outlaw-adventurers" known in Balzac as the Treize. On issues of method, Shapiro's critique could well be lodged against Rougemont. The strategy of indirection, "looking always for the psychological, the mythical, the vestigial, and metaphoric" in historical processes, an attachment to "the piquant and little detail, the amusing analogy," all aspects that seem to look ahead, are roundly condemned in Caillois— as indeed they might be in Rougemont (37). But the political resonances are the most telling. While condemning fascism, Caillois is said also to condemn democracy "as the seed of fascism" (31). Moreover, the plunge of "great masses of people" into the present war is said to be viewed by Caillois as "a kind of social vertigo, the fascination of the deadly, and transposes to the social group the psychological process of

17. Jean-Paul Sartre, "Denis de Rougemont: 'L'amour et l'Occident,' " in *Situations* (Paris: Gallimard, 1947), 1:58.

18. Meyer Shapiro, "French Reaction in Exile," *Kenyon Review* (winter 1945): 29.

the desperate gambler and the mad lover who pursues the woman who will lead him to destruction" (35). We have already encountered both motifs in Rougemont (who was as much a Gaullist as Caillois). By essay's end, Shapiro, writing before the war was over, recalled in a monitory note texts that we have already encountered, the harshly reactionary writings of Renan after the 1870 war. They are said to have inspired both Caillois and de Gaulle as much as they did Pétain. Whereby we encounter once again the tutelary grip of the 1870 paradigm in the New York of the 1940s, and the uncertainties surrounding de Gaulle and his supporters—Caillois, but potentially Rougemont as well—in the New York intelligentsia.

"Angérone," accompanied by a drawing by André Masson, was Rougemont's contribution to the second issue of the New York surrealist journal *VVV*. It is a two-page lyrical meditation on Angérone, goddess of silence. The author of *L'amour et l'Occident* begins with an expression of distrust toward all who would define—or even speak of—love. "All eloquence is of love, excited by the love that makes it flourish. But love itself is a thing of silence. *That* which I cannot speak of without offending its greatness is what ignites my thought. Nothing can be said of love itself, but neither can anything be said, except by love, if indeed something is truly said."[19] At the heart of love, then, is silence in that nothing can be said of it. But also because "when desire seizes on a man, it sometimes makes him mute. It even happens that desire first manifests itself by precisely such muteness." Now this central silence is said to be in some way linked to the phenomenon of hypnosis. Whereupon we recall that the specific technique of Hitler in the 1941 article was hypnosis. Might it be that the silence to which Rougemont pays homage in this lyrical text is related to a certain unspeakability of the bond between the phenomenon of passion whose very core he would celebrate in "Angérone" and the political monstrosity whose affinity with that "passion" he pretended to demonstrate in "Passion and the Origin of Hitlerism"? A page later we read: "This knowledge is forbidden. And it is the approach of the violation of the interdiction that imposes on lovers their silence, the fascination of a sacred horror, and

19. Denis de Rougemont, "Angérone," *VVV* 2 (March 1943): 69. On Rougemont's dealings with the surrealists, see Bruno Ackermann, "Amitiés surréalistes," in *Denis de Rougemont: Une biographie intellectuelle* (Geneva: Labor et Fides, 1996), 751–55.

the attraction of mortal fear."[20] In his *Journal d'Allemagne,* those words were applied to Rougemont's experience of a Nazi rally in Frankfurt. As the Horst Wessel Lied rises from the masses, their arms outstretched, Rougemont, his hands in his pockets, understands what he is witnessing: "It can be understood only by way of a particular kind of shudder and heartbeat—while the mind remains lucid. What I experience at present is what must be called *l'horreur sacrée.*"[21] From one sacred horror to the other, the spark has been communicated. Call it a loss of innocence.

For all his activity, Denis de Rougemont frequently found New York a depressing experience. A stroll in Times Square on a rainy evening after a dinner by himself, for example, struck him as the opposite of a spiritual exercise: "Une véritable centrifugation de l'être" (460). But the aspect of America that most troubled him was an inability to believe in evil. He mentioned this reservation one evening at the home of the theologian Reinhold Niebuhr, editor of the journal *Christianity in Crisis* (465). But it was at the Cosmopolitan Club, a few days later, in conversation with Jacques Maritain, that the project of a book took shape. Both were in agreement that what is lacking in America (and democracies in general) is a belief in the devil. From this perspective Maeterlinck, doyen of the Francophone writers in wartime New York, had been thoroughly Americanized. His *Jugement dernier* had revealed a hell totally uninhabited, a heaven whose all-welcoming portals bore an inscription from the cemetery of Palm Beach. Rougemont, at the risk of being regarded as the madman who saw the devil everywhere, would be the anti-Maeterlinck of the New York colony. But there were other risks as well. By speaking to the Americans of evil, might one not come to be viewed as the devil himself? Maritain encouraged him to run the risk, recalling the case of the Irish evangelist who, having told the Swiss that martyrs were our best intercessors with God, was in short order killed by his interlocutors—who ended up becoming excellent Christians in the process (469). The meeting in the Cosmopolitan Club was transposed as the beginning of *La part du diable* and established the tone. The book at its most characteristic

20. Rougemont, "Angérone," 70.
21. Rougemont, *Journal d'une époque,* 320.

aspires to being a set of paradoxical parables in the service of an unsettling thesis.

La part du diable is in its way also a theory of the unconscious. The devil's primary stratagem, we are told, was identified by Baudelaire: his "cleverest wile is to convince us that he does not exist."[22] He is never more diabolical than in effacing his own traces. In this, he is the consummate trickster, *un homme à trucs,* a double or triple agent. Indeed, so devious is he that his existence can be neither demonstrated nor portrayed. To draw his—presumably anthropomorphic—portrait is already to grant him a victory. He is the "absolute anti-model," a principle disruptive of the very category of form itself. As for demonstration, Rougemont makes clear that his interpretive essay is commanded by the imperatives not of logic but of *jouissance.* "It is no more than an attempt to interpret certain shortcomings [*déboires*] of our time by referring them to the activity of the only being to whom these can give cause for rejoicing [*le seul être qui s'en réjouisse*]" (13). This principle of unconsciousness, allergic to anthropomorphic form, commanded by considerations of extreme pleasure, moreover, is linguistic. "The great satanic ambition must be to seize our speech in our mouths, in order to distort the witness we bear at its source. And this is why the Bible energetically affirms that when we lie 'it is the Devil himself who sticks out his tongue in our own' [*qui tire sa langue dans notre langue*]" (30). Our language, by virtue or vice of Satan, is from its inception doubly inscribed.

Yet it would be wrong to underestimate the theological dimension of Rougemont's phenomenology. Lucifer is a fallen angel or inadequate messenger, but the opacity of this rebellious signifier, its refusal to transmit the divine news as emitted, is, by definition, heretical. And the particular heresy pinpointed by Rougemont is familiar to us: "At the root of every temptation lies the glimpse of the possibility of reaching divinity by a shorter road than that of reality" (23). Or, in Eve's terms, the sin is the very idea of "divinizing oneself," becoming like a god. Wherein we rediscover the principal motif of Catharism as analyzed in *L'amour et l'Occident.* The simulacrum that had worked its way into our language at the outset, passing itself off as second nature, effacing its presence but affording—on some other extra-

22. Denis de Rougemont, *La part du diable* (New York: Brentano's, 1942), 17.

human scene—effects of *jouissance*, is the twelfth-century heresy central to Rougemont's masterwork of 1939.

That the devil is presented to us—via Baudelaire—as a principle of unconsciousness (to the extent that there might be no finer figure of the devil, we are told at one point, than a liberal intellectual denying the devil's existence) means that an author of Rougemont's sophistication would inevitably confront the general question of the relation of his essay to psychoanalysis. Rougemont's elliptical answer to those who would "drown the Devil in the murky waters of the unconscious" is a curious fable told by Jung about a patient suffering from a paralyzing bird phobia. The analysis, based on a clear sense of what birds so often symbolize, advanced rapidly; the patient's general state improved considerably, but she continued to be unable to take a step into the street without fearing that she would immediately be attacked by birds. After a year without progress on the bird front, Jung began to despair and was about to terminate the analysis. What was to be a final session took place on a day of such extreme heat that Jung decided to hold it outdoors in a small pavilion, beside his villa, on the Zurich lakeshore. "They went out, the lady leading the way. No sooner were they in the garden, Jung concluded, than . . . well, *the birds attacked her*" (42). Thus, without further comment, ends the first section of Rougemont's essay.

Plainly the effort has been to affirm a realm beyond the mirages of subjectivity and its projections, accidents "irreducible to psychology," "let us say tiles [*tuiles*] that fall from roofs, which fall equally on a normal man and on a man tortured by complexes" (41). The fall of Lucifer would be just such an accident supervening on world history. A half-century later a psychoanalytical commentator would define the Lacanian register of the *real* in terms of just such a "coincidence that takes us by surprise and produces a vertiginous shock."[23] It is as though it had taken psychoanalysis, which had always had its own reservations about the limitations of psychology, just that long to catch up with Rougemont's parapsychoanalytical theology. More significantly coincidental still, the characterization of the *real* just invoked takes place in the course of an essay on the stunning parallels between the thought of

23. Slavoj Zizek, *Looking Awry: An Introduction to Jacques Lacan through Popular Culture* (Cambridge: MIT Press, 1991), 33.

Jacques Lacan and the films of Alfred Hitchcock—of which the most
notorious remains *The Birds.* Early in the second section of his essay
on the devil, Rougemont returns elliptically to the Jung anecdote. The
emptiness of prewar liberal cant is hinted at in the following sentence:
"Over our heads, in the sky of our cities, great birds circled with a
sinister droning, and those birds were attacking us!"[24] The birds of
phobia had become menacing planes. Now it happens that our psychoanalytical commentator, charting the structure of Hitchcock's
films, zeroes in on the same transformation: "In *North by Northwest*
we have what is perhaps the most famous Hitchcockian scene, the
attack by the plane—a steel bird—that pursues the hero across a flat
sunbaked landscape."[25] So the coincidence within Rougemont's extra-
psychological theology and the coincidence within Slavoj Zizek's ex-
trapsychological psychoanalysis (a meshing of Hitchcock with Lacan)
at this point coincide. All this in a world, according to Rougemont, in
which "people live by movies as they once lived by religion."[26]

The reference to movies, then—in completing the associative chain
of psychoanalysis, terrifying bird, and murderous plane in Rougemont's Franco-American essay of 1942—seems a compelling anticipation of the very same chain in Zizek's Franco-American (or Lacano-
Hitchcockian) excursus a half-century later. It effectively compounds
the coincidences insisted on within each text by a supreme coincidence between those very coincidences. In *La part du diable,* however,
that reference to movies is to the degraded or "depersonalized" realm
within which passion, having abandoned the private sphere, survives.
The point had already been made in "Passion and the Origin of Hitlerism": "Modern man lives more and more in a world of collective
bewilderment, in a world in which he participates in forms of living
foreign to his individual experience. The cinema offers a good example of this. There everyone can 'by proxy' live adventures which never
happen to him."[27] The movies, that is, offer a degraded version of the
process of transfer of the passions to the nation, a process whose most
stunning exemplar, alas, remained Nazism. All of which is to say that

24. Rougemont, *La part du diable,* 45.

25. Zizek, *Looking Awry,* 99.

26. Rougemont, *La part du diable,* 58; see also the English-language translation by
Haakon Chevalier, *The Devil's Share* (New York: Pantheon, 1944).

27. Rougemont, "Passion and the Origin of Hitlerism," 77.

the reference to movies is a reminder of just how continuous certain cultural impulses remain between the world of Nazism and that of the democracies.

Significantly, the reference to movies comes in a section titled "Hitler or the Alibi." Its theme is that one of the devil's greatest ruses is to convince us that he is Hitler himself, a figure of absolute evil or alterity. For the belief that evil is the province of the other (and not of ourselves) is not merely false, according to Rougemont; it is the elective means through which evil is able to sustain itself. He had argued vigorously, it will be recalled, that Nazism drew its energy from that same libidinal energy historically unleashed—as "passion"—by heresy during the "psychical revolution of the twelfth century." And the *horreur sacrée* celebrated by the sometime surrealist Rougemont in the pages of *VVV* was plainly in substantial contact with the same "sacred horror" experienced in the Nazi rally at Frankfurt and reported in the *Journal d'Allemagne.*

In the chapter "The Fatal Error of the Democracies," we read: " 'You see, I am only Hitler!' Satan tells us. We see only Hitler. We find him terrible. We detest him. With more or less determination we set up against him our old democratic virtues. We are no longer able to see the Demon among ourselves. The trick has been played. We're trapped. If the Devil is Hitler, that means we are on the right side? Quits? The Devil could ask for nothing better: he loves our good conscience. It is the wide door through which he prefers to enter us, announcing himself under a false name."[28] That page constitutes the book's fulcrum: "The precise point where everything becomes reversed, the point where our accusations, abandoning the Führer and his people, become leveled with their full impact against ourselves."

La part du diable, for all its antifascism, is above all an essay written against the moral complacency of the democracies. If "our adversaries do not differ essentially from us"; if "the adversary is always within us"; if "we here too are already more or less Hitlerized in our ways and in our thoughts"; if "Hitlerite arbitrariness [*l'arbitraire hitlérien*] translates into politics the same principles which authorize the anarchy of our private morals," then it may be asked "in the name of what our moralists of passion pretend to combat Hitler" (68, 70, 116, 117).

28. Rougemont, *La part du diable,* 66.

Alterity—evil—is lodged in the core of identity itself. The demonic temptation to which the Cathars (after Eve) yielded—*eritis sicut dii*—is already present in the "Babelization"—excelsior!—of the material conditions of everyday life in the West (108). The corrupting will to divinity—or superhumanity—is by no means a monopoly of the Hitlerites.

Stylistically, Rougemont, whose essay begins with a crucial borrowing from Baudelaire's *Petits poèmes en prose,* illustrates his point with a series of unsettling fables or parables. I have already noted the Hitchcockian tale—intended to "confound" the psychoanalyst—that he borrowed from Jung. Another, which might have been called "Baudelaire in New York," deals with a philanthropist strolling down Fifth Avenue, dispensing charity to assorted refugees, his cigar smoke rising like incense—a sign that he is in good odor with the Eternal. The devil, when questioned about how formidable an adversary such an individual must be, says between his teeth: "I'll take care of that fellow! Here is his plan, which he let drop as he gave the beggar a quarter. The plan is perfect, as you feared. *But I am going to organize it!*" The deflationary puncturing of charity was the Baudelairean gesture par excellence.

The culminating fable is titled "Woman Beats Man (*An Animated Cartoon*)." Here is how it begins: "They loved each other so much that they could not stop saying, 'How can one love so much?' One fine evening she began to beat him and left him for dead on the bedside rug. Then she went to sleep, all tired out. The next day he was still alive. 'Why did I beat you?' she asked him. 'If you don't know, it's because you don't love me very much.' Disfigured by his beating, he opened his eyes balefully and said, 'I still love you. Spare me.' She turned away to hide the smile that twisted her lips, and to weep" (142). As the story progresses and she becomes more desperate to decipher the link between her love and the need to beat him, more frustrated at his inability to help her in that quest, and more aggressive in her *bastonnades* as a result, his perplexity—and bruises—reduce him to silence. Whereupon: " 'This man doesn't love me,' thinks the woman. 'Let's go and beat another one.' " At which point Rougemont proffers his moral: "If he had beaten her first. . . ."

As a phenomenology of the sadomasochistic couple, "La Bastonnade" is not without perspicacity. The sequence of non sequiturs that "he" and "she" address to each other, facilitating the downward spiral of violence, is particularly effective. But psychology is the least of the concerns of Rougemont's cartoon. The relation of power in the couple recalls that *vasselage amoureux* whereby a man, in the world of *cortezia*, becomes servant to his lady. Or perhaps, more allegorically, "she" here figures the destructiveness of the "eternal feminine," the extreme romantic posture against which Rougemont argued just before presenting his cartoon. The chapter immediately after the cartoon, however, begins by offering a somewhat different interpretation: "The above story may be that of a couple, but it is also in a certain way that of the relations of Germany and Europe" (145). To the extent that Germany figures the romantic posture at its most extreme, there is no contradiction. What remains troubling, however, is the moral of the story. It may be a call to European harshness toward Germany, but it takes the allegorical form of condoning spousal abuse: "If he had beaten her first. . . ." At this juncture Rougemont's essay, in reaction against the "feminine" excesses of romanticism, lapses into a misogyny that is not merely allegorical. "The woman who is no longer dominated by man—whether the fault be man's or her own—loses her femininity or becomes its slave" (142). "Woman is not more diabolical than man, but more easily led astray, because she lacks objectivity, coldness of appreciation, perspective in relation to the real, or in a word, rhetoric. . . . She lacks form, and it is up to man to give it to her" (140).

Agape here seems to be preparing its entry and triumph over eros under the banner of the most conventional of doctrines: Saint Paul's assertion that "the husband is the woman's chief, and that woman without man cannot be saved" (141). The vertiginous spiral of the "cartoon" and the myriad interimplications of democratic and Hitlerite "passions" give way to the affirmation of an absolute difference. Before fleeing toward what he will call "le Bleu du ciel," Rougemont takes one final step toward the "last circle" of his hell (146). In an odd prose poem, "Le coup de pistolet," the "she" and "he" of the cartoon appear to have been transformed into "she" and "I." At the poem's end, the narrator lies in bed with his partner. "She is delirious [*elle délire*] and I have this bullet in my heart." He is nevertheless sufficiently aware to engage in a sequence of sophisms that reduce him to the same silence found in the case of the male at the end of "La Bastonnade." "La Bastonnade": "He remains silent. . . ." "Le coup de pistolet": "And here I am, *no longer able* to ask any question"

(148). With the sadomasochistic "he" become "I," Rougemont, having reached his last circle, brings in the most conventional of celestial choirs, in a section titled "Le Bleu du ciel," to announce the road to salvation. Saint Michael makes an appearance to remind us that the meaning of his name—*Quis sicut Deus?* [who is like unto the Lord?]— is a refutation of the demonic promise of the moderns: "You will be like gods." It was a passage Rougemont knew would appear insane to the "liberal intellectuals" of New York, and he delighted in the prospect.[29] After an entirely conventional eulogy of the virtues of responsibility, freedom, and "sense of one's fellow man," the book comes to a close with an affirmation. Against the devil, Rougemont would oppose the blue skies that he has loved—those of the Ile-de-France, the Alps, and, now, Manhattan, "bursting [*fusant*] like an inexorable joy between the silvery verticalities of its skyscrapers."[30]

La part du diable thus ends with a lyrical passage that seems in every sense a flight from the vertiginous depths it had plumbed. After the devil as implicit theory of the unconscious and the devil as that pocket of alterity disfiguring every claim to identity, the bromides about Christian virtue in the final section are even more disappointing than the final marriage-affirming sections of *L'amour et l'Occident*: Kierkegaard had somehow evacuated the premises. It was as though Rougemont's residual Manicheanism, a sense of the irretrievably fallen nature of humanity, had allowed him to see through the shallowness of the Manichean vision of World War II: neither side was bereft of evil. But that same residual Manicheanism dictated the flight upward (toward a *bleu du ciel* fundamentally at odds, in its purity, with Bataille's), a sublimation that seems in flight from the very complications Rougemont had charted so intriguingly in the first part of his book.

The New York intellectuals were sensitive to Rougemont's accomplishment in the book even as they reacted against it. Hannah Arendt wrote in the *Partisan Review* that she knew of very few recent publications "that come so close to the experiences of modern man."[31] The

29. Rougemont, *Journal d'une époque*, 504. On the American reception of *The Devil's Share*, see Ackermann, *Denis de Rougemont*, 776–78.

30. Rougemont, *La part du diable*, 190.

31. Hannah Arendt, "Nightmare and Flight," in *Essays in Understanding* (New York: Harcourt, Brace and Co., 1994), 133.

future author of *The Banality of Evil* concluded her article: "Whether one agrees with Denis de Rougemont or not, he belongs to those who, in his own words, 'are all in the sinking ship, and at the same time . . . are all in the ship that has launched the torpedo.' Those who know this, who do not want to get away from this not very comfortable position, are not numerous, and they are the only ones who matter" (135). And yet Arendt found the book "confused." "Much against his will and though fearing and predicting 'modern gnosticism,' he falls into the worst pitfalls of gnostic speculation." The anti-Catharist of *L'amour et l'Occident,* that is, has ultimately yielded to a will to sublimation that we too found to be a flight from Rougemont's own discovery. This, more than complaints about the sub-Nietzschean or sub-Chestertonian literary quality of certain parables (specifically "La Bastonnade"), more than the surprising claim that Rougemont's devil is "nothing but a personification of Heidegger's Nothingness" (37), form the heart of Arendt's critique.

Lionel Trilling, writing in the *Kenyon Review,* had words of praise for *La part du diable:* "I am glad Rougemont wrote this book. I hope it will be read, for, where it succeeds, it brings acutely into question a great many of the liberal-progressive assumptions we all too blandly accept."[32] Yet he too had reservations. Arendt threw Nietzsche and Chesterton against Rougemont; Trilling throws Dostoyevsky and Shaw. For Shaw's Don Juan (in *Man and Superman*), "Hell is the home of the unreal," a realm in which there is "nothing but a perpetual romance, a universal melodrama." The critique of "perpetual romance" and the call to reality sound very much in line with the arguments of the author of *L'amour et l'Occident.* But Trilling's perfidious critique lies in lodging the accusation of "unreality" against Rougemont himself. "As a celebrant of the moral life, Rougemont is suave and beguiling; but he talks about it like a public person, all external; with a sense of its drama—he is one of those whom the word *tragedy* charms too much—but not of its pain; with no sense of its contradictions, of the human being in growth and in life. In short, he speaks of it with no sense of its reality" (502). Suave, beguiling, excessively charming: Rougemont, it appears, would be a very French Mephistopheles indeed. But the passage just cited follows directly a

---

32. Lionel Trilling, "A Derivative Devil," *Kenyon Review* (summer 1945): 498.

critical allusion to Rougemont's treatment of psychoanalysis, the same parable that suggested how anticipatory of later developments in analysis that apparent critique seemed, in retrospect, to be. The vertiginous coincidence of Jung's tale of a bird phobia seemed, in its over-determination, to announce the category of the *real*.

No, if Trilling insists at such length on the "dashing way" and "urbane bravura" of Rougemont in his treatment of the devil, if he all but argues that Rougemont, in his intolerance of reality, is at some level the devil, is it not because he is all too aware that the dandyish Baudelaire is the tutelary presence hovering over Rougemont's book? While setting forth his Shaw-Dostoyevsky subtext, he, in fact, acknowledges that the book to all appearances has been written somewhere between the Bible and Baudelaire.

But Rougemont was not alone, among those setting out for New York during the war, to have pitched his thought somewhere between Baudelaire and the Bible. In a celebrated essay, Gershom Scholem comments that Walter Benjamin derived his sense of the devil, for all its affinities with the cabalist tradition, from Baudelaire.[33] The comment is made on the subject of a cryptic Benjamin text entitled "Agesilaus Santander," after a secret second name to which Benjamin laid claim and which was an anagram, according to Scholem, of *Der Angelus Satan*. Somewhere, then, between Baudelaire and the mystical interpretation of the Bible, a critic, secretly identifying with the devil, makes plans to leave for New York. Rougemont, February 22, 1942: "I enter by chance a small restaurant on lower Madison Avenue. The narrow, deep room seems empty. It must be about 9:30 at night. I hesitate at the threshold: will they still be serving? At the other end of the room, two men and a woman, seated at a table, are talking and drinking. I hear one of the men, who has just noticed me, say: 'There's the devil!' They turn around and laugh. I have already fled."[34] It was as though the risk Maritain suggested that Rougemont might run in writing *La part du diable* had been successfully assumed. Might Trilling have been one of the diners?

33. Gershom Scholem, "Walter Benjamin and His Angel," in *On Jews and Judaism in Crisis* (New York: Schocken, 1976), 213: "The Luciferian element, however, entered Benjamin's meditations on Klee's picture not directly from the Jewish tradition, but rather from the occupation with Baudelaire that fascinated him for so many years."

34. Rougemont, *Journal d'une époque*, 502.

And what if the vertiginous coincidence of what the psychoanalyst calls the *real* were one that failed to occur? Two critics, sometime presences at the Collège de Sociologie, inclined to identify with the devil, pitching their work somewhere between Baudelaire and the mystical (Catharist, Sabbatian) interpretation of Scripture, decide to leave Paris, war-torn Europe, for New York: Rougemont, Benjamin. Only one would make it. The failure of the other would become the stuff of literary legend. But lest that failure be swept up into the "universal melodrama" that Trilling, quoting Shaw, took to be the touchstone of the demonic, it is good to pause (as we have) to consider the achievements and shortcomings of the more successful of the pair.

FIVE

Simone Weil
Letters from Harlem

There is a love in whose light our deepest intuitions are revealed as partial glimpses of paradoxes more wonderful than any we dare conceive. —LESLIE FIEDLER, "Simone Weil: Prophet Out of Israel"

"I am not at all of the opinion of Denis de Rougemont," Simone Weil wrote to Boris Souvarine in an undated letter now in Harvard's Houghton Library.[1] The Albigensians, she explained, struck her as increasingly "sympathiques." She had not yet made her way aboard the *Serpa Pinto* from Casablanca to New York, where she would move with her family to 549 Riverside Drive off 125th Street. Souvarine, her close friend and sometime editor at *La critique sociale*, was, for his part, still in Nice, and had yet to secure the visa allowing him to settle on Perry Street in Greenwich Village. The attraction to the Albigensians was a characteristic affinity on Weil's part. Shortly before her arrival in New York in early July 1942, she had written two memorable texts on the civilization of medieval Languedoc that would appear (under an anagrammed pseudonym) in *Cahiers du Sud* while she was still in Manhattan. Leslie Fiedler, introducing her to the readership of *Commentary* some years later as a "saint of the absurd," characterized the texts on medieval Provence as central to an understanding

1. The letter has been published in "Lettres de Simone Weil à Boris Souvarine," *Cahiers Simone Weil* 15, no. 1 (March 1992): 17–19.

of her legacy, and it is those essays, with their implied polemic against Rougemont, that will offer us an entry into the thought of this woman of genius, as T. S. Eliot called her, whose "genius was akin to that of the saints."[2]

For Rougemont, as we have observed, the Albigensian or Catharist passion was construable as the "Oriental temptation of the West."[3] The mystical propensity to fuse with divinity had come to Provence from the East (Persia and the Middle East). Catharism was also known as Bougrerie because it was said to come have come west via the Bulgarian Balkans.[4] For Weil, Catharism was rather the Eastern salvation of the Western church. Weil's Languedoc had witnessed a veritable blossoming of Eastern spiritual influences. Did one not see sculptural motifs evocative of Egypt in Saint Sernin and Toulouse? "However little we know of the Cathars, it appears that they were in some way heirs to Platonic thought, to the initiatic doctrines and mysteries of that pre-Roman civilization which embraced the Mediterranean and the Middle East; and either by chance or for some other reason, their doctrine recalls on certain points, along with Buddhism, along with Pythagoras and Plato, the doctrine of the Druids, which had impregnated that same land in a previous age."[5]

Weil's South was drenched in Eastern spirituality, but this was in no way a contamination of Christianity, as Rougemont would have it, but rather a restoration of the Eastern—and specifically Greek—roots of a Christianity that had been violently separated from its own past. "The Greek spirit was reborn in the Christian form which is its truth." In this the Catharist civilization of Oc was a resurrection of the Greek "miracle," a renaissance altogether more authentic than the counterfeit humanist Renaissance that traditionally bears that name.[6] Here we touch on Weil's religious syncretism, the speculative bent that had her

2. Leslie Fiedler, "Simone Weil: Prophet Out of Israel," *Commentary* (January 1951): 40; T. S. Eliot, preface to *The Need for Roots* by Simone Weil (New York: G. P. Putnam's Sons, 1952), vi.

3. Rougemont, *L'amour et l'Occident*, 344.

4. Georges Duby, preface to *La chanson de la croisade albigeoise*, edited by Henri Gongaud (Paris: Livre de poche, 1989), 7.

5. Simone Weil, "L'agonie d'une civilisation vue à travers un poème épique," in *Ecrits historiques et politiques* (Paris: Gallimard, 1960), 69.

6. Simone Weil, "En quoi consiste l'inspiration occitanienne?" in *Ecrits historiques et politiques*, 78.

ranging the world's religious mythologies for regions of resonance
between them and Christianity.

But how did the continuity between Christianity and Eastern spirituality come undone in the first place? Weil's answer is: through a *coup
de force*. Rome, the incarnation of imperial statism, ripped Christianity from the spiritual fabric that sustained it, and reinterpreted it
spuriously as the heir of the this-worldly religion of Israel and its god
of vengeance. To think religiously for Weil meant to undo, in terms as
Greek as possible, and if need be against the Church itself, the Judaiza-
tion of Christianity. That heresy, the will to affirm a crucial discontinuity or incompatibility between the Old and New Testaments, was
known in the Church as Marcionism, and T. S. Eliot, among others,
thought Weil had fallen into "something very much like the Mar-
cionite heresy."[7] But the Catharists were already party to the effort.
The letter to Souvarine spoke of the "scant respect" the Albigensians
had for Jehovah. In January 1941, Weil had written to Déodat Roché, a
scholar of Catharism, that one of the principal reasons for her attraction to the Cathars was "their opinion concerning the Old Testament,
which you express so well in your article ['Les Cathares et l'amour
spirituel'], where you so rightly say that the worship of power had
caused the Hebrews to lose the notion of good and evil. . . . The
influence of the Old Testament and that of the Roman Empire, whose
tradition was continued by the papacy, are in my opinion the two
essential causes of the corruption of Christianity."[8] Israel, in sum, had
been Rome's instrument in creating a fictive enclave or discontinuity
within the continuum of Christianity and the Eastern spirituality that
it inherited from Egypt by way of Greece. And the enclave was beginning to come undone in the Catharist South of the twelfth century.

Then that renaissance was crushed. The Albigensian Crusade of the
thirteenth century had effectively dismembered Catharist culture.
And it was no doubt the pathos of that circumstance that led Weil to
regard the *Chanson de la croisade albigeoise* (and not the poems of the
troubadours) as the masterwork of the literature of the South. Toulouse was for her the French Troy, and the epic a lasting testimony to

7. Eliot, preface to Weil, *Need for Roots*, viii.
8. Quoted in Jean Riaud, "Simone Weil et les cathares," *Cahiers Simone Weil* 6, no.
2 (June 1983): 108.

the greatness of a civilization even as it was being destroyed. This meant that Simone Weil arrived in New York in 1942 lamenting a holocaust of sorts. But it was the holocaust of the 210 Catharist faithful who offered themselves up on the stake at Montségur some seven hundred years earlier rather than abjure their faith.[9]

That in turn meant not only that Weil's holocaust, the crusade against the Albigensians, was a massacre of the self-proclaimed adversaries of the Jews, but also that the "Unoccupied Zone" (or "Free France," as it was called)—the refuge of such Jewish families as that of Dr. Bernard Weil, her beloved father—was in reality occupied Languedoc. "The contradictions with which the mind collides, the sole realities, the criterion of the real," as she put it in a fragment published in *La pesanteur et la grâce*.[10] It would be hard to imagine a situation less auspicious for a thinker contemplating joining the Resistance. That de Gaulle, in his historic appeal of June 18, 1940, had invoked the resources of an intact colonial empire as the key factor enabling further French resistance to the Nazis was already troubling enough for an anticolonialist of Weil's stripe. But her attachment to the lost Romanesque civilization of the South meant that the anticolonialist thrust was to be visited deep within metropolitan France itself. Such was the upshot of her conviction that unoccupied France was occupied Languedoc.

An example of Weil's speculative exegesis of Scripture will help illuminate matters at this point. In "Les trois fils de Noé et l'histoire de la civilisation méditerranéenne," an essay included by J.-M. Perrin in his collection *L'attente de Dieu*, Weil tackles the legend of Noah, one of the few figures to whom she attributes nobility in the Old Testament. Noah planted the first vineyard after the flood, drank of his wine, became drunk, "and lay uncovered in his tent" (Genesis 8:20). Tradition has humorously cast him in the role of patron saint of alcoholics. (Chesterton assigned him the memorable line, "I don't care where the water goes if it doesn't get into the wine.") For Weil, though, the wine-drinking hero is a mythological cousin of Dionysos. This in turn enables a dismantling and reversal of the biblical narrative of Noah's three sons and their fates. Ham, father of Canaan, it will be recalled,

9. Michael Zink, introduction to *La chanson de la croisade albigeoise*, 15.
10. Simone Weil, *La pesanteur et la grâce* (Paris: Plon, 1947), 115.

saw his father's nakedness and was punished as a result. His two brothers, Shem and Japheth, averted their eyes and would henceforth be masters over the progeny of the accursed Ham. Weil sweeps the biblical version contemptuously away and affirms that Ham's observation of the intoxicated Noah-Dionysos in his nudity was tantamount to absorbing the divine mystery incarnated by both. Whereas Shem and Japheth stand accused of rejecting the very revelation whose repression the biblical version of the tale consolidates.

But the three sons of Noah were key markers in the racial terminology of the nineteenth century. Gobineau identified blacks as "Hamites" and Caucasians (or Indo-Europeans) as "Japhetids."[11] Shortly thereafter, Shem would be identified as the forefather of the "Semites." We thus find the narrative of Noah's sons reinterpreted as a fable of black pride: Ham alone gazed on the mystery. . . . But the descendants of Ham were more subtly ramified than might be expected. Weil's letter to Souvarine is above all concerned with demonstrating that the Phoenicians are not Semites at all. ("Moreover, I don't ask for anything better than to be descended from the Phoenicians. You know my sympathy for Carthage. . . . If I thought I descended from the Phoenicians, I would have a racial awareness and would vigorously lay claim to superiority for that race. Instead of which, I am paralyzed by the sentiment that I am accused of descending from people who couldn't find anything better to give to humanity than Jehovah.") In the essay on Noah, moreover, the Phoenicians are identified as Hamites, and thus play the role of key link in the chain of cultural transmission, following Herodotus, that went from the Egyptians to the Phoenicians to the Pelasgians to the Greeks.[12] Weil was an adept of what would later be called "black Athena"—or perhaps, better yet, "black Dionysos."[13]

The Albigensian Crusade, moreover, the crushing of the only worthy Renaissance (or rebirth of Greek spirituality) we have known, was a victory of Japheth over Ham: "It has thus been given us to see wars between Christians in which the spirit of Ham was on one side and

11. See Pierre-André Taguieff, *La couleur et le sang: Doctrines racistes à la française* (Paris: Mille et une nuits, 1998), 29.

12. Simone Weil, "Les trois fils de Noé et l'histoire de la civilisation méditerranéenne," in *L'attente de Dieu*, edited by J.-M. Perrin (Paris: Fayard, 1966), 233.

13. Martin Bernal, *Black Athena: The Afroasiatic Roots of Classical Civilization* (New Brunswick, N.J.: Rutgers University Press, 1987).

that of Japheth on the other. Such was the case for the Albigensian war. It is not for nothing that there is Romanesque sculpture in the Egyptian style to be found in Toulouse."[14] The history of the West, that is, has been that of the crushing of the black Dionysians or Hamites by the Japhethids (or Semites) enabled by the Semitic myth of Noah. As for the situation in 1942: "Today the sons of Japheth and those of Shem are far more clamorous. One side is powerful, the other persecuted; but they are brothers and resemble each other a good deal" (243). For Weil, Aryan and Jew, Japhethid and Semite, Rome and Jerusalem would always be joined, whichever side might temporarily be victimizing the other, in their joint victimization of the Hamite.

It is time to join Simone Weil in her family's apartment on Riverside Drive, at that extreme stretch of the (eminently Jewish) Upper West Side that begins to merge with (black) Harlem. From a letter to Dr. Louis Bercher: "I explore Harlem. I go every Sunday to a Baptist church in Harlem where, except for me, there's not a single white. After two and a half hours of service, once the atmosphere has been established, the religious fervor of the pastor and the faithful explodes into dance (of the Charleston variety), shouts, and spirituals. It's really worth seeing. One is transported with faith. Genuine faith, it seems to me."[15] It was Bercher's opinion that "if she had stayed in America she would surely have become a black."[16]

With her Hamite allegiances and anti-Jewish antipathies, Simone Weil seems a living anticipation of the black-Jewish tensions that would not explode on the Upper West Side until many years later. But she was a Jew who, in that conflict, had at the outset switched sides. The undated letter to Souvarine (on which this chapter is in many ways a commentary) invoked the exemplary testimony of Flavius Josephus, who betrayed the Jewish cause in the middle of the Roman-Jewish wars: "When it comes to historians, none are as good as the traitors." Or perhaps her true legacy as a political thinker lay with the anti-Semitic Third Worldism of a figure such as Jacques Vergès, the lawyer who would defend Klaus Barbie, the "butcher of Lyon," in the 1980s. For surely Weil's searing line on the occasion of the Nazi entry

14. Weil, "Les trois fils de Noé," 241.

15. Jacques Cabaud, *L'expérience vécue de Simone Weil* (Paris: Plon, 1957), 310.

16. Simone Pétrement, *Simone Weil: A Life,* translated by Raymond Rosenthal (New York: Pantheon, 1976), 478.

into Paris ("a great day for Indo-China") deserves to be paired with the half-Vietnamese Vergès's quip during the Barbie trial to the effect that his mother did not have to wear a yellow star because she was yellow from head to toe.[17]

Weil, was not principally a political thinker, however, but a religious one. Her theology, moreover, resonated in crucial ways with the theme of exile. The world for her was essentially exile from God. God's creation of the world was to be understood as his withdrawal or "abdication" from it. Our task under such circumstances is to "de-create" the world, to work toward that decimation of what is, and above all of the opacity that is ourselves, that would allow for their luminous reabsorption into the God whose withdrawal is our best description of creation itself. Here is a particularly resonant evocation of Weil's theology from La connaissance surnaturelle: "We are in relation to God as a thief permitted by the goodness of the person whose house he has entered to make off with his gold. That gold, from the perspective of its legitimate owner, is a gift; from the point of view of the thief, it's a theft. He is obliged to return and make restitution. Thus it is with our being. We have stolen a bit of being from God in order to make it ours. God gave it to us. But we stole it. It must be returned."[18]

If return was the imperative of the greater exile of existence, it was even more pressingly that of the lesser exile of her four months in New York. A common motif of her life on Riverside Drive was that her sole purpose in joining her parents, fleeing Marseille, in their transatlantic escape to America was to facilitate a return to Europe—and specifically occupied France—by way of the Gaullist movement in London. As she wrote (July 30, 1942) to a former classmate at the Lycée Henri IV, Maurice Schumann, who had become an official in the Gaullist organization: "Despite the pressure of my parents, who wanted to escape anti-Semitism and did not want to be separated from me, I would never have left had I known how difficult it is to make it from New York to London."[19]

The theologian of excruciating exile, with the exception of her

17. George Steiner, "Sainte Simone—Simone Weil," in No Passion Spent (New Haven: Yale University Press, 1996), 172; Jacques Vergès, Le salaud lumineux: Conversations avec Jean-Louis Remilleux (Paris: Michel Lafon, 1990), 14.

18. Simone Weil, La connaissance surnaturelle (Paris: Gallimard, 1950), 232.

19. Simone Weil, Ecrits de Londres et dernières lettres (Paris: Gallimard, 1957), 186.

forays into "Hamite" Harlem, found her exile in a sixth-floor apartment overlooking the Hudson excruciating. To look out every day on Grant's Tomb, the monument to the military defeat of the South, must have seemed a cruel parody of that other defeat of another South—Catharist Languedoc—whose memorialist she had recently made bold to become. Justice, she knew, was in any event always a fugitive of the camp of the victors.

The *New York Times* of July 15, 1942, the day after Bastille Day, was awash with French-related news. On the local scene there was first of all a report of the speech of Secretary of the Interior Harold Ickes to the Free French rally at the Manhattan Center, a meeting at which Simone Weil had met Jacques Maritain. More interesting because of the division in American policy it betrayed was a spat between Mayor Fiorello La Guardia and Secretary of State Cordell Hull over whether to accord a tax exemption to the French embassy for the property at 934 Fifth Avenue it was eager to acquire. The mayor responded to a diplomatic inquiry by stating curtly that he knew of "nothing in international law or custom which gives to a vassal State under the domination of a nation at war with our country the rights and privileges of its predecessor government." The *Times* nonetheless opined that the mayor would soon defer to the secretary of state, who was not of his opinion. Most heart-wrenching was the news of the new severity of measures against the Jews timed to coincide with Bastille Day. The list of prohibitions was such "that Jews have nothing left but to remain at home or walk aimlessly in the streets." But the item that devastated Simone Weil was not specifically related to the Jews. It was rather the report that two women had been killed during a July 14 demonstration in Marseille, the city she had left because of its political inertness: "The demonstration at Marseille . . . consisted of a 'spontaneous' parade up the Cannebière [*sic*], the main thoroughfare of the city, by thousands of French citizens bearing small French flags. Traffic in Marseille was held up for hours as the police vainly tried to break up the demonstration, making many arrests. Two women were killed and five other persons were hurt during the Marseille demonstration." Simone Weil identified not with the persecuted Jews straying "aimlessly" through the city but with the women who had been stripped of their very being in Marseille. Self-obliteration as a return from exile, after all, had been a principal motif of her theology: "If only I knew how to disappear, there would be a union of perfect love between God and the earth."[20] New York in the summer of 1942 was emphatically the wrong place, the wrong time (not) to be. She immediately fell sick upon reading the news of the slain women in Marseille and stayed in her room for two days without eating.

The letter of July 30, 1942, to Maurice Schumann was an effort to implement a return trip across the Atlantic, to join the Gaullists in London with the hope of making her way into occupied France. She had long been entertaining a plan to spearhead an elite group of Front Line Nurses, adept at performing emergency first aid in cases of shock, exposure, and hemorrhage, and capable of inspiring the Allied war effort through their exemplary performance. Weil, who had worked in a Renault factory and joined the Republican forces in the Spanish civil war, had written her plan as a formal proposal, which she sent off to Schumann—and to anyone else (including Roosevelt) who might support her plan. That proposal is remarkable above all for the author's will to present her elite female unit as the Allied counterpart to Hitler's elite *Schutzstaffel* (S.S.). Both would be buoyed by an almost religious will to self-sacrifice, and both would be the exemplary organizations of their respective regimes. But was it so sure that Weil's female masochists would be a match, even at the level of inspiration, for the Hitlerian sadists of the *Schutzstaffel*? The suggestion, toward the end of the proposal, that the ancient Germanic seminomads, never defeated by the armies of Rome, had understood the exalting potential of a female presence on the battle front no doubt left more than one reader with the impression that this particular proposal was prepared to understand Germanic excellence (from Teutonic tribes to the *Schutzstaffel*) in ways so pronounced as to be alarming. The proposal was never acted on.

Simone Weil, however, was serious in her quest. After she died, Leslie Fiedler, eager to cast her in the role of holy fool, went out of his way to insist on her incompetence. "During the Second World War, desiring to participate again, she worked out a plan for being parachuted into occupied France to bring to the wounded members of the

20. Simone Weil, *Cahiers* (Paris: Plon, 1953), 2:394.

Resistance—not medical care, for she lacked even the simplest skills of healing, but her mere presence as a woman!"[21] Whereupon the reader was invited to smirk at what the military authorities might have made of that offer. But Weil did not lack credentials as a healer; she had taken a first-aid course in Harlem. Her friend Simone Dietz recalls serving as Weil's dummy for exercises in artificial respiration and dressing wounds, sharing disbelief at such questions on the written exam as "Is iodine a disinfectant or a plant?"[22] Amid the rhetoric of Free French rallies that even now read as raw material for a neo-Flaubertian satire, in sum, Simone Weil was doing all she could to rejoin the battle.

But she was prepared to see her project rejected, whence an alternative plan she presented to Maurice Schumann in her letter of July: "My second thought was that I could perform more effectively in clandestine work if I were to leave France and return there with precise instructions and a mission—preferably, a dangerous one."[23] The theological will to make oneself the locus where being self-destructs in its repatriation by divinity here turns into a paramilitary strategy. A second letter to Schumann comes close to careening out of control: "I beg you to procure for me, if you can, the quantity of useful suffering and danger that will save me from the sterility of being consumed with grief. I cannot live in the situation in which I find myself at present. It drives me to the brink of despair" (199). Her humility is such that she is prepared to accept almost any useful task temporarily, she writes (although considerations of utility always seem an afterthought in her letters). Then the condition: "Only, if it is a task that does not bring with it a high degree of suffering and danger, I would be able to accept it only on a temporary basis; otherwise the same grief that is consuming me in New York would consume me in London and would paralyze me" (200).

She would eventually make it to London, if not France, and accomplish the "more-than-suicide" she had been craving.[24] Schumann put her in touch with André Philip, commissioner of the interior and labor in the National Committee of the Free French movement, and

21. Fiedler, "Simone Weil," 37.
22. Jacques Cabaud, *Simone Weil à New York et à Londres* (Paris: Plon, 1967), 34.
23. Weil, *Ecrits de Londres et dernières lettres*, 186.
24. Fiedler, "Simone Weil," 41.

it was agreed that she would join his staff in London.[25] After four months in New York, she was retraversing the ocean, apparently making good on the *reculer pour mieux sauter* that she had always said was her only reason for going to New York in the first place. Dying as she did, in the summer of 1943 in rural England, of complications relating to the near-starvation diet she imposed on herself lest she be more comfortable than those subjected to food rationing in martyred France, Simone Weil has been viewed by some as a patron saint of anorexia. It is a cavalier view, willfully dismissive of the circumstance to be examined that French starvation during the war had become a subject of political debate and was linked to the controversial blockade, imposed by the Allies, of foodstuffs from the empire. Simone Weil was distrustful of the all too official myth of Joan of Arc. Her brand of heroism no doubt entailed an identification with that anonymous woman who cast the stone that killed Simon de Montfort, the Inquisition's military leader in the crusade against the Catharist heresy.[26] But that her decision to give up the relative comfort of life in the French colony of New York entailed a form of heroism should not be doubted.

Which is why the major text she wrote in New York, a long letter to the Dominican priest Father Couturier, sent just before she left for England in November 1942, is all the more stunning. For it is one of the abiding paradoxes of the French wartime emigration to New York that the figure most deeply committed to risking her life in the struggle against Hitler did so out of a sense of things so profoundly anti-Semitic as to set the mind reeling.

The link with Father Couturier was by way of Jacques Maritain, whose connections with the Committee on Social Thought of the University of Chicago had made him in certain respects the most prestigious of the French intellectuals in New York. The Maritain household, an apartment at 30 Fifth Avenue in Greenwich Village, was a center of émigré life. Maritain, whose *A travers le désastre*, to the extent it could be found and read, was an inspiration in Nazi-occupied Europe, had himself been resisting . . . de Gaulle's letters and telegrams urging him to join the Free French in London. (In the inimitably

---

25. Pétrement, *Simone Weil*, 482.
26. See her remarks on the episode in "L'agonie d'une civilisation," 72.

eloquent punctuation of de Gaulle's telegram: "DESIRERAIS BEAU-
COUP QUE VOUS PUISSIEZ VENIR LONDRES PLUS TOT POSSIBLE
STOP".)[27] In making her desperate way to London, in sum, Weil
sought out the help of a philosopher desperate not to go to London.

In his reply to Weil of August 4, 1942, Maritain commented on the
"nobility" of her project for an elite front-line nursing corps, and
recommended that she get in touch with one of his colleagues at the
New School, Alexandre Koyré, the distinguished historian of science,
who was about to leave for London in the coming days. But he was
above all struck by Weil's predicament in relation to the Church—her
conviction, voiced in her letter, that in remaining outside the Church
she was "obeying God."[28] "You have truly received the gift of faith," he
wrote her, "but you are burdened by a conceptualization which is as
yet inadequate" (72). Surely, she would do well to confer with his dear
friend Father Couturier, who was lecturing in Baltimore at the time,
but would soon be back in town. Thus began the contact that would
issue in Weil's hundred-page *Lettre à un religieux*.

Weil's letter to Couturier, which was never answered, is a protracted defense of her decision not to convert to Christianity. As such,
the circumstance dictating it has been misleadingly compared to that
of Henri Bergson, another French thinker of Jewish origin who was
drawn to Christianity, but declined to undergo conversion under the
troubled circumstances of World War II.[29] For Weil was in many ways
an anti-Bergson. Whereas Bergson's refusal to convert was born of a
residual fidelity to a people undergoing unprecedented persecution at
the time, Weil's refusal, as Martin Buber has pointed out, was dictated
by a sense that the Church was all too Jewish.[30] Indeed, Weil's letter,
written upon her departure from New York, is dominated by her
polemic against Judaism.

It is a phantasmagoria of sorts, a "tissue of suppositions,"[31] dictated

27. Jean-Luc Barré, *Jacques et Raïssa Maritain: Les mendiants du ciel* (Paris: Stock,
1995), 492.

28. "Un Echange de Lettres entre Simone Weil et Jacques Maritain," *Cahiers Simone Weil* 3, no. 2 (June 1980): 70.

29. Jean-Pie Lapierre, preface to *Lettre à un religieux* by Simone Weil (Paris: Gallimard, 1951), 8.

30. Martin Buber, "Bergson et Simone Weil devant Israël," *Cahiers Simone Weil* 6,
no. 1 (March 1983): 48.

31. Weil, *Lettre à un religieux*, 95.

by a compulsion of which Weil herself seems intermittently aware. She was of the opinion that nothing of what she was writing could be affirmed outright or be subject to any sort of verification: "The opinions that follow have for me differing degrees of probability or certitude, but all of them are accompanied in my mind by a question mark. I shall enumerate them in the indicative only because of the intrinsic poverty of language; I would need language to contain a supplementary mode" (14). One is reminded (once again) of Freud writing *Beyond the Pleasure Principle* in a mode, he wrote, similarly resistant to criteria of verification.

Of the thirty-five entries in Weil's brief for considering herself a Christian outside the Church, the first, whose shadow runs through the letter, pertains to Judaism. In the years prior to Christ's advent, she writes, "Israel possessed less of a share in God and divine truths than several neighboring peoples (India, Egypt, Greece, China). For the essential truth concerning God is that He is good. To believe that God is capable of ordering men to performs deeds of such atrocious injustice and cruelty is the greatest error one can commit concerning Him" (15). The slide from the comparative to the superlative in the passage is significant, for soon Israel, undergoing what Emmanuel Lévinas has called an "élection à rebours," a reverse selection, takes on the role of a principle of malfeasance in the spiritual fabric of Weil's world.[32]

The lives of the patriarchs, beginning with Abraham, are said to be "sullied with atrocities." The Hebraic intolerance of idolatry is for the most part "a fiction of Jewish fanaticism."[33] In fact, "were the Hebrews of the heroic era to be resuscitated, were one to arm them, they would exterminate all of us, men, women, and children, for the crime of idolatry" (18). The Hebraic brief against idolatry was for Weil the cruel mystification through which the Jews worshiped the only idol worth resisting, the all-importance of the collectivity, be it nation or race. In a borrowing from book 4 of Plato's *Republic,* she referred to that idol— "an ersatz for God"—as the Great Beast ("le gros animal").[34] In the letter to Couturier, the theme is voiced as follows: "The real idolatry is

32. Emmanuel Lévinas, "Simone Weil contre la Bible," in *Difficile liberté* (Paris: Albin Michel, 1963), 180.

33. Weil, *Lettre à un religieux,* 17.

34. Weil, *La pesanteur et la grâce,* 180.

covetousness . . . and the Jewish nation, in its thirst for fleshly goods, was guilty of it in the very act of worshipping its God. The Hebrews had as their idol not metal or wood, but a race, a nation, something equally earthbound. Their religion is inseparable from that idolatry in its essence because of the notion of the 'chosen people.' "[35] The Jews, in sum, historically the first polemicists against idolatry, at a time when they were facing extermination in Europe, were accused by Simone Weil of having pioneered the politics of extermination in the service of the only idolatry worth resisting.

But there was a subversive countertradition of pure charity and respect for—indeed, love of—suffering. It flourished in Greece, where Zeus was potentially present in every beggar, but stemmed from Egypt and was transmitted to the Greeks via the Philistines, the Phoenicians, and the Pelasgians. References to Herodotus are made to bear more weight than they can reasonably bear. Before Weil's letter is over, Greek geometry, Hindu meditation, and native North American myth have all been enrolled speculatively into the countertradition. But before the Egyptians there was Noah, as we have already seen, or rather Ham, the son who did not turn his back on the intoxication and unadorned nudity—of doctrine—of his father, twinned with Dionysos, as a prefiguration of Christ. If the tradition has been lost, it can only be, Weil writes, because the twin Hebrew techniques of extermination and cover-up were effective: "In this case, the Hebrews would have distorted history, as Semites and murderers of the Canaanites" (47). After Christ, there was that rare break with the Judeocentrism of the Church, the short-lived Catharist heresy, the only Renaissance worthy of the name, with its receptivity to the Egyptian roots of Greek spirituality. Which more or less brings us to 1942 and the corner of Riverside Drive off 125th Street, the apartment from which the inspired anti-Semite would make her forays into the long-suffering, occasionally Dionysian world of the people she was enough of a student of Gobineau to identify as the blessed descendants of Ham. Might Simone Weil have been New York's first Afrocentric anti-Semite?

There is, however, a turning point in Weil's history of the West. It comes with the objective complicity between two historic adversaries,

---

35. Weil, *Lettre à un religieux,* 19.

Rome and Jerusalem. In a letter to Déodat Roché (January 23, 1941), she had opined that the joint influence of the Old Testament and the Roman Empire was the principal cause of the "corruption of Christianity."[36] In her letter to Couturier, she fleshes out the supposition. Having subjugated the lands of the spiritual countertradition, Rome, which worshiped Plato's Great Beast in its materialist-atheistic mode, converted to Christianity: "But it was in neither the interest nor the dignity of the empire for its official religion to appear to be the continuation and culmination of the centuries-old traditions of countries that had been conquered, crushed, and degraded by Rome—Egypt, Greece, Gaul." And it was here that the Jews proved their usefulness in what can only be termed an act of historical distortion. "For Israel, it had no importance; first, the new law was quite distant from the old one; and then, above all, Jerusalem no longer had any existence. In addition, the spirit of the old law, so far removed from any mysticism, was not that different from the Roman spirit. Rome could accommodate the Lord of Hosts."[37]

The Romans thus succeeded in their revisionist writing of history. To "deracinate" the conquered meant effectively to teach them that their own indigenous spirituality was an afterbirth of Judaism. (It would take Lévinas, years later, to lodge a critique of Weil's metaphorics of *enracinement* every bit as effective as—though quite different from—Gide's critique of "rootedness" in Maurice Barrès.) With a fraudulently Judaized Christianity, Constantine had succeeded in foisting on the empire the "fausse mystique" it had been seeking since the days of Claudius (88, 93). All of which, Weil admitted in concluding, might be "a tissue of suppositions." But one thing seemed virtually certain to her: "There has been an effort to conceal something from us; and it has been successful. It is not by chance that so many texts have been destroyed, that so many shadows obscure an essential part of the story" (95).

Thus runs Weil's deconstruction of the course of Western history. The thought that Judaism was the enabler of the "false mystique" needed by the empire is strikingly reminiscent of a development in the much admired (though admittedly quixotic) proposal for an elite

36. Riaud, "Simone Weil et les cathares," 108.
37. Weil, *Lettre à un religieux*, 93.

front-line corps of nurses that Weil sent around New York. In that case, Weil had all but congratulated Hitler on establishing in the *Schutz-staffel* the "ersatz religion" the Reich needed to inspire its forces.[38] But the Roman Empire, she wrote to Couturier, was "a crudely materialist and totalitarian regime, . . . like Nazism."[39] Hence the need for a "fausse mystique." In sum, the Romans seized on Judaism (as evoked in *Lettre à un religieux*) the way Hitler seized on the *Schutzstaffel* (as evoked in "Projet d'une formation d'infirmières de première ligne"). The call for heroism against Hitler and the espousal of values Hitler might well endorse seem inextricably entwined.

To be sure, Weil's thought would flourish in many an acknowledged and unacknowledged legacy. The complicity of specular opposites (Rome and Jerusalem) in the service of the repression of an infinitely more tenuous play of difference (say, in Weil's case, the Greco-Provençal mix of *douleur* and *joie*), not to mention the undoing of the ego's defenses as an affirmation of that latter play of difference, would serve as the elements of a problematic that would thrive in French thought (in its para-Freudian phase) long after Weil's death. Michel Serres, to cite a case of acknowledgment, refers to his reading of *La pesanteur et la grâce* as the single event that turned him into a philosopher ("She was the only philosopher to have truly influenced me").[40] And how can we attend to Foucault's notion that the French Revolution was a pale statist parody of the "revolution" staged in the discourse of the reactionary nobility at the beginning of the eighteenth century without being reminded of Weil's reading of the humanist Renaissance as a pale satire of the Catharist renaissance of the eleventh century?[41] In the rush to extrapolate from her work what seems pregnant with future development, though, one risks eliding what this visit to Weil in New York has allowed us to glimpse: the devastating meshing of what is best and worst in her thought.

That circumstance would inevitably have raised many an eyebrow among those who knew her in wartime New York, and such is the focus of an important second letter, mailed just prior to her departure for England, to the philosopher Jean Wahl. The letter is divided

38. Weil, *Ecrits de Londres et dernières lettres,* 191.

39. Weil, *Lettre à un religieux,* 88.

40. Michel Serres, *Eclaircissments* (Paris: Flammarion, 1992), 33.

41. Foucault, *Il faut défendre la société,* 193.

into two: a first part addressing contemporary realities and a second, whose "indirect relation" to matters of the day she is willing to entertain, which deals with her own speculative thought in a manner far less tentative than in the letter to Couturier. (Jacques Cabaud has referred to the letter to Wahl as the "perfect vade mecum for Simone Weil's 'syncretic' thought.")[42] Wahl himself had just escaped Drancy, the concentration camp outside Paris, and, after a stay in Toulouse (the Languedocian "Troy" of Weil's imaginings) had made his way to the United States. The Office of Strategic Services was particularly interested in the Sorbonne professor because his assessment of the French political reality had made him the only prominent intellectual present at the 1942 summertime colloquium at Mount Holyoke College (an effort to revive the celebrated Pontigny colloquia in exile) to have fully endorsed the basis of America's Vichy policy. In its confidential report, the Office of Strategic Services evoked Wahl's views, which would have made him a rather sympathetic interlocutor for Weil, in these terms:

Professor Wahl, who is, of course, anti-Vichy, rejects, however, any accusation of treason leveled against Marshal Pétain. While he condemns his policies, he believes that some of the Marshal's points of view can be justified. He points out that at the time of the armistice one could, indeed, honestly believe (a) that England was about to fall or surrender and (b) that for the government to escape to North Africa in order to continue the fight from there would only have drawn the Germans to follow them, which the French might not have been able to avoid. That would not only have put all of France, and all or part of her North African empire, under German occupation, but also would have weakened the Allied position in Africa and the Mediterranean. He points out, furthermore, that while it is true that whenever the Germans insist with finality on a certain demand, the Marshal grants it, he has frequently resisted demands not so insistently put forward. He has, in fact, kept a part of France and North Africa free from German occupation and has kept the French fleet out of the hands of the Germans, until the Allied invasion of North Africa. Thus, Professor Wahl was almost the only one [at the Mount Holyoke colloquium] who fully accepted the basis of the Allied Vichy policy.[43]

Despite his minority political stance, Wahl would cut so impressive a figure at the gathering that he would be offered (and would accept) a

42. Cabaud, *L'expérience vécue de Simone Weil*, 335.
43. Richard Lachmann, OSS Report FR-529, "Symposium of the French University in New York at Mount Holyoke College, August 17 to September 11, 1942," 22.

position on the Mount Holyoke faculty, whence, presumably, his absence from New York, where Simone Weil regretted missing him once
again.

Weil's letter begins with a forthright inquiry into rumors related to
her by Wahl concerning alleged Vichy sympathies: "You speak ob-
scurely, implying that there are individuals spreading bizarre rumors
about me? Might it by chance be claimed that I have sympathies
leaning toward Vichy?"[44] She recalls that despite her past as a pacifist,
she had not budged from the anti-Hitlerian line she adopted once
Hitler entered Prague. "In June 1940, I ardently desired the defense of
Paris, and left only after seeing with consternation the signs announcing that Paris was an open city." Given her clandestine activity in
Marseille and the notorious nuisance she had made herself in New
York with her unrelenting requests for any means of getting to London, there could be no doubt of her sympathies. "I beseech you,
consequently, to deny any rumors to the contrary."

In fact, though, Weil was far less hostile toward those agonizing in
Vichy than toward the self-contented, manifesto-brandishing advocates of the Resistance in the French colony of Manhattan. "What may
have given rise to such rumors is that I don't much like hearing
individuals who are completely at ease here qualify as cowards and
traitors those in France who are muddling through as best they can in
terrible circumstances" (2). (It is a position we will encounter again in
the case of the most celebrated of French writers in New York, Antoine
de Saint-Exupéry.) Finally, there was no guilt or burden that interested
her that she could not assume as her own. Whence the judgment that
despite her consternation at the armistice, she believes that "every
Frenchman, including myself, bears as much responsibility for it as
Pétain." At this point the will to assume a devastating burden takes the
form of effectively exonerating Pétain. Anything is to be preferred to
fusing with the self-contented moralists adjusting their armchairs, in
Camus's memorable phrase, in the direction of history: "I believe that
Pétain has done just about everything that his own physical and mental state allowed him to do to limit the damages." She is even willing to
concede that working with the Germans might, under certain circum-

44. Simone Weil, "Lettre de Simone Weil à Jean Wahl (New York 1942)," *Cahiers Simone Weil* 10, no. 1 (March 1987): 1.

stances, be honorable. The adversary that most upsets her is the Great Beast, the braying crowd with its calls to unanimity echoing down Fifth Avenue: "Most of the people who set themselves up as judges here have never had a chance to test whether they themselves are heroes. I am horrified by facile, unjust and bogus attitudes, above all when the pressures of public opinion seem to make them virtually obligatory" (3).

At this point Weil offers as succinct and affirmative a statement of her mythologically grounded scheme of history as may be found in her work. The Catharists of Languedoc, to be sure, constitute a kind of perfection. As for the Jews, she is of the opinion that Moses rejected the spiritual mystery streaming out of Egypt for the reason that "like Maurras, he conceived of religion as a simple instrument of national greatness." Once again, Jew and anti-Semite are conflated. In the words of *La pesanteur et la grâce*, "the anti-Semites naturally propagate the influence of the Jews."[45] Yes, there might be some elements—Job, the Song of Songs—of the Old Testament worthy of admiration, but they have manifestly been imported from extrinsic sources. All the rest are no more than a "tissue of horrors."[46]

The author then turns to the sole saving remnant in humanity, "the Hamitic strain of thought," which is to be found like a "luminous thread" woven through human history. "But everywhere pride and the will to domination, the spirit of Japheth and Shem, tend to destroy that thought" (5). Seen from 125th Street, Japheth and Shem, Rome and Israel, Aryan and Jew, whatever their conflicts, whichever of each pair might deflect an intended extermination back on its would-be perpetrator, .were in the last analysis joined in the will to destroy the black descendants of Ham. For all Weil's efforts to link up with the Resistance in London, the central horror of World War II struck her as almost beside the point. One imagines her, after posting the letter to Wahl, taking a final stroll in Harlem before the Swedish freighter ending her American exile set sail.

45. Weil, *La pesanteur et la grâce*, 190.
46. Weil, "Lettre de Simone Weil à Jean Wahl," 4.

George Steiner at the Lycée Français

"Dans l'Orient désert. . . ." One must be in a desert. For he whom one must love is absent. — SIMONE WEIL, *La pesanteur et la grâce*

What mattered most was the ultimately inexplicable wonder of the sixth verse, talismanic to the French language and to French poetry after Racine: the understated infinity of desolation in the tension between the opulence of *Orient* and the barrenness of *désert*.

— GEORGE STEINER, *Errata*

It was the suddenness of the French emigration to New York that distinguished it from the exile of German-speaking intellectuals. The Germans who escaped had six years of increasingly severe restrictions (or outbursts), a crescendo of torment, during which they were more or less free to bail out of a painful situation and arrange (if they had not wagered on a new career in France) for a better situation abroad. This was, in fact, a source of some resentment on the part of the Francophones in New York. Henri Grégoire, the eminent Belgian Byzantinist and president of the Ecole Libre, noted that whereas German scholars had succeeded in infiltrating a broad range of academic institutions and departments, French scholars, whatever their distinction or discipline, were invariably taken in as so many "native informants" and assigned to teach French language or literature. Nothing could be further from the experience of German émigré scholars,

Grégoire wrote in the Ecole Libre journal *Renaissance,* whom no one would dream of assigning to the "concentration camp of a German department."[1] The phrase was still usable in this benign sense—such is the myopia of academic resentment—in 1945.

Of all the tales of sudden emigration from France, few are as gripping as the Schindleresque anecdote recorded by George Steiner—who was ten years old but already being strenuously groomed for the life in literature that would be his—regarding his family's migration. Steiner has presided for so many years, in English of such virtuosity, over the diverse strands of Western literature that it may come as a surprise that he was born in Paris in 1929 and spent his formative years in the Lycée Français of New York. The city, moreover, retained a fascination for him. Years later he would write of what had become in his eyes its emblematic center: West 47th Street. For that street managed to house contiguously the Hasidic tribes—"out of Babel"—of diamond dealers, on the one hand, and, on the other, the glorious Gotham Book Mart, to which he often repaired and on whose walls hung portraits of the modernist "minstrels"—Pound, Eliot, Céline—of anti-Semitism.[2] New York, that is, played out in the *unité de lieu* of its secret center a literary (and extraliterary) conflict between anti-Semite and Jew that would be elaborated with growing intricacy in a number of Steiner texts and whose source, to all appearances, lay in those war years spent in the French colony of New York.

The decision to migrate to New York was stunning in its suddenness. Steiner's father was a cultivated Viennese banker of the sort who was obliged (such were the pressures of the time) to create a new career for himself upon emigration—to France, as it happens—in 1924. (His acerbic wit is nicely captured by Steiner, who evokes him muttering under his breath that "all nationalities would sell you their mothers, but the French delivered" [9].) During the "phony war," Steiner *père* was commissioned by Paul Reynaud, who had just become prime minister, to journey to New York and negotiate the purchase of fighter planes from Grumman. At a luncheon with the French mission, Steiner noted several tables away a group of American bank-

1. Henri Grégoire, "Introduction," *Renaissance* 2–3 (1944–45): 8.
2. George Steiner, *Errata: An Examined Life* (London: Weidenfeld and Nicolson, 1997), 147.

ers lunching with several German bankers sporting swastikas on their lapels. New York was a neutral city at the time, and the Germans were presumably negotiating their war needs much as Steiner *père,* on behalf of the French ministry, was. But Steiner recognized one of the Germans from a loan transaction involving Siemens they had together negotiated in the past. During the meal, a waiter delivered a message to Steiner from his former German associate. The Frenchman ripped up the message and headed to the men's room, where the German awaited him. Grabbing him by the lapel, the German informed him that the killing had already begun in the east and that he, Steiner, had little time to get his family out of Paris. The date was—presumably—early 1940.[3] It was shortly thereafter that the Steiner family, reluctantly heeding the German's advice, left the comfort of an apartment overlooking the Pont Alexandre III and headed for New York. It was a prescient move and a telling confirmation of the quaint notion of class solidarity.

There is a turning point in Steiner's evocation of his years in the French Lycée in New York. It pertains to the central role played by Racine's *Bérénice* in his initiation to "the long noon of French literature" and in the evolution of his literary sensibility more generally.[4] By the end of Steiner's evocation of Racine's immense "minimalism," *Bérénice* has become for him something of a talisman, an urtext, and the play around which, it appears, he might be willing to renew the age-old polemic of Racine versus Shakespeare in the hope of winning the fray, this time, for France (34–35). Indeed, such a wager soon comes to inform his sense of vocation. If Steiner's plea for the "essentiality" of *Bérénice* can only seem "bizarre" to readers of English, then his vocation will be to serve as a "double or triple agent" seeking to communicate the imperative presence of one great literature in and to another. "Comparatism"—or translation, understood in its most exalted sense—is a form of "honest treason" (36). As the crucial case of *Bérénice* demands. . . .

But it is here that Steiner's moving analysis of a few lines of the play

3. George Steiner with R. Jahanbegloo, *Entretiens* (Paris: Editions du Félin, 1992), 30. The text tells us that the scene took place during the "phony war," then "in early 1939." In resolving the discrepancy, I draw on Steiner's elaborations on the episode during a memorable visit to Boston (April 1997).
4. Steiner, *Errata,* 28.

are curiously exceeded by the plain sense of the myth of Bérénice and its history. For it is as though the love tragedy—"the centrality of love and of its inevitable contract with separation"—were far less apposite to Steiner's argument than the issues of "double or triple agency" with which the case of Bérénice is awash. Bérénice is the tale of a Jewish queen of Caesarea who pleads for her people during the Roman crushing of the Judaean rebellion, but then chooses to side with the Romans. She ends up the concubine of Titus at the time of the destruction of the Second Temple, only to be dismissed by him— "against his will and against hers [*invitus invitam*]" in Suetonius's phrase—out of his newly achieved sense of responsibility to Rome once he ascends to the august rank of emperor.

The question underlying the myth of Bérénice is Simone Weil's: the terms of the compatibility (or incompatibility) between the apparent adversaries Rome and Israel, emblematized respectively by Titus and Bérénice.[5] It is thus quite significant that the principal historical source for Bérénice is the Jewish historian Josephus, whose opposition to the zealotry of those resisting Rome was enough to send him directly into the camp of the Romans. His *Jewish War*, largely written during Titus's brief reign, was to a significant extent an exercise in Roman apologetics. And it was Josephus, it will be recalled, whose treachery—the practice of what Steiner, discussing Racine in English, calls "honest treason"—recommended him to Simone Weil as an exemplary historian.

Steiner, zeroing in expertly on celebrated lines of Racine about ramparts buried under their own ruins, is, of course, aware that they could not have been received by his own lycée class without some vague thought of the war going on in Europe, but his comments on the centrality of *Bérénice* seem curiously indifferent to the fact that the wars in question—in both the play and the period in which he read it—were preeminently wars against the Jews. The relation between the Racine masterwork and the historic interlude of World War II, however, was twofold, and more specific.

5. Behind Titus and Bérénice, as Racine saw, lay Virgil's Aeneas and Dido, the tragic couple who serve in the *Aeneid* as a prefiguration of Anthony and Cleopatra. For Weil, as we have seen, it was crucial to affirm that there was an essential distinction between "Hamites" such as the Phoenician-Carthaginian Dido and "Semites" such as Bérénice.

On the one hand, *Bérénice* echoed the drama of Jewish deportation from France. The best readings of the play have tended to unsettle its apparent symmetry (*invitus invitam*) and insist on the apparent hypocrisy of Titus. Given his absolute power, Titus might well have come up with a solution allowing the Jew to remain. In Charles Mauron's apt terms, if Bérénice is "genuinely unhappy," Titus comes across as "falsely Cornelian."[6] At this point, however, Mauron's reading of the play appears to be staging an allegory of recent scholarship on Vichy and the Jews. Specifically, the heart of Robert Paxton and Michael Marrus's argument is the insistence that Vichy was busy promulgating its own anti-Semitic statutes "in rivalry and competition with" the policies imposed by Germany.[7] The hypocrisy that many a reader of Racine has sensed in Titus (in the dismissal of *his* Jew) would be parallel to the hypocrisy of Vichy in its zealous policing of the deportation of some seventy-six thousand Jews.

But if *Bérénice* may be read as an allegory of Jewish deportation, it was, paradoxically, also readable in those years as an allegory of collaboration with the occupier. In 1940, Robert Brasillach, still a prisoner of war, wrote a rather polished version of *Bérénice,* which was published after the war (and after his execution for crimes of collaboration with the enemy) under the title *La reine de Césarée.* Brasillach's version of the play was ultimately inspired by Giraudoux, whose leading disciple he was intent on being, and specifically by his *Judith:* the play would affirm the ideal possibility of love against the imperatives of "racial" incompatibility, but be forced to witness the breakup of the ideal couple because of the instability inherent in the temporality of love itself. Nonetheless, Brasillach's Bérénice is acutely aware that hers is a drama of collaboration. Her most remarkable speech—to her confidant—reads as follows: "My people, ten years ago, your emperor defeated us, sacked our cities, razed even the most sacred memories of our ancestors. It was in the red heat of war that I met Titus. That I fell

6. Charles Mauron, *L'inconscient dans l'oeuvre et la vie de Racine* (Aix: Ophrys, 1957), 86. For a discussion of Mauron's *Bérénice* as it impinges on an understanding of Jean Giraudoux's recourse to the play during World War II, see Jeffrey Mehlman, *Legacies of Anti-Semitism* (Minneapolis: University of Minnesota Press, 1983), 53.

7. See Robert Paxton and Michael Marrus, "Quand Vichy déportait ses Juifs," interview in *Le nouvel observateur,* June 1–7, 1981, 63, and Paxton and Marrus, *Vichy et les Juifs* (Paris: Calmann-Lévy, 1981); see also the English-language translation by Marguerite Delmotte, *Vichy and the Jews* (New York: Basic Books, 1981).

in love with him. It does not make me blush today, and I have no sense of having betrayed my race in joining my fate to one who momentarily was my people's enemy."[8] Whereupon there follows an evocation of just how useful her "people"—"a ragtag lot of merchants, philosophers, usurers, revolutionaries, and bankers"—can be even to their conquerors. Bérénice here appears to be not so much the Jew dismissed (or deported) as the would-be collaborator—as much a practitioner of what Steiner calls "honest treason" as, say, Josephus.

What is most remarkable about Bérénice's speech from Brasillach's play is that years later, as German defeat loomed inevitable, the rabidly anti-Semitic Brasillach would virtually repeat Bérénice's lines in his own defense. On February 19, 1944, he would write in *La révolution nationale:* "Frenchmen of any depth during these last years will have more or less slept with Germany, not without quarreling, and the memory will remain sweet to them."[9] One is hard put to imagine Brasillach penning those lines without thinking of the passage quoted from his *Bérénice.* But if that echo were present, he would be defending his collaboration with a monstrously anti-Semitic regime virtually in the words of a Jew. Unless, of course, the absolute Frenchness of Racine—an author whom no Jew, according to Maurras, could understand—were a potent enough solvent to cleanse any character created in his shadow of the putative sin or crime of being Jewish.

Perhaps Steiner's apparent indifference to the anti-Jewish subtext of *Bérénice,* the Roman destruction of Jerusalem, in his recollection of his overwhelming exposure to the play at the French lycée in New York is to be understood in those terms: to read Racine in wartime was no doubt the highbrow equivalent of singing the "Marseillaise," a sublimely patriotic exercise capable of obliterating every other political or ethical imperative. And yet we are left with both the major historical latencies of the play—*Bérénice* readable as (1) allegory of Vichy's hypocritically autonomous anti-Jewish policy and (2) myth of the charms of collaboration with the occupier—and Steiner's own finely suggestive definition of a classic as "a signifying form which 'reads' us."[10] There is a sense, that is, in which Steiner could not be more on the

8. Robert Brasillach, *La reine de Césarée* (Paris: Plon, 1954), 59.
9. Quoted in Pascal Ory, *Les collaborateurs* (Paris: Seuil, 1976), 116.
10. Steiner, *Errata,* 18.

mark in positing the "essentiality" of *Bérénice* (where one might well have expected *Antigone*) in his memoir, because there is a sense in which the ambiguities of that text, the twin latencies I have adduced, provide a remarkably cogent reading of a significant strand of Steiner's own work.

Consider the fiction. *Return No More* is an early novella, written in 1964, that recounts the return to Normandy, years after the war, of a crippled former German officer who had been billeted in the home of the Terrenoire family during the German occupation. On the day of the Allied invasion, he had ordered the hanging of a Terrenoire son suspected of sending signals to the approaching forces. But now, with a desire to make amends, and above all with a deep sense of the vital possibilities he had known and shared with the Norman family, he comes hobbling back to France to propose marriage to the younger Terrenoire daughter, Danielle, who, after a few cavils of an entirely material nature are answered, accepts. With the turbulence of the ambient seascape woven deftly into its fabric of images, *Return No More* would appear to be Steiner's counterproposition to that classic of the Resistance, Vercors's *Le silence de la mer*. The young woman, long after the fact, responds to the gentlemanly German officer stationed in her home. By the end of his novella, Steiner, the expert reader of Flaubert, gives us a Norman wedding worthy of the most devastating pages of *Madame Bovary*. But it is here that disaster strikes. An unforgiving brother of the bride draws the (crippled) groom into a collective wedding dance that, with a "single screeching note" blown by a local musician and the "mad round" that ensues, turns into a Dionysian romp in which the groom, Falk, falls and is then trampled to death.

The impossible erotic union of the occupier and the occupied, the fantasy at the heart of *Bérénice*, thus figures at the center of Steiner's novella. There is, however, something willfully centrifugal or un-Racinian about his treatment of the subject. Although the author was aware by 1964, to the point of obsession, that the central horror pitted Nazi against Jew, *Return No More* seeks to overcome the bitter but less wrenchingly ultimate opposition between German and Frenchman. Then there is the temporal issue. The tale's last line, uttered by Terrenoire before Falk's bloodied corpse, is: "You came back too soon,

Monsieur Falk, too soon."[11] No compaction or unity of time here; the novella envisages some form of resolution—or avoidance of catastrophe—in the fullness of time. Finally, there is the fact that whereas love's "contract" with separation seems of the essence in Racine, it is visited, however frenetically, from without—by an unforgiving brother—in the novella.

In the fullness of time. . . . Steiner's most important work of fiction, *The Portage to San Cristobal of A.H.,* was published fifteen years later, in 1979. It might well have borne the title *Return No More,* for it is once again a tale of resistance to the postwar return of a Nazi. The central conceit entails the extreme discomfort of the elites of a variety of Western capitals, given the compromises and hypocrisies of all contemporaries of the war, at the news that the Israeli secret service has retrieved a quaking ninety-year-old Adolf Hitler from deepest Amazonia and is bringing its precious cargo back for trial. At the novella's conclusion, after the expert comedy of international manners we have been treated to, capital by capital, Steiner allows his Hitler to speak. His message could well have been scripted by Simone Weil. It is that the Nazis learned everything from the Jews: "Your invention. One Israel, one *Volk,* one leader, Moses, Joshua, the anointed king who has slain his thousands, no his ten thousands, and dances before the ark. It was in Compiègne, wasn't it? They say I danced there. A small dance."[12] Falk's failed marriage dance—of occupier and occupied, German groom and French bride—here modulates to the limit case: Hitler's horrendously triumphant dance celebrating the union of Nazi and Jew. And since, in Weil's terms, Hitler figured nothing so much as the apotheosis of Rome, and Rome ("the great atheistic beast") and Israel ("the great religious beast") were twin cultural formations, Steiner's troubling novella effectively ends in affirmation of Weil's thesis.[13] "My racism was a parody of yours, a hungry imitation," as Steiner's Hitler tells his Israeli captors.

But the nightmare fusion of Nazi and Jew, (Hitlerian) Rome and Jerusalem, returns us to the historical backdrop of *Bérénice* (the Ro-

11. George Steiner, *Return No More,* in *The Deeps of the Sea* (London: Faber and Faber, 1996), 196.

12. George Steiner, *The Portage to San Cristobal of A. H.,* in *Deeps of the Sea,* 142.

13. Weil, *La pesanteur et la grâce,* 183.

man decimation of the Jews) and the fantasy (of a union between Rome and Jerusalem, Titus and Bérénice) whose thwarting is the core of Racine's tragedy. It was not for nothing that Falk, the protagonist of *Return No More* and Hitler's predecessor in Steiner's personal mythology, enters our purview muttering a tag in Virgilian Latin.[14] The "essentiality" of *Bérénice,* in sum, its ability, in Steiner's terms, to read us, was for him simultaneously an ability to write—or at least underwrite—his fiction at its most disturbing, most gripping, most Weilian.

And beyond the fiction? Steiner is famously the author of *After Babel,* surely the most intriguing and richly textured study of literary translation we have. In his recent memoir, he suggests that the biblical myth was a "cover-up" (as Weil said of so many other episodes of the Hebrew Bible), what Freud might have called a "screen memory." The multiplicity of tongues, that is, is not a curse, but our principal and incommensurable blessing.[15] Now in making the case for Babel-as-blessing, Steiner compares the mushrooming plethora of languages to the multiplicity of species—say, "100,000 species of insects in a corner of Amazonia"—and proceeds to press a para-Darwinian argument: our "polyglot condition" is the "pre-eminent adaptive agency and advantage of the human spirit" (89). All of this is preeminently an émigré's perception. Let us retain, however, the Amazonian metaphor. Might it not bear some relation to the teeming region out of which the agents of Steiner's principal fiction negotiated Hitler's "portage"? The heart of Steiner's argument in *After Babel* entails the delineation of a fourfold "hermeneutic motion" governing literary translation. In their most lapidary form, the four moments of the dialectic are listed as "trust, penetration, embodiment, and restitution."[16] Together they narrate a "dialectic" whose moves are an act of faith in the worthiness of whatever is to be retrieved from Babel, a violent and disorienting incursion into the foreignness of the text, a will to "naturalize" the content of the source text, and, finally, a restoration of "parity" in relation to the source language.

It is not our purpose in this context to gauge the multiple translucencies of Steiner's defense and illustration of the "exact art" of trans-

14. Steiner, *Portage to San Cristobal of A. H.,* 152.

15. Steiner, *Errata,* 85.

16. George Steiner, *After Babel: Aspects of Language and Translation* (New York: Oxford University Press, 1977), 303.

lation. Rather we would insist on the uncanny resemblance between the narrative of the "hermeneutic motion" and that of *The Portage to San Cristobal of A.H.* For it is not for nothing that Steiner finds himself, at a key juncture of his argument, quoting Saint Jerome on meaning being brought home as a captive by the translator. Consider, more specifically, the following:

1. Amazonia, the site of the secret Israeli mission, is, as we have seen, Steiner's metaphorical equivalent for Babel in his memoir *Errata*.

2. The author makes use of the key term in the novella's title in characterizing the third moment in the hermeneutic motion: what translation negotiates is "the portage home of the foreign 'sense' and its domestication in the new linguistic-cultural matrix" (333).

3. To the extent that the final moment entails an enactment of reciprocity, parity, or equilibrium between the two languages or texts ("source" and "target" in the translator's jargon), the hermeneutic motion culminates in a gesture precisely parallel to that of Hitler's diatribe at the end of the novella: a "parity" between hunter and hunted, Nazi and Jew, is affirmed (300).

In summary, then, at the core of Steiner's masterwork, *After Babel*, we find the "portage" of a "captive" (meaning) out of "Amazonia" (qua Babel) that culminates in a bizarre statement of equilibrium between the subject and the object of the ("hermeneutic") aggression. We find, that is, an oblique version of the plot of *The Portage to San Cristobal of A.H.* At which point we would be inclined less to adjudicate between one version and the other in terms of primacy than to recall the prototextual role of a reading of *Bérénice* in wartime New York in the elaboration of the "Hitler" novella. But then *Bérénice*, a myth of putatively "honest treason" for whom the principal source is the "honest traitor" Flavius Josephus, was the text that launched Steiner, we learn from *Errata*, into the "honest treason" of comparative literature or higher translation. From which it follows that the subject of *Bérénice* was in any event never far removed from the topos of translation in the first place.

A final station in the evolution of *Bérénice*. After the failed erotic union of occupier and occupied (*Return No More*) and the Weilian affirmation of the fundamental identity of Nazi and Jew, Rome and Israel (*The Portage to San Cristobal of A.H.*); after the plot of the latter novella was detected in displaced form as the radiant core (or "herme-

neutic motion") of *After Babel,* we encounter the improbable book of
dialogues, principally on the myths of Antigone and the sacrifice of
Abraham, between Steiner and the philosopher Pierre Boutang. Boutang was the fair-haired boy of 1930s street fascism, a man whose
reputation has never recovered from the extravagant praise lavished
on him by Lucien Rebatet, Brasillach's coeditor at *Je suis partout,* in his
Mémoires d'un fasciste, and long *persona non grata* (before his reinstatement in 1967) in the French academic establishment. Boutang was
secretary to Charles Maurras and, by Steiner's admission, a sometime
"pamphleteer against Jews."[17] Their friendship is an "obvious im-
probability" (138).

What drew Steiner initially to Boutang was Steiner's admiration for
the latter's *Ontologie du secret,* whose importance, he claims, will one
day make it "seminal."[18] The friendship between the two crystallized,
however, around Boutang's angry rejection of Steiner's dedication of a
copy of his famed study of the myth of Antigone. Steiner, no doubt
drawing on Anouilh's wartime recasting of the myth, dedicated his
book to Boutang, "Creon's unfaithful ally."[19] The implication was that
if Creon represented the business as usual of Collaboration (and Antigone the passion of Resistance), then Boutang was on the side of
Creon, but so unreliably as to be absolved of all accusations of collaboration. The philosopher's response was to remind Steiner that
Maurras, his master, remained a quirky devotee of Antigone all his
life. But the full piquancy of the circumstance does not emerge until
later in the volume, when Boutang lets it be known that it is precisely
to the extent that he has been an unrepentant admirer of Pétain and
has even risked his career fighting for the marshal to be accorded
proper burial rites that he too should be recognized as a devotee of
Antigone. The reversal of Anouilh's famed scenario is complete: Antigone's struggle is precisely that of the principled patriot or collaborator. Steiner, a consummate ironist, was apparently hooked.

The volume of dialogues is nominally about two myths, one Greek,
one Hebrew, but is, as well, most interestingly about the meshing of
absolute friendship on the one hand and Catholic anti-Judaism (and

17. Steiner, *Errata,* 137.

18. See George Steiner's article in the *New York Times Book Review,* July 5, 1998, 13.

19. Pierre Boutang and George Steiner, *Dialogues: Sur le mythe d'Antigone, sur le
sacrifice d'Abraham* (Paris: Lattès, 1994), 10.

its catastrophic sequels in modern Europe) on the other. Steiner's friendship, we read, is rooted—a "troubling source"—in his sense of Boutang's physical courage, the legacy of a youth militating with the anti-Semitic "Camelots du roi," and his own suspicion that under threat of physical danger, he would react in all probability "abjectly"—as a coward (39). What we are served, in sum, is the confession of a Jewish intellectual's subservience to the intimidating strength of a former fascist militant become metaphysician. The resulting friendship is nonetheless so valuable to Steiner as to lead him to reserve for it Montaigne's celebrated line concerning his absolute bond with La Boétie. In the final struggle, Steiner opines, though they be on opposite sides, the mere presence of Boutang will be such as to inspire the Jew he knows himself to be to feats of courage, lest he court the contempt of his superior friend.

But even as he affirms the friendship, Steiner is eager to set it within the broader context of the war against the Jews. Now it happens that Simone Weil is a constant reference in the dialogues. For Boutang she was a modern Diotima, our initiator to the mysteries of Plato, but also our best guide to Antigone. Indeed, on the crucial case of the proper burial of Pétain, the philosopher observes: "Here Simone Weil would be on our side" (57). Steiner, while acknowledging that there are sentences, even whole pages, in Weil's writings "which make one's blood stop," would write elsewhere that she evidenced "the traits of classical Jewish self-loathing . . . carried to a fever pitch."[20] (But he would also write less dramatically that his own admiration of Boutang might well be the fruit of a "self-disdaining fascination.")[21] Finally, in the *Dialogues*, Steiner challenges Boutang about his constant references to Simone Weil. He suggests that the "disappearance" of the Jew is no doubt precisely what Boutang, in his Catholicism, desires. The philosopher claims to be horrified, remonstrating that at no point could he have desired such an occurrence. Steiner retreats to an evocation of two statues at the entrance of the cathedral of Strasbourg: the Church triumphant and the Synagogue in shackles. Surely this was the program of Catholicism from the outset. . . . Boutang demurs.

What the Steiner-Boutang dialogues give us, then, are the two di-

---

20. Steiner, *No Passion Spent*, 177.
21. Steiner, *Errata*, 139.

mensions of the Bérénice myth: a bond of absolute affection, physically rather than erotically rooted, between Jew and anti-Jew is pursued against (or within) a will to recall, even reactivate, the war against the Jews whose prime executant was Titus. Steiner to Boutang: "But have the courage, good God, to say that for you the disappearance of the Jew would be finally. . . ." Boutang interrupts: "The contrary of my thought. . . ."[22] Within the medium of Simone Weil, something on the order of a transference is enacted before being rejected by Boutang. *Bérénice,* far more than *Antigone,* reads, and even writes, Steiner as only a "classic" (in his sense) can. It is a legacy of the instruction of the Lycée Français in wartime New York whose implications for the literate world, in a series of exquisitely erudite volumes, continue to unfold.

22. Boutang and Steiner, *Dialogues,* 135.

SEVEN

Louis Rougier and the "Pétain-Churchill Agreement"

After Simone Weil's death—from complications brought on by willful starvation—there remained the painful task of conveying the news to her family in New York. A cable was sent to André Weil, her brother and a prominent algebraist who had been teaching in Pennsylvania, but though he rushed back to New York, he did not have the heart to tell his parents the news.[1] Instead, he asked Louis Rougier to call them. And it was through Rougier's call the following day that Selma and Bernard Weil heard of the illness of their daughter (about which she had kept them in the dark); then, after a confirming cable to London, they learned of her horrid death.[2]

1. André Weil, who in later years was frequently called the "world's greatest living mathematician," was notoriously frustrated by his underemployment in America during the war (Paul Hoffman, "Numbers Man," *New York Times Magazine,* January 3, 1999, 39). He was persuaded to omit from the preface to the book on algebraic geometry he submitted to the American Mathematical Society a statement of gratitude "to those few who strove to liberate me from the distasteful and humiliating duties of a job that my position as a refugee in the United States compelled me to accept." See André Weil, *Souvenirs d'apprentissage* (Basel: Birkhäuser, 1991), 195. Jacques Hadamard, Weil's inspiration as a mathematical generalist, also spent the war years in the United States and experienced similar frustrations. While being interviewed for a modest post at a modest university, he observed his own portrait—part of a series of great mathematicians—on the wall of the chairman's office. Upon informing the chairman that he was the man whose picture graced the office wall, he was told to come back in a week. When he returned, the portrait had been removed and he was told that there was no job for him. See V. Maz'ya and T. Shaposhnikova, *Jacques Hadamard: A Universal Mathematician* (Providence, R.I.: American Mathematical Society, 1998), 239.
2. Simone Pétrement, *Simone Weil: A Life* (New York: Pantheon, 1976), 539.

Rougier was in many ways a curious choice to bring down the curtain on Simone Weil's life. A professor of philosophy at Besançon, he had made a mark in the 1920s as a historian of religion, and had edited a series at the Éditions du siècle provocatively titled "Les maîtres de la pensée antichrétienne." His own principal contribution to the series was a study of Celsus, the late-Roman philosopher who wrote a polemic against the new dispensation of Christianity that survives only in Origen's refutation of it. Rougier's sympathies were plainly with Celsus's "alert critique" and with Rome, a position that could not have been more un-Weilian.[3] It might well have been characteristic of the notoriously contrarian André to introduce an anti-Christian eulogist of Rome on the last page of Simone's biography. Still, Rougier was in many respects a formidable individual. In 1935, he presided over the first colloquium on the philosophy of science ever held at the Sorbonne. Perhaps whatever complicity joined Rougier and André Weil in this delicate task lay in shared mathematical and scientific endeavors. It was not for nothing that Aldous Huxley, in the introduction to his *Proper Studies,* had invoked his considerable debt to Rougier's *Paralogismes du rationalisme,* a book he regarded as woefully unrecognized.[4]

But no; what makes Rougier's presence at the end of, say, Simone Pétrement's monumental biography of Weil oddly appropriate is neither his differences with her on the subject of Christianity and Rome nor his affinities with her brother on issues of mathematics and philosophy. Nor is it the reflection of André's contrarianism, or even Rougier and the Weils having been neighbors on Riverside Drive during the war. No: what set Simone Weil and Louis Rougier apart in the French colony of wartime New York was the utter seriousness with which they took the rampant hunger in metropolitan France. The tubercular Weil, refusing to eat during her doomed English convalescence lest she ingest sinfully more than the millions of French living on rations in metropolitan France, died as a result. In the archaic formula of her British death certificate: "The deceased did kill and slay

---

3. Louis Rougier, *Celse ou le conflit de la civilisation antique et du christianisme primitif* (Paris: Éditions du siècle, 1926), 316.

4. Quoted in Maurice Allais, *Louis Rougier, prince de la pensée* (Lourmarin: "Memor et Gratus" des Terrasses de Lourmarin, 1990), 40.

herself by refusing to eat whilst the balance of her mind was dis- turbed."[5] Rougier, in his New York years, pursued a single journalistic obsession: the hunger induced by the Allied blockade of France was wreaking a demographic catastrophe that would ultimately be of greater consequence than any political victory the Allies might achieve. In the eloquent title of an article he published as late as February 26, 1944, in *Pour la victoire,* the devastating prospect opened by the Allied blockade was that of "La paix sur un cimetière d'enfants."[6] The starvation of a hostage nation was, in sum, the shared obsession that earned Rougier his place—in a New York running to fat—on the last page of Simone Weil's life.

The rationale for the British blockade, which as of July 12, 1940, was applied to both occupied and unoccupied France, was simple enough to fit into a slogan: "To feed France is to feed Germany." The implication was that if it was necessary to starve France in order to defeat Germany, so be it. The issue lent itself to gender conflict. "Sentimental" females (with one notable exception) pleaded for relief for the starving French, while "hard-headed males" responded that war was war, and the French would have to assume responsibility for its human cost. Sarah Delano Roosevelt, the president's granddaughter, was said to have forgone Fourth of July fireworks in order to contribute fifteen dollars to the purchase of cookies for "the children of France." Clemenceau's daughter Germaine Frank, the wife of an American industrialist, attempted in vain to bring shiploads of French children to the United States. The philanthropist Anne Morgan campaigned successfully for food relief; eventually, after an intervention by Cordell Hull, two ships—one of which (too little too late?) bore the tragicomically appropriate name *Exmouth*—sailed to Marseille freighted with foodstuffs.[7]

On the other side, the *Herald Tribune* editorialized (on August 12, 1940) against any food shipments to France. The prosecution of the war was too important an aim to be compromised by the pleas of sentimentalists. Within the cabinet, Henry Morgenthau, secretary of the treasury, did his best to stymie the Quakers, who led the battle for

5. Pétrement, *Simone Weil,* 537.
6. The article has been republished in Rougier, *La défaite des vainqueurs,* 53–62.
7. Fritsch-Estrangin, *New York entre de Gaulle et Pétain,* 99–111.

war relief, by blocking international payments. (Might there be a link between that stance and a remarkably skillful Vichy propaganda device? Apparently genuine dollar bills could, with effort, be peeled open, and just when the recipients prided themselves on discovering the fake, the inner surface of the bills afforded them an "explanation"—the signature of the "Jew Morgenthau"—of the "deception.") A New York congressman, Sol Bloom, went so far as to accuse Herbert Hoover, who supported relief, of being the "unwitting accomplice" of the Nazis (103).

There was as well an intellectuals' manifesto, spearheaded by the playwright Robert Sherwood, against sending food relief to France. But it was no doubt the surprising unanimity (or indifference) of the French émigré community in opposing such relief that Rougier found most galling. In the celebrity battle that the issue had become, Eve Curie, daughter of the renowned scientists, led the opposition. Her position, voiced in an interview in the *New York Times,* was that because Britain had assumed the responsibility for combating Hitler, it would be indecent for a Frenchman to recommend any modification of the strategically motivated blockade. (Twenty years after the war, a commentator on her position would evoke a measure of responsibility for what he did not hesitate to call a "genocide sponsored by Great Britain" [106].) Finally, the backdrop of Rougier's campaign is rendered in starkest terms by the attitude of the Gaullist-sympathizer organization France Forever (which also went under the tellingly different French name, "La France quand même"). The menu of the Philadelphia banquet at which the organization passed a resolution requesting Britain not to lift the blockade of France survives:

> Hors d'oeuvre variés
> Potage Saint-Germain
> Steak avec deux légumes
> Plateau de fromages
> Glace
> Fruits rafraîchis
> Vins et liqueurs (109)

If Simone Weil felt uncomfortable at the speed with which her fellow émigrés indulged in every luxury a transatlantic liner might offer,

Rougier's distaste at the indulgences of those he called "Eve Curie and her whole shrill band of Harpies" was no doubt even greater.[8]

Rougier's point of departure in his New York articles was Renan's observation, in a letter of 1871, that any insistence on categories of "race" in political matters would lead to a new, nightmarish sort of war: wars would no longer be "political" but "zoological."[9] Their aim would be demographic, the prosecution of a policy of depopulation that would be situated on a different plane from those of conventional political wars. Whence the paradox of 1944: Germany was about to lose the war militarily, but win it demographically. Worse yet, one of the principal weapons in Hitler's demographic war against France had been the British blockade, a weapon that had proved politically and militarily ineffective in advancing British aims, but demographically devastating in advancing those of the Germans. The (British) blockade, that is, was not an effective (or ineffective) weapon against such horrendous policies as those of the (gradual or accelerated) death camps. It was rather a weapon whose effects were fully consistent with (and in some ways even more efficient than) those resulting in the death camps. Statistical details would invariably follow. "In February 1942, the mortality rate in the Seine Department had risen 53 percent in relation to 1939. What did it become two years later? Child mortality for ages one to nine years had gone up 45 percent. In hospitals, the death rate went from 3 percent to 50 percent. The number of deaths from tuberculosis had risen 50 percent in April 1941" (46). In 1944, Rougier was using the word "holocaust" to describe the French situation (48).

Consider now a second article by Rougier for *Pour la victoire*, "Physiologie de la dictature." The author, a Tocquevillean liberal who had organized a colloquium in Paris before the war on Walter Lippmann, was intrigued that the passing of Europe's monarchies had for the most part given rise to an era not of parliamentary democracies, as might have been expected, but of dictatorships. Drawing on the work of Wladimir Drabovitch, a student of both Pavlov and Janet, Rougier evokes an anomaly encountered by Pavlov in his celebrated

8. Louis Rougier, *Les accords Pétain-Churchill: Histoire d'une mission secrète* (Montreal: Beauchemin, 1945), 257.
9. Rougier, *La défaite des vainqueurs*, 40.

experiments on conditioned reflexes in animals. One day, a new dog brought to his laboratory proved particularly refractory. The offspring of two feral dogs, he flashed his fangs and seemed prepared to attack the experimenters. In Rougier's terms, he had retained a quite vigorous "instinct for freedom" (87). The surprise came when Pavlov discovered that the most effective way of reducing that "instinct" was through "undernourishment." Examples from Janet (on the "specular imitation of cataleptics") and Gustave Le Bon (on the "gregarious" propensities of crowds) were further adduced in support of the argument that there is a biology or "physiology" of dictatorship. Beneath a certain level of caloric intake, individuals would fall short of the threshold of psychic energy requisite to the exercise of the complex function called freedom—the capacity, in Clemenceau's definition, for self-discipline.

Walter Lippmann, Rougier's old associate, was thus doubly wrong in suggesting that the best refutation of Rougier's fears concerning the long-term perils of the blockade was the resplendent youth of the Nazi shock troops, who had emerged from the starvation conditions of 1917, 1918, and 1919. First, he was wrong because the children of the aggressor nations of the First World War had never been subjected to the famine currently affecting the children of the victimized nations of the Second. Second, he was wrong because the young wolves ravaging their way through the sheep pens of Europe, for all their renewed physical strength, were in no way exemplary practitioners of the self-discipline that lay at the core of freedom. No, it was an illusion to believe that one might graft "democratically minded *esprits*" on "dictatorially fitted bodies" (91). But time was running out. Only a quick end to the blockade would ensure the demographic—indeed, the physiological—conditions in France that would make the political and military victory that seemed in the offing worth achieving.

The argument, which Rougier ran through as many permutations as his fertile mind could come up with, was worth, as the French say, whatever it was worth. What makes it extraordinary, however, was that Rougier, under remarkable circumstances, shortly after the fall of France, succeeded in placing it before none other than Winston Churchill—and that the British prime minister responded affirmatively. That, at least, was the substance reported in a stunning volume published in Montreal during the last months of the war, which provoked a considerable debate reported extensively in the pages of the *New York Times*. Both the meeting with Churchill, just before Rougier's arrival in New York, where he had a Rockefeller grant to teach at the New School, and the book, which he would rewrite and republish several times in his later life, were turning points in the existence of the most nonconformist of the French intellectuals spending the war years in New York. They would result in his ostracism in New York, and his being driven from the French university system after the war. We turn then to Rougier's version of events as reported in his provocatively titled volume of 1945, *Les accords Pétain-Churchill: Histoire d'une mission secrète.*

Rougier, as we have said, was a Tocquevillean liberal. (When he arrived in New York in December 1940, he would claim to be appalled by the utter conformism of the American press, which he saw as intent on rehearsing the horrors of a kitsch melodrama, with conventional villains, titled *The Fall of France,* and utterly uninterested in the complexities of France's tragic situation.) From his own perspective, France's defeat had been a function of its inferior armaments, a largely technical question. If betrayal there had been, it was on the part of the British, who called Lord Gort and his troops, nominally under the command of General Weygand, back to England in the middle of the Battle of France and who refused to commit British Spitfires in sufficient number to the defense of France. As for Pétain, there was little he could do. To continue the war, perhaps staging a "Mediterranean Dunkerque" and setting up a government in exile in North Africa, would have meant to court disaster. The Italians in Libya and the Germans in Spain would have descended on that government in a pincer movement and occupied French Algeria. There would have been no "Unoccupied Zone" and no possibility for a "Mediterranean strategy" of the sort that eventually led to an Allied victory. The Franco-German armistice of the summer of 1940, which was not a peace treaty, was, in sum, not a betrayal on the part of Pétain, but a strategic error on the part of Hitler.

Still, it became imperative for the French to keep this perspective in view and above all to reassure the British that under trying circumstances, the armistice in no way constituted a reversal of alliances.

Rougier's position, as outlined in his book, was, that is, a form of principled *attentisme*. He journeyed to Vichy with the intention of offering his services, and above all his British connections at the London School of Economics (among them Lionel Robbins), to the end of keeping the Franco-British alliance secretly alive. In the "disconcerting euphoria" that he discovered in Vichy in July 1940, an effervescence born of the sense that real change would at last be possible in France, Rougier immediately identified the enemy, Marcel Déat, the neosocialist *normalien*. Déat had been trained in philosophy by the illustrious Célestin Bouglé, and was fighting at the time for the establishment of a one-party system, modeled on Germany's, in France. Rougier, whose native talents appear to have won him surprisingly quick access to the emerging power elite, made the case to General Weygand against Déat's proposal, about to be submitted to a vote by Pétain's cabinet. His argument is almost operatic in its stylistic effects, and is worth citing as an introduction to the philosopher's political liberalism and to his powers of persuasion: "The single French party would be modeled on the Nazi Party. But it would resemble it the way a black mass resembles a white mass. The Nazi Party was founded on an obstinate rejection of the Versailles diktat; the French party would be founded on the unconditional acceptance of the defeat and its implications. The Nazi Party was founded on the myth of the innocence of Germany in the war of 1914; the French party would be founded on the myth of the unilateral responsibility of France and England in the war of 1939. The Nazi Party was founded on a demand for vital space; the French party would be founded on our resignation to become a small agricultural country, the orchard and amusement park of Hitleria."[10] Eventually, Weygand interrupted Rougier, indicating that he had "understood," and that there would be no single state party in France. Rougier chalked it up as a personal victory.

There remained the matter of reinitiating contact with the British, a task all the more daunting in that Laval, whom the philosopher regarded as a nemesis, would plainly block any such initiative. (In his memoirs, Moulin de Labarthète, a Vichy minister, recalls Laval's reaction upon learning that Rougier's passport to England was being re-

10. Rougier, *Les accords Pétain-Churchill*, 94.

newed: "Nice work! If you want to experience the fate of Poland some day, just keep it up.")[11] Pétain, in Rougier's telling, was won over. In a meeting with the philosopher on September 20, at the Pavillon Sévigné in Vichy, he made no secret of his contempt for Laval, commissioned Rougier to act on his proposals, and eventually presented him to his cabinet as "a Frenchman who, instead of asking what is to be done, proposes solutions."[12] Thus began Rougier's "secret mission" to London.

He found the city positively exhilarating. An ambient sense of the enormous burden shouldered by England, and England alone, imbued every aspect of British life with a kind of "frenzy" that Rougier found particularly tonic. (He later joked that the best way to bring America into the war would be to offer free weekends to London and allow the wartime enthusiasm everywhere in evidence to work its charms [148].) Rougier arrived in London on October 22, 1940, and with almost picaresque rapidity found himself in dialogue—the first Frenchman on an "official mission" from Vichy France—with Churchill.[13] He assured the prime minister that France was committed to an Allied victory, and laid down the argument he would elaborate at such length in the French press of New York about the demographic catastrophe wreaked by the British blockade. Churchill was impressed. Eventually, a summary of the talks was written up, and emended in a hand Rougier has always claimed was Churchill's (although Rougier was not present when the emendations were made).[14] The principal terms of the "gentlemen's agreement," as Rougier referred to it, were as follows. The French would cede neither their (undefeated) fleet nor their colonial bases to the Germans. In exchange, the British would relax the blockade on foodstuffs from the French empire, put

11. Quoted in Ferro, *Pétain*, 304.

12. Rougier, *Les accords Pétain-Churchill*, 115.

13. Subsequent commentators have questioned whether the letter of introduction Pétain gave Rougier in any way granted the philosopher's trip the status of an official mission. See Jean-Baptiste Duroselle, *L'abîme* (Paris: Imprimerie Nationale, 1982), 277.

14. Robert Frank believes that the handwritten annotations in English on the Rougier text were not by Churchill himself, but by his aide, William Strang, of the Foreign Office. See Robert Frank, "Vichy et les Britanniques, 1940–1941: Double jeu ou double langage?" in *Le régime de Vichy et les Français*, edited by Jean-Pierre Azéma and François Bédarida (Paris: Fayard, 1992), 148. My thanks to Robert Paxton for directing me to Frank's essay.

an end to *ad hominem* attacks on Pétain over the BBC (which the French found utterly demoralizing), and allow de Gaulle to take military actions against as many Germans and Italians as he might like, but—such was in any event de Gaulle's original charter—not against Frenchmen. Tucked unobtrusively into part II, section A, paragraph 3 of Rougier's text was the explosive statement that the French government would recommit the empire to the war as soon as the British "or their eventual allies" were in a position strong enough to stage a landing and equip French colonial troops. The British appended one crucial stipulation: Rougier was not to make any contact with the Gaullist camp or divulge the substance (or even the existence) of the agreement to the Gaullists.

In the middle of Rougier's negotiations with Churchill, a diplomatic bombshell was detonated. News was released that Pétain was even then meeting with Hitler, in what was in some ways a "photo opportunity" engineered by Laval, at Montoire. The photograph of the celebrated handshake at Montoire, offered by the octogenarian marshal more in disorientation than in collaboration, was distributed worldwide and became the kitsch emblem of French "collaborationism." Worse yet, news, published in the *New York Times,* reached London that a "separate peace treaty" was being signed; Tunisia would be partially ceded to the Italians, Morocco to the Spanish. According to Rougier's account, Churchill, exasperated, threatened to bomb Vichy. Rougier concluded that the news was false—disinformation spread by Goebbels through Bern. He offered himself up to Churchill as a hostage if the reports were not disconfirmed in twenty-four hours. Churchill was assuaged, the reports were disconfirmed, and the negotiations, which could not be made public, were brought to completion. Rougier left London for Lisbon (where he claimed to be impressed by Salazar's "astonishing erudition"), then Tangiers, and Algiers, where he met with Weygand. On November 11, he was received by Pétain at the Hotel du Parc. The marshal was so adamant in his lack of confidence in Laval that Rougier would later write to Churchill (December 26, 1941) that their negotiations had been responsible for the (temporary) "downfall" of the dauphin. Rougier was asked to submit receipts for his travel expenses—an apparently trivial detail that would nonetheless authenticate his trip as "official business." The following day, Colonel Fonck informed Rougier that Pétain had given the order to "ratify" the agreement.[15] A few weeks later, Rougier left for New York.

Consider the politics of wartime France in terms of two quite different trips to London. The first, de Gaulle's in June 1940, is the stuff of legend, but precisely to that extent, of kitsch as well. The second, Rougier's in October of the same year, is far less available to the sort of mystique that Rougier—in his liberalism, but also in his scholarly career as a historian of the impasses of Christianity—seemed intent on demystifying. More interestingly, whereas the second trip, in Rougier's telling, entertained as one of its aims and provisions control over all that might be at stake in the first (de Gaulle was not to attack Vichy France), the first trip could be sustained only through its innocence (or ignorance) of the second (Rougier's trip and what it portended was not to be divulged in any way to de Gaulle).[16] It is as though the *image d'Epinal* of Gaullist resistance were the local economy or limit case within a far broader—but fundamentally "secret"—economy figured by Rougier's principled *attentisme.* (*Principled:* action was to be deferred not in order to see which way the wind was blowing, but in order to prepare conditions for a resumption of combat once, say, the Americans joined the fray.)

One can further discriminate between the two missions to London. Whereas the Gaullist case entailed a frontal opposition or antithesis between "resistance" and "collaboration," for Rougier feigned collaboration was no doubt the subtlest ruse of resistance. De Gaulle might have the luxury of a certain political purity, but he ran the risk of political and military irrelevance (as the Gaullist absence from the invasion of North Africa made clear). The Rougier strategy, on the other hand, ran the risk of being so embroiled in its undecidabilities between feigned collaboration and genuine resistance as to be fundamentally compromised. The point was succinctly illustrated in the

15. In times of fatigue, Pétain was notoriously inclined to agree with all requests in order to be free of petitioners. On these grounds, Gaston Schmitt has challenged any "alleged ratification" of Rougier's "protocole." See Schmitt, *Les accords secrets franco-britanniques de novembre-décembre 1940: Histoire ou mystification* (Paris: Presses universitaires de France, 1957), 79–97.

16. According to Frank, "Vichy et les Britanniques," 151, however, de Gaulle was kept fully informed by the English. At the time of Rougier's visit to London, de Gaulle was in Africa.

1998 trial of Maurice Papon, where it became clear that one could just as well argue that feigned resistance, given the sentiments of the French populace, might be the most effective tactic of genuine collaboration as the reverse: nothing smoothed the departure of a convoy of future deportees more expeditiously than Papon's apparently solicitous distribution of blankets at the Bordeaux train station. In formal terms, the Gaullist dispensation affirmed a binary opposition (between collaboration and resistance) that the Rougier-Pétain model adeptly claimed to scramble.

That model entailed an extraordinary ethical dilemma: in the strictest sense, French national honor could be maintained only insofar as French hypocrisy (the feint of collaboration) could be affirmed. In short, the French, in the postwar world, could be viewed as honorable only to the extent that they could be viewed as hypocritical. Such was the thesis of Pétain's *double jeu*. It was a staggering burden, from beneath which the French are still extricating themselves. But that dilemma mediated a theoretical model whose generalized extrapolation in the postwar period attained remarkable currency. The frontal, binary opposition between "resistance" and "collaboration" was no more than the impotent (because illusory), idealist misreading of a configuration that unsettled the distinction between the two. It was as though Rougier's London mission, secretly reinscribing de Gaulle's, establishing (or attempting to establish) the parameters within which de Gaulle's might function, figured nothing so much as its unconscious. Or rather, as though the secret memorandum Rougier had claimed to negotiate on Pétain's behalf, offering himself as a hostage to Churchill in the process, was the unacknowledged text in terms of which the entire French trauma of World War II was to be understood and by means of which it might be redeemed—an "unconscious" text, to the extent that Rougier was honor-bound to secrecy. Whereupon, he left for New York City.

Vichy had disconcerted Rougier with its "euphoria" in the summer of 1940, and London had braced him with its enthusiasm; New York, where he arrived in December 1940, immediately depressed him with its conformism. The Tocquevillean, as we have observed, took to neither America's sentimental obsession with the "Fall of France" nor its melodramatic assessment of the villainy of those who had "betrayed" his country. A first misencounter concerned the French fleet, regarding which he had hammered out a key provision in his secret memorandum. What struck Rougier was not merely that Vichy's "delivery of the French fleet" to the Germans had become a leitmotif of émigré rhetoric, but that the frequency with which the fleet's surrender was reported in major American periodicals so defied common sense as to lead him to doubt the good faith of those disseminating a patently fallacious rumor. One could not, after all, deliver up the same fleet every two months.[17] A run-in with Gustave Cohen, the eminent medievalist and jovial cofounder of the Ecole Libre, involved Cohen's announcement that there were fifty German submarines at Dakar. Untrue, as it happened, and Rougier was able acidly to refute Cohen's rumor on strategic grounds. "Dare I, *cher maître*, remind you of the excellent lectures on the criticism of testimony that you dispensed to your students at the Sorbonne?" (180). Rougier would not be forgiven. On March 9, 1942, a few months before the French fleet in Toulon was scuttled rather than allow it to be turned over to the Germans, Jean Perrin, the distinguished Sorbonne professor and Nobel Prize–winning economist, addressed the inaugural banquet of the French-American Club in these terms: "And we tremble endlessly at seeing our splendid fleet, sullied by German uniforms and led to wage infamous battle. . . ." (372). The philosopher could only blanch.

In retrospect, one reads much of the rhetoric of the New York Gaullist rallies a bit as one might the speeches of Flaubert's Comices agricoles. *Genre oblige.* But the circumstance must have been particularly galling to Rougier, who found himself being recruited by a "colony" so impassioned in its denunciation of the "Vichy traitors" as to make his recent trip to London virtually inconceivable. The émigrés, "les obésités de la Cinquième Avenue," were for the most part vigorously in favor of the British blockade (186). Above and beyond Rougier's pledge of silence to the British, there must have been times when the atmosphere in French New York made his London journey unspeakable, indeed unimaginable even to himself. And these were the people eager to welcome the distinguished philosopher, recently arrived from France, into their impassioned ranks.

Rougier refused. The principal occupations of those he called the "counterfeiters of patriotism" seemed to him the dissemination of

17. Rougier, *Les accords Pétain-Churchill*, 179.

false news and the preparation of blacklists. (A particularly shaky example of such a list appeared in *Life* on August 24, 1942: several of those named would end up as cherished members of the Resistance.) Here is Rougier's evocation of the *cour des miracles* Gaullist New York had become:

> A kind of miraculous pool, in which rebels, deserters, those who had fallen afoul of the Code, those who had exported their capital at a time it was forbidden by French law, those who had immediately taken flight in the hour of their country's distress discovered a new virginity. The crippled began to walk, the blind could see, the deaf hear. Monsieur Bernstein, the author of the famous letter to Urbain Gohier, spoke of country and honor and dispensed lessons in courage to General Giraud. [The playwright Henry Bernstein, bête noire of Drieu la Rochelle, who had attacked him physically in the Tuileries on May 22, 1940, was rumored to have been a deserter in World War I.] For which reason he was elected president of the French-American Club. Frenchmen from France were stripped of their rights, to the benefit of a noisy emigration with a pronounced taste for night spots and a propensity to take the lobbies of luxury hotels for the catacombs of the resistance. (190)

This was Rougier's nightmare vision of the French colony—"parvenus of the defeat, the faith-healed believers of Gaullism"—in wartime New York.

He resisted the advances of France Forever. One evening at a dinner, a message from the British ambassador was relayed to the host: no personal attacks on Pétain were to be made at the Free French rally scheduled for Carnegie Hall that evening. Rougier could not suppress his satisfaction: here was one more sign that the London agreement he claimed to have negotiated was being implemented (191). There was visible discomfort around the table. Finally, the hostess let him know that he had been "chloroformed," like all the others who had come from Vichy. It would pass; he would be given a month to complete "detoxification" at France Forever—as though the Gaullist movement had become a branch of Alcoholics Anonymous. He courteously declined an offer of membership.

That decision would cost him in his academic career. Mirkine-Guétzévitch, dean of the Ecole Libre, let him know confidentially that his decision to join neither Free France nor France Forever had been poorly regarded, and that he would do well to write directly to Henri Focillon, president of the Ecole Libre, explaining his position. Rougier, who had known the eminent Focillon for twenty years, agreed, and explained (a) that he was opposed to a diplomatic break between Washington and Vichy, because it would be welcomed by the Germans even more enthusiastically than by the Gaullists; (b) that he was for sending food to the children of France, under careful supervision, lest a demographic catastrophe ensue; and (c) that he felt that France's responsibility in its military defeat was amply shared by the entire Allied community. "I beg your pardon," he wrote in conclusion, "but as a Frenchman I consider myself neither defeated nor ashamed" (201). Focillon replied with a surprisingly agitated letter on November 2, 1941:

We met yesterday. I insisted on presenting your credentials in terms that did honor to your scholarly merit and your personal qualities, which are beyond discussion. I read your letter to those assembled and should say that on more than one score we share your opinion.

Nonetheless, the majority of our colleagues are of the opinion that for the moment they are not in fundamental agreement with you. We are initiating a labor that requires absolute cohesion. But there is absolutely nothing in this decision that would be injurious to your person or your talent. An academic foundation is free to recruit as it wishes after an honest discussion [*une discussion loyale*]. I can assure you that ours was so in all respects . . .

I look forward to seeing you again in New York or Washington and resuming the discussion begun at Walter Lippmann's. (202)

Rougier replied on November 3, 1941, in a letter that mercilessly pinpointed the political pressures under which the Ecole Libre would soon come to grief:

I have received your reply, which informs me that the majority of my colleagues, after honest discussion, are of the opinion that they are not in fundamental agreement with me. You don't tell me wherein the disagreement lies. You call a discussion honest in which the person under consideration is not heard! This is not even an attack against an opinion, but against a person. It is true that you remind me that an academic foundation is free to recruit as it wishes. Is it free to usurp the title of "French" before American popular opinion, when, excluding in advance authentic Frenchmen [*des Français authentiques*], while welcoming a majority of foreigners and naturalized Frenchmen, it practices a kind of reverse racism [*racisme à rebours*]? Does it have the right to call itself free [*libre*] when it begins by establishing a crime of opinion? Is it a very auspicious beginning for its struggle against totalitarianism, which is, on the intellectual level, the politicization of culture, when it demonstrates through its recruitment criteria that, in the guise of an institution of higher learning, it is intent on being an instrument of political propaganda? You had a choice between two conceptions: establishing in America a French institute, open to all competent individuals, proclaiming in resounding manner the ecumenical character of French culture; or engaging in a partisan endeavor, based on discrimination among individuals, marked by a spirit of rancor, vitiated from the outset by concealed political agendas. You have chosen the narrow solution: have you emerged anything but diminished in the process?

What you reproach me with is a refusal to accept the intellectual and moral paralysis which, in the days of Joan of Arc, was called the quarrel of the Burgundians and the Armagnacs, and today, the quarrel of the Gaullists and the Vichyssois. I know only one France, but one French people, bruised, mutilated, suffering, unjustly treated, iniquitously condemned, craving respect and deliverance. I shall recognize but one legal government, concerned less with its form than its content: one that the people of France will be called on to freely choose when it will have the freedom to express itself.

Between your attitude, which excludes me without giving any reason, and my attitude, which offered to collaborate while giving my reasons and taking my risks, where is the genuine freedom, dignity, and equity? All things considered, I prefer having to write this letter to having had to sign yours, something you could not have done, knowing you as I do, without a certain malaise. (204)

Thus spoke the lonely French voice of what I am inclined to call principled Pétainism in wartime New York. It should be noted that the prescient reference to "reverse racism" was the complaint of a French nationalist and in no way that of a racist. Rougier, in his meeting with Pétain, had waxed indignant on the regime's inability to defend the rights of foreign refugees in the "Unoccupied Zone." (In December 1942, he married Lucie Herzka, who was Jewish, in New York.)[18] One imagines the effect of the last letter. Rougier had seized the ethical and rhetorical high ground in a manner that would not be forgiven.

The paradox was that Rougier's position on maintaining an American presence in Vichy was at the time the American position. More interestingly, Rougier's invocation of the broader question of academic freedom and its subversion by political agendas ended up being

18. Allais, *Louis Rougier*, 33. Nonetheless, in a letter of December 5, 1940, Rougier appears to have advised Churchill and Halifax against allowing "Communists, Socialists, and Jews" to speak on the BBC lest the French population be alienated. See "Despatch to His Majesty's Ambassador in Paris," July 13, 1945, in *State Papers* (London: His Majesty's Stationery Office, 1946), 25:31.

the stumbling block on which the Ecole Libre would eventually come to grief. On August 23, 1944, during the liberation of Paris, a confidential report was filed with the Foreign Nationalities branch of the Office of Strategic Services under the title "Politics versus Academic Freedom in the Ecole Libre." It delineated an institution at odds with itself over the pressures denounced by Rougier. According to the report, a "de Gaullist" faction, spearheaded by Lévi-Strauss, had been functioning so openly as an agent of de Gaulle's French Committee of National Liberation that the Department of Justice requested that the Ecole Libre register under the Foreign Agents Registration Act.[19] That request, in turn, "stunned" a second faction, headed by Jacques Maritain, who felt that acceding to the American request would be a de facto admission of abandonment of the principle of academic freedom: it amounted to a "slur" on their academic integrity. The members of the Maritain group were prepared to curtail their overtly political activities in order to qualify for an exemption from registration under the American statute. The Gaullists countered that it was time to drop the pretense of academic neutrality and announce themselves openly as an arm of the French committee. *Pour la victoire,* whose early Gaullism had cooled considerably by 1944, lamented the "spectacle of French spiritual deterioration" and accused the Gaullist faction of wanting to turn the Ecole Libre into a "veritable propaganda agency" (10). Finally, in a tumultuous board meeting in June 1944, Maritain resigned as president (which he had wanted to do on personal grounds in any event), but Alexandre Koyré was "ousted" as secretary-general of the Ecole Libre, and the administration was taken over by Lévi-Strauss and his associates, Louis Rapkine and Jean Benoit-Lévy. Alvin Johnson, director of the New School, was prepared to dissolve the Ecole Libre, and a tentative compromise formula was put together at the time of filing. It was, in sum, as though the issues raised by the Rougier case had come back to haunt the Ecole Libre, but they did so long after the philosopher's indignant letter to Focillon effectively sealed his ostracism in the French intellectual community of New York.

Excluded by the French for espousing a position that was, after all,

---

19. OSS Report FR-873, "Politics versus Academic Freedom in the Ecole Libre," August 23, 1944, 9.

until 1942 that of the State Department, Rougier found himself increasingly in dialogue with Americans. Shortly after his arrival, Walter Lippmann arranged for him to recount his London mission to Chief Justice Felix Frankfurter, who asked him to write the matter up so he might communicate the report directly to the president. Rougier accepted a teaching appointment at Saint John's College in Annapolis. And he continued to write—on the blockade, but also, on occasion, about the history of science—in the leading New York French weekly of Henri de Kérillis and Geneviève Tabouis, *Pour la victoire.*

Kérillis, who describes himself as having been a "De Gaullist" before de Gaulle, but also long after him, had early on been identified by the general for his vigorous resistance journalism. De Gaulle wrote him, suggesting it was his destiny to be to the new war what Maurice Barrès had been to the previous one. In a volume translated by Harold Rosenberg in 1946 under the title *I Accuse de Gaulle,* Kérillis recounts the episode that sealed the break between *Pour la victoire* and the Gaullists. The New York newspaper was affiliated with the London Gaullist newsletter *La Marseillaise* (which the *Herald Tribune* qualified as a Free French counterpart to *Stars and Stripes*) and regularly received copy from it.[20] Shortly after the American landing in North Africa, in the course of which the French ship *Jean-Bart* was sunk, *Pour la victoire* received a piece from London containing the following paragraph: "No matter how much we are assured that Algeria, Tunisia, and Morocco will be restored to us intact, that the Senate will not nullify Roosevelt's promises as it did Wilson's in 1918, and that the *Jean-Bart* will be replaced with a brand-new ship, we are nevertheless convinced that France has suffered a grave injury. Viewed in the light not of our passing generation but of History, the occupation by our American friends of a land that has cost us so much blood is actually a more serious blow to our country than Nazi occupation of French departments, because it is a blow to our honor" (49). Although the article came after a series of more or less cordial skirmishes over *La Marseillaise*'s anti-American line, the editors of *Pour la victoire* in New York were astonished, and refused to publish the passage. Efforts at mediation failed. De Gaulle intervened to reaffirm his confidence in

20. Henri de Kérillis, *I Accuse de Gaulle,* translated by Harold Rosenberg (New York: Harcourt, Brace, 1946), 43.

François Quilici, editor of *La Marseillaise,* and insist on unexpurgated publication of the material from London. *Pour la victoire* held fast, and on January 13, 1943, Quilici cabled the New York editors to indicate that all collaboration between the two papers would be terminated. Kérillis, almost in spite of himself, had been cast into the anti-Gaullist camp. He figures in Rougier's memoirs as a rare ally in French New York.

In the spring of 1945, as America prepared to savor the fruits of victory, readers of the *New York Times* were treated to an astonishing public drama in which an obscure French professor, Louis Rougier, referred to inaccurately in one letter as a "modest law professor," appeared to take on Winston Churchill and the British Foreign Office. Given the political circumstances, the match was astonishingly uneven. Here was one David whom no one thought was up to slaying Goliath. But such was Rougier's eloquence (and such the stash of photostatic copies of documents he had saved) that the debate gave every indication of turning his way before the *Times* precipitously shut it down. One might have expected that the news story of May 30, 1945—"Vichy-British Pact Alleged by Book: Professor Who Worked for Pétain Repeats Story but London Denies It"—would have put an end to the matter. After all, what match for "London" might a mere professor (and a Pétainist professor at that) be in the closing months of World War II? The story, however, issued in a second rebuttal by the Foreign Office, which resulted in a lengthy *Times* article on July 17. It was titled "Pétain 'Pact' Data False, Say British: Foreign Office, Denying Any Churchill Agreement with Marshal, Attacks Emissary." Four days later, Rougier, accused of foisting a hoax on the foreign-relations community, responded. The *Times,* which might have preferred to put the issue to rest, covered the story, which was centered on Rougier's refutation of the British position, in an article titled "Rougier Reiterates He Carried On Secret Vichy-British Negotiations: Challenging British Foreign Office Statement, He Declares He Has Halifax Letter Referring to Talks with Pétain."

Plainly, the Rougier matter would not go away. Worse yet, Rougier seemed prepared to make the documentary case not merely that he was not lying, but that Churchill—for electoral reasons?—had now become party to a forgery. The details emerged in a statement by

Rougier that appeared in the article of August 8: "Rougier Accuses Britain of Forgery: Declares White Paper Lied to Disprove His Account of Secret Vichy Pact." The *Times* had had enough. If one had to swallow the story of a Churchill-Pétain "pact," it might at least be separated from the irrepressible figure of Professor Rougier. The day that Rougier's statement about a British forgery was printed, the *Times* ran a second story titled "Vichy Aide Claims Pact with Britain: Minister of Education Says He Negotiated It for Pétain—Calls Him Pro-British." Then in striking uppercase letters: "BRANDS ROUGIER FAILURE." Jacques Chevalier, the Vichy minister of education, was said to have been Pétain's secret conduit to Churchill by way of his old Oxford friend, the earl of Halifax. Rougier's effort was at best a dress rehearsal for the Chevalier-Halifax agreement and itself yielded no practical results. After this, the name Rougier disappeared from the *New York Times*.

Consider how the Rougier story played out in the pages of New York's newspaper of record. Rougier's story initially appeared in the *Times* in a context stacked against it. Pertinax, the French journalist and author of *Les fossoyeurs*, wrote a curiously personal news article ("Pétain will Face Merciless Court," May 4, 1945) in which Rougier's alleged mission was introduced, with great skepticism, as the principal piece in Pétain's defense. Rougier himself, whom Pertinax had "heard out" early in the war, was referred to as "one of those college professors who try to meddle with diplomatic affairs." In a subsequent article in the *Times* (July 29, 1945), Paul Winkler, "director of the French feature news agency," would cite Rougier's profession as prima facie evidence for the falsity of his claims: "He said he had been suspicious of Professor Rougier because 'I couldn't understand why a university professor should be entrusted with a diplomatic mission.'" Pertinax's dubious refutation of Rougier's claim consisted of saying that even if, "in an unguarded moment," Churchill had received the itinerant professor, the agreement had no validity because "Pétain never appended his signature to the draft." But Vichy was, of course, in no position to engage in open diplomacy with the British. It was of the essence of Rougier's recourse to the term "gentlemen's agreement" that no signatures would be appended. Whereupon Pertinax invoked Rougier's anticipatory jubilation at the American invasion of North Africa and recounted Pétain's crucial failure to travel to Algiers, which was, to be sure, the turning point in his historic destiny. Properly understood, the journalist writes in an oddly self-contradictory formulation, the Rougier incident will bring "additional evidence of Pétain's vicious political vision and faint-heartedness." Exit Pertinax.

The readers of the *Times* were not convinced. After the contents of Rougier's book were revealed, Charles Upton Clark wrote a letter of praise on June 2, 1945. The book was "a 'must' for every student of propaganda, with its wealth of illustrations, involving numerous well-known commentators; but its chief value is to enhance the enlightened patriotism of Churchill and Pétain and to justify completely our much maligned policy toward Vichy." The Foreign Office, which would have been horrified by Clark's enthusiastic pairing of Churchill and Pétain had it read his letter, began the counterattack in a "4,000-word statement." The central claim of the British refutation was that the memorandum drawn up by Rougier in the course of his London trip was not at all the record of a negotiation with Churchill, but rather a series of talking points to be presented to General Weygand in North Africa. Indeed, quite significantly, on the first page of the memorandum copied by Rougier, which did indeed correspond to a page in the archives of the Foreign Office, in the titular phrase "Entretien avec Weygand," the name Weygand had been blacked out (so that Rougier might perfidiously pass his memorandum off under the title "Entretien avec Churchill"). As for the remainder of the "protocole," it is quite different from the text retained by the British and bears not at all on such questions as diminishing the blockade, avoiding attacks on Pétain, keeping the fleet and the colonial bases out of German control, and so forth.

Four days later, on July 21, the *Times* made Rougier's response the centerpiece of its article:

The British Government has several times denied that secret negotiations had taken place between the British Prime Minister and the Vichy Government in the autumn of 1940. Marshal Pétain and the French Ministers Flandin and Peyrouton have testified that such negotiations had occurred and had been brought before the Council of Ministers at the end of December 1940.

In contradiction with its preceding denials, the British Foreign Office, in a 4,000-word statement, now admits that negotiations took place in London and in Madrid. [In Rougier's version, the Madrid negotiations were to determine the precise modalities through which the blockade was to be dimin-

138

ished, in accordance with the London agreement.] However, the British Foreign Office states that these negotiations took place, through me, not between Mr. Winston Churchill and Marshal Pétain, but between the Prime Minister and General Weygand [who was heading a token French army in Tunisia and whom Churchill would have called on to raise the standard of rebellion], and that the text of the gentlemen's agreement which I have published in my book . . . is not the draft of an agreement between two Chiefs of State, but the draft of what I had been requested to convey to General Weygand regarding "the state of affairs both in this country and at Vichy." It is further stated that the name which I crossed out is not "Churchill" but "Weygand," and that the marginal corrections are not in the handwriting of Mr. Churchill [as claimed by Rougier] but in the handwriting of Mr. Strang or Lord Halifax.

This new interpretation, which would absolve the British Government of any compromise with the Vichy Government, raises certain difficulties. For the present I shall leave to handwriting experts the task of arguing about whose handwriting appears in the margin and whose name is crossed out. But why should I have been requested by the Prime Minister to explain to Weygand the "state of affairs at Vichy"? Weygand knew far more about it than either the Prime Minister or I did. Why should I have been requested to explain to Weygand the viewpoint of France? He would have stopped me with one word: "I know it better than you do."

But what is decisive is the letter from Lord Halifax to me dated Dec. 29, 1942: "I have now received a telegram from the Foreign Office confirming that, as I had anticipated, they cannot agree to your publishing anything about the confidential conversations which you had in the autumn of 1940 with Marshal Pétain and with the Foreign Office." [That letter had come in response to a request from Rougier, who was eager to disseminate in America the facts of his mission.] Lord Halifax wrote "with Marshal Pétain" and not with General Weygand. The Prime Minister would do well to be in agreement with his Ambassador beforehand.

The British Government no longer challenges the existence of the telegram which it sent me on Nov. 21, 1940, when I was in Geneva. [The telegram, according to Rougier, was to confirm the acceptance and implementation of the terms of the agreement.] But it gives it an unexpected interpretation. According to this latest version, the telegram did not refer to my conversations in London but was a summary of the negotiations which were going on at that time in Madrid. Why should the Foreign Office have deemed it expedient to send me a summary of these negotiations to Geneva if it had never mentioned them to me and if I had been unaware of their existence until that day? In that telegram reference was made to economic negotiations in Madrid, but only at some future time. Part of the telegram follows: "On this understanding we are prepared to begin economic discussions with the Vichy Government at Madrid, trade between French North Africa and ports in unoccupied France being first reviewed, and are prepared to send a representative from this country to meet a representative from Vichy in Madrid." It will be observed that the negotiations were to be with the Vichy Government and not with General Weygand. This new interpretation offends, not only common sense, but grammar. It has its tenses, present, past, and future, somewhat mixed up.

The British Government denies that it ever instructed the BBC to "refrain from personal attacks on Marshal Pétain." Here I am compelled to summon the testimony of General de Gaulle against the Prime Minister. General de Gaulle sent me last month an emissary to tell me that he was thoroughly convinced of the existence of the accords, because at the end of October 1940, the British Foreign Office had requested both the General and the de Gaullists in London to refrain from personal attacks on Marshal Pétain.

The British Government denies that it ever agreed to refrain from winning over the French colonies remaining under Vichy control. What a pity that the telegram of Nov. 21 states precisely the opposite!

What the British Government does not explain is why it enjoined me to remain silent if there was nothing to conceal. Why it imposed the conditions that neither I nor other emissaries from Vichy, such as Colonel Groussard, should contact any of the de Gaullists. De Gaulle's envoy said to me, "Had we met in London at that time we certainly would have come to some understanding." Was Mr. Churchill bent on dividing the French?

The response was, to all appearances, devastating, and resulted in a carefully reasoned letter to the *Times* (from the historian A. de Montmorency, on August 1) endorsing Rougier's position. His conclusion: "Winston Churchill's vehement denial of any pact with Pétain seems to have been motivated by strong electoral reasons, rather than by historical truth." Rougier's next foray in the *Times* was in response to the British government's publication of its version of the memorandum in contention. Rougier had claimed that the deleted name in the title phrase ("Entretien avec . . .") was Churchill, and that he had blacked that name out lest the person making the copies learn of his secret mission. The British claimed the deleted name was Weygand (these were to be "talking points"), which meant (if the British version were a forgery) that the British had to come up with a reasonable agenda for the "Rougier-Weygand talks." They could not, and Rougier, in a dazzling display of irony, showed just how implausible it was for the British to commission a French philosopher to convey philosophical banalities—for example, that "a German peace means accepting the triumph of ideologies which have been denounced as anti-Christian by the Church"—to the head of the residual French forces in North Africa. "I can assure Mr. Churchill," Rougier told the *Times,* "that if I had engaged in such odd conversation with General Weygand, I should have been put out in less than two minutes."

The documentary evidence, the inconsistency of the British refutation, and above all the stipulations of the agreement having been loyally implemented on both sides as of November 1940 (as the letter writers to the *Times* were able to attest) all ended up supporting Rougier's case. The statements in the *Times,* however, added a rhetorical dimension to the demonstration that was irresistible. It was difficult to imagine a man of Rougier's obvious intelligence engaging in the discussions (with Weygand) that the British version of the memorandum had scripted for him, and it was hilarious to hear the philosopher hinting at what those discussions might have been like.

The *Times,* as we indicated, put an end to its season with Rougier by running a story about yet another Pétain-Churchill agreement (negotiated—if never quite ratified—by the Vichy education minister Jacques Chevalier and Lord Halifax). For all Rougier's faith in his memorandum (and for all his exegetical mastery of its implications and terms), that document, said Chevalier, was a failure. Historians, at least initially, were less unkind. In *Our Vichy Gamble,* written at the behest of Cordell Hull with full access to the State Department's archives, William Langer comes down largely on Rougier's side (observing that the "extensive *démentis* of the British government" indicate that the discussions with Rougier must have been "of some importance") before subsiding into a face-saving compromise for Churchill.[21] Gaston Schmitt, in a volume published in 1957 under the auspices of the Comité d'Action de la Résistance, concedes that the British Foreign Office blundered seriously in its responses to Rougier, but produces a devastating letter from Pétain to Weygand claiming that in Vichy, Rougier was commonly regarded as a British agent.[22] Might the marshal have simply consigned the professor's memorandum to the oblivion of some drawer? Jean-Baptiste Duroselle, who published in 1982 what is in many ways the definitive account of Vichy's "residual

---

21. William Langer, *Our Vichy Gamble* (New York: Knopf, 1947), 88.
22. Schmitt, *Les accords secrets,* 80.

relations" with Great Britain, has complete confidence in the "good faith" of the itinerant professor, but sees him as a hopeless naïf in the world of high-stakes diplomacy. With his assurance that his tattered and heavily emended pages embodied the secret honor of France, Duroselle's Rougier comes across as a prototypal text-fetishist.[23] Finally, one is left by Robert Frank, who suspected that Rougier had doctored his text in 1945, with this intriguing exercise in ambivalence: "The difficulty with Rougier is that he combined with consummate art truth and falsehood, sincerity and sham, good faith and fraudulence."[24] There was, in the last analysis, a certain perverse moral grandeur in the claim Rougier never tired of pressing. The British version of his adventure, after all, cast him in the role of failed hero of the Resistance: he would have gone off to Africa in the hope of inspiring a resistance movement under Weygand's leadership. To have been assigned such a role by America's principal ally at the end of the war was as enviable a fate as an opportunist might wish for. But Rougier was anything but an opportunist. He wanted no part of a resistance that did not include Pétain.

There was much talk of the Rougier documents at the time of the Pétain trial. They were to constitute the decisive proof of Pétain's inspired hypocrisy or *double jeu*. But somehow they never made it to the trial. Instead, it was another argument out of French New York, André Schwob's in his *L'affaire Pétain*,[25] that provided significant material *for the prosecution:* Pétain as longtime conspirator against the republic, working hand in glove with the sinister left-wing Hitlerian Gustave Hervé, the principal provisions of the Vichy constitution already in place before the war even began. Rougier was certain that de Gaulle had intervened to confiscate the documents.

Shortly after Roosevelt died, Commandant John Grombach invited Rougier, who was by then working "with the American services," to

23. Duroselle, *L'abîme,* 276.
24. Frank, "Vichy et les Britanniques," 146. Robert Paxton, for his part, is dismissive, noting merely that "the notations on Rougier's document are not in the handwriting of Winston Churchill, as he claimed" (*Vichy France: Old Guard and New Order* [New York: Norton, 1972], 88).
25. André Schwob, *L'affaire Pétain* (New York: Editions de la Maison Française, 1944).

lunch at the New York Athletic Club.[26] In the course of the meal, Grombach requested permission to photograph the Frenchman's documentation. Because such photographs had already been taken several times over by American government agents, Rougier expressed mild surprise. Grombach explained his request. There were indeed two sets—"un double jeu"—kept in the White House, one in the president's safe, the other in that of General Watson. Both men had died, and both sets were nowhere to be found in their safes. Not only was Pétain's *double jeu* fading into invisibility; the *double jeu* in Washington on which, for Rougier, that *double jeu* rested had also disappeared.

It remained for Rougier's adversaries to take their revenge. The illustrious Thomist philosopher Etienne Gilson had never forgiven Rougier his polemic against scholasticism. Upon assuming the directorship of the Institut Franco-canadien in Montreal, he denounced Rougier ("a world-class liar") and *Les accords Pétain-Churchill* and withdrew the lecture invitation that had already been extended for the winter of 1945–46.[27] The Rougier disinvitation became a theme of student protest.

In 1948, he was called before two academic commissions of inquiry to determine his fitness for teaching in postwar France. The second was so manifestly incompetent that Rougier, denouncing the judge, called the proceedings to a close himself: "I hereby adjourn the session, since you have neither the serenity of a judge nor the objectivity of a historian. I pity you" (121). Additional witnesses against Rougier were sought. Maritain and Gustave Cohen both obliged. Cohen described the reasons for the decision to exclude Rougier from the Ecole Libre: "The reason for the hostility lay in the stories, which seemed quite implausible to us, of Rougier's discussions as an envoy of Pétain. Moreover, that element alone sufficed to provoke in us a legitimate distrust resulting in a complete and definitive break" (122). French New York had become a nightmare. In an affidavit filed for the defense, Jacques Chevallier, then a *député* from Algiers, recalled meeting

26. Rougier was, in fact, interviewed with some regularity by the Office of Strategic Services starting in July 1943. Eleanor Clark, his principal handler, describes him as "very intelligent and somewhat repulsive," a skeptical supporter of Giraud, and a man with whom "it is sometimes a little hard to see where he draws the line." OSS Reports FR-606, July 13, 1943, and 611, July 15, 1943.

27. Louis Rougier, *Les accords secrets franco-britanniques de l'automne 1940: Histoire et imposture* (Paris: Grasset, 1954), 204.

Rougier in 1944 and affirmed that it was impossible to evaluate Rougier's situation during the war "without having oneself lived in the particular atmosphere of division, irritation, and even at times hatred prevailing in New York among members of the French colony" (129). According to a leak from the Federal Bureau of Investigation, he continued, of the three thousand cases of French espionage brought to the attention of the FBI between June 1940 and November 1942 not a single one was retained. Chevallier's testimony proved ineffective. Rougier was placed on retirement by order of the Ministry of Education on July 23, 1949.

He drifted further to the right and could soon be found signing articles alongside those of the unrepentant fascist Maurice Bardèche. Lionel Robbins of the London School of Economics, his conduit to Churchill in 1940, blackballed him from attending the major conference organized by Robbins and Friedrich Hayek.[28] His crime: lèse-Churchill. . . . Eventually, he would be discovered by Alain de Benoist and the "New Right": his early polemics against Christianity stunned the neopagans around Benoist with their pertinence. Alain de Benoist: "There are intellectual masters, cherished ideas, and professors and teachings worthy of admiration. But there are also, though they are increasingly rare, it should be said, masters such as lived in ancient Greece, as simple in their manners as they were subtle in their thoughts, simultaneously intimate and distant, and who, beneath the porticoes where paths crossed, taught their disciples to forge that strength of character without which intelligence is naught. For the author of these lines, Professor Rougier was one of them."[29]

And might there be an intellectual legacy of Rougier before, in his embitterment, he was swallowed by the Right? In *La France jacobine*, he published (in Switzerland) a curious essay titled "Psychanalyse du peuple français." Harking back to his own experience in the war, he presented an image of France in terms of a split consciousness that political analysis ought to be able to reconcile with itself. Perhaps, he suggests at one juncture, France has to "work through" a still-earlier trauma, the French defeat of 1870 and its sequels. It is a somewhat

28. Allais, *Louis Rougier*, 34.
29. Alain de Benoist, introduction to Louis Rougier, *Le conflit du christianisme primitif et de la culture antique* (Paris: GRECE, 1974), 12.

different scenario than that equating Pétain and Bazaine, which we encountered earlier. Thiers, in July 1870, pleaded with the imperial government not to go to war, and was accused of cowardice. The Prussians were delighted. Thiers's residence was attacked. "And yet it was he who was right." Meanwhile, Gambetta, refusing to yield an inch to the Prussians, had already discovered the rhetoric of Paul Reynaud on June 13, 1940: "So long as there is an inch of sacred soil beneath our soles, we shall hold aloft the glorious banner of the French Revolution." What is striking is that Gambetta would live to bestow on Thiers, "enemy of the people," the title of "liberator of the land."[30] Time had allowed Thiers and Gambetta to perceive that they were fighting—differently—the same battle on the same side. Might the same be in the offing for *gaullistes* and *maréchalistes*?

Rougier's memorandum, we observed earlier, figures something on the order of a French unconscious, a well-nigh fetishized text within which the most sacred oppositions of the society come undone. Embracing (but crucially exceeding) the opposition between resistance and collaboration, Rougier's text offers the essential deferment of *attentisme*, a realm in which feigned collaboration is the subtlest ruse of resistance. Juxtapose what one had until now solemnly opposed; that was Rougier's most constant lesson during the war. It is a fundamentally analytic lesson. Jean Laplanche on psychoanalytic interpretation: "Such an interpretation implies that, as in the case of the analysis of dreams, all the elements be juxtaposed so that nothing be eliminated, that the *either/or* be retranslated into an *and*."[31] Louis Rougier never ceased being the analyst of the nightmare that wartime New York had become for him.

---

30. Louis Rougier, *La France jacobine* (Paris: La Diffusion du Livre, 1947), 219.
31. Jean Laplanche, *Life and Death in Psychoanalysis,* translated by Jeffrey Mehlman (Baltimore: Johns Hopkins University Press, 1976), 74.

EIGHT

Saint-Exupéry
Between Breton and Maritain

In aviation circles, one habitually smiled when referring to Saint-Exupéry as a great pilot. Indeed, for his biographer, he was less a heroic aviator than a heroic survivor of his numerous crashes.[1] But at the time he landed in New York aboard the American export liner *Siboney* on the last day of 1940, Saint-Exupéry was the most celebrated Frenchman of the exile. The "Conrad of the skies," as he was known, had been plucked from relative obscurity by André Gide, who had written a preface for *Vol de nuit,* a volume about the sacred quality of life among those opening the skies of South America to air mail. Henry Miller dubbed him a "Jack London superman, with more sophisticated ruminations."[2] Sartre, in flight from bourgeois comfort, declared himself "under the spell" of the writer-machinist.[3] Indeed, Saint-Exupéry's eminence as a pilot-poet was such that his entire stay in America, which evolved from a projected "three or four weeks," as he told the *Times* on arrival, to more than two years, was recorded, commented on, and in part lived as a function of its coverage in the pages of New York's newspaper of record.

If one were to delineate the structure of Saint-Exupéry's stay, it might be organized around two strikingly symmetrical scandals provoked by comments he made to the *New York Times.* The first, a

1. Stacy Schiff, *Saint-Exupéry: A Biography* (New York: Knopf, 1994).
2. Henry Miller, *Letters to Anaïs Nin* (New York: Putnam, 1965), 28.
3. Jean-Paul Sartre, *Witness to My Life: The Letters of Jean-Paul Sartre to Simone de Beauvoir, 1926–1939* (New York: Scribner's, 1992), 371.

146 demurrer on the occasion of his appointment to a national advisory post at Vichy (about which he had apparently not been consulted), was reported on January 31, 1941, shortly after Saint-Exupéry's arrival in the United States, and provoked the wrath of André Breton and the surrealists. Saint-Exupéry would respond in an angry letter, never sent, to which we shall attend shortly. The second, "An Open Letter to Frenchmen Everywhere," appeared in the *New York Times Magazine* on November 29, 1942, shortly after the Allied invasion of North Africa, and prompted a memorable polemical response from the Catholic philosopher and spiritual guide of the exile community, Jacques Maritain. Saint-Exupéry would respond publicly to Maritain in the pages of *Pour la victoire,* the anti-Vichy weekly, and additionally in a pained letter. The symmetry of the occasions lay in the fact that our author, as we shall see, was as dispirited by the necessity of responding to Maritain as he had been invigorated by the imperative of answering Breton. It was not so much that his time in New York, which he lived as a kind of season in hell between two bouts of service as a reconnaissance pilot, had exhausted him. Rather, he had taken the measure of both men and decided that beyond any issue of politics or ideology, whereas he could not be diminished by conflict with Breton, a man for whom he evinced utter contempt, he could only be diminished by a break with Maritain, for whom his esteem was "absolute."[4]

The trip to America was from the outset fraught with significant—and infelicitous—resonances. Saint-Exupéry, after all, had made a name for himself with the Compagnie Générale Aéropostale at a time when air mail was something of an international French-run franchise. He witnessed the foundering of the company into bankruptcy in the wake of a politico-financial scandal of the sort that wracked the Third Republic during its last decade. The United States would pick up the pieces as air mail became American. The Compagnie Générale Aéropostale, it has been suggested, was Panama revisited. As in the case of the construction of the canal, a French fiasco that had become the center of a political scandal had turned into an American success. Now Saint-Exupéry, in the wake of a new French failure, the battle against Hitler, would once again, in the best of cases, be constrained to

4. Antoine de Saint-Exupéry, *Écrits de guerre, 1939–1944* (Paris: Gallimard, 1982), 230.

see the United States succeed where France had failed. One of the most memorable lines of his New York years was a rejoinder to de Gaulle's legendary "We have lost a battle, we have not lost the war": "Tell the truth, general. We lost the war; our allies will win it" (119). In the wake of a resounding French defeat, in sum, an Allied victory would be bittersweet at best.

Upon arrival in New York, Saint-Exupéry, the winner of the National Book Award of 1939 for *Terre des hommes* (translated as *Wind, Sand, and Stars*), expatiated on the reasons for France's defeat, which he attributed principally to Germany's superior industrial power and France's utter failure to "recognize the nature of modern warfare."[5] These were sentiments worthy of de Gaulle at the time. There were two ominous notes, however, in the *Times* article. First, the man who had given new meaning to the phrase "lyrical flight" was said to have "submitted graciously to a long series of questions, replying frankly to those regarding France's collapse and avoiding others, including one about his opinion of Marshal Henri [*sic*] Pétain." In émigré New York a willingness to denounce Pétain's treachery was as de rigueur as a willingness to dismiss Potain's diagnostic capacities in the salon of Marcel Proust's Mme Verdurin. The hesitation would have raised hackles. Then: "M. de Saint-Exupéry said he still had faith in democracy, but not in the kind of democracy practiced in France at the outbreak of the war." This particular émigré had little sympathy for the *ancien régime* of the Third Republic. The political scandals in which Aéropostale had become embroiled and the utter inadequacy of French preparation for the war were sufficient grounds for that demurrer. He would later attempt to clarify his antidemocratic democratic stance in a long letter to his translator Lewis Galantière: "I could thus be the most ardent democrat and still claim to be speaking unambiguously in telling you that it was democratic tendencies that ruined Aéropostale."[6] In addition, Saint-Exupéry had developed the conviction that liberty, equality, and fraternity were so frequently at odds with one another that only a new and more exalted sense of their articulation held hope for the future of those sonorous abstractions. Finally, one should not underestimate the political resonances in the

5. "France's Fall Laid to Military Chiefs," *New York Times*, January 1, 1941, 20.
6. Antoine de Saint-Exupéry, "Lettre à Lewis Galantière," in *Écrits de guerre,* 151.

148   1930s of the paramilitary discipline that had become part of the pilot's ethos. Saint-Exupéry came to think of Aéropostale as a kind of
airborne monastery on whose austerity and fraternal solidarity he
thrived. The aspiring fascist Robert Brasillach was an admirer, and
regarded him as a neo-Nietzschean.[7] And then there was his friendship with Drieu la Rochelle, future editor of the collaborationist *Nouvelle Revue Française*. Was it known that Drieu had personally accompanied Saint-Exupéry through the formalities at Vichy requisite for
his journey abroad? Surely there were those who saw Saint-Exupéry's
ethos of transcendence through discipline as an apprenticeship in
fascism. However opposite his politics might be from Charles Lindbergh's—the Frenchman wanting the United States to enter the war
and the American to keep his country out—the omnipresence in the
press of America's most celebrated flyer and the notoriety attached to
the decoration he had received from Hitler could not but inflect the
perception of France's most celebrated flyer once he became a New
York personality.

   A mere two weeks after arriving in New York, Saint-Exupéry was
the guest of honor at a gala "book and author luncheon" at the Hotel
Astor. There were fifteen hundred persons in attendance. They had
come to see the author receive the National Book Award for 1939, an
honor that his service flying reconnaissance missions had prevented
him from receiving earlier. The moviemaker Jean Renoir, who had
sailed to America with Saint-Exupéry, recalled whole shopwindows
devoted to the novelist's works. He was a celebrity, perhaps America's
favorite Frenchman, residing on Central Park South in the first of
several sumptuous American lodgings he would come to occupy. If
any of his fellow citizens were in any way jealous, an opportunity to
strike back, as it happened, was provided by Saint-Exupéry himself in
what turned out to be, in its very desultoriness, an inflammatory
article in the *Times* of January 31, 1941. The bland compound headline
was like a red flag: "St. Exupery Dislikes Vichy Appointment; Writer-
Aviator Says He Would Have Refused If Asked." To "dislike" an appointment is far weaker than to turn it down. The conditional of the
subordinate headline, moreover, suggested that it was by now too

---

7. Robert Brasillach, "Terre des hommes," in *Les critiques de notre temps et Saint-
Exupéry*, edited by B. Vercier (Paris: Garnier, 1971), 68.

late—*politesse oblige?*—to turn down anything. Worse yet, the body of the brief article made it clear that his reason for rejecting the appointment to Vichy's national council was a discomfort less with the policies of Vichy than with politics per se.

In an extended letter to André Breton, Saint-Exupéry makes annoyed reference to a rumor, apparently spread by the surrealist "pope," according to which the writer would not himself have penned the demurrer, but would merely have acceded to it once it had been issued in his name. The aviator-writer then proceeds to give the names and addresses of all the friends, aides, and translators who were party to his efforts in issuing it. Saint-Exupéry casts himself in the role of the victim of a shoddy policelike persecution. And he takes particular glee in casting Breton in the role of public accuser—indeed, inquisitor. It is a particularly shrill statement, in the course of which public accuser Breton (a role he cultivated in his manifestoes) emerges as a man of profoundly Nazi sensibility: "It is glaringly obvious that your action could have been advocated by Goebbels himself. There is no doubt that if such an action were still in his power, he would subsidize the American publication *in toto* of the political and social texts of your surrealist journals."[8] Saint-Exupéry initially takes up an argument that Jean Paulhan would espouse at the end of the war: given the flag-trashing pacifism of certain leftist groups (including the surrealists) before the war, one is hard put to fathom Breton's nerve in claiming a higher moral ground in the name of a newfound patriotism. Before long, however, Saint-Exupéry, qualifying Breton as "the most intolerant man" he knows, evokes the surrealist's profound affinity with the very enemy toward whom Breton had claimed the poet-pilot had been all too indulgent: "You are the man of concentration camps of the spirit" (132). The parallels between surrealism and Nazism continue. Breton's publication in *La révolution surréaliste* of a photograph of the poet "Benjamin Péret insulting a priest" is said to be worthy of Nazi photographs of storm troopers insulting Jews in the street. And the only material in print rivaling in baseness the surrealists' leaking of the serendipitously discovered treatment for venereal disease of a sometime adversary, according to Saint-Exupéry, is the anti-Semitic pornography of the Nazis.

8. Antoine de Saint-Exupéry, "Lettre à André Breton," in *Ecrits de guerre,* 130.

The last point is crucial for the aviator-writer. It is as though psychoanalysis, with its obsessive interest in sexual secrets, had allowed the tyrannical bent of surrealism to attain unprecedented levels of persecutory maleficence. Whence the following evocation of a "solemn session" of the surrealist group intended to discipline Roger Vailland for departing from the group line: "Your assembly of torturers—happily for him without any real power—picked him apart down to the root. The Holy Inquisition was not familiar with psychoanalysis. That ignorance made it more timid than you, more respectful of a man's utterances. It is a weapon which is never idle in your hands" (133). It is as dark a perspective on surrealism as one could encounter in wartime New York, to which Breton had repaired and where he was working toward the survival of the movement by writing prolegomena to his third surrealist manifesto. After the war, Sartre, who rightly saw in Saint-Exupéry a protoexistentialist and the inventor of a "literature of construction," would return from a visit to the United States with a comparably sinister sense of surrealist politics: he opined bizarrely in *Qu'est-ce que la littérature?* that the best one could expect from a politics of surrealism is "a primitive and secret society on the model of the Ku Klux Klan."[9] But Saint-Exupéry's sinister sense of the movement—a persecutory tyranny exacerbated by psychoanalysis—had a predecessor on the Right. The central section of Drieu la Rochelle's important *Bildungsroman Gilles* (1939) was a rewriting of Dostoyevsky's *Possessed,* with the surrealists in the role of the "possessed." Paul Morel, the Oedipally driven son of the president of the republic, is encouraged by the surrealists in his erotic transgressions, but the surrealists, we eventually learn, have no interest in the "liberation" of young Morel. On the contrary: they are working hand in glove with the police in the hope of attaining power by blackmailing the president of the republic. The orgies in which his son was nabbed were staged by the police for sinister political ends. The Freudian (or Oedipal) reference was a sham, a decoy mobilized by the police, in their collusion with the surrealists, as part of a panoptic strategy of domination.[10]

It is this view of psychoanalysis as a tool of persecution in the hands

9. Sartre, *Qu'est-ce que la littérature?* 191.
10. For further discussion of *Gilles,* see Jeffrey Mehlman, "On Literature and the Occupation of France: Blanchot vs. Drieu," *Substance* 27, no. 87 (1998): 6–16.

of the fundamentally tyrannical surrealists that Saint-Exupéry appears to share with—or to derive from—Drieu's major novel. At the end of *Gilles,* Drieu's hero paradoxically escapes from the panoptic police state . . . to a redemptive vision of a fascist Europe. For Saint-Exupéry, the police state was fascism. But what bound the two visions together was the sense that psychoanalysis allowed the ills of authoritarianism, with which surrealism was already rife, to attain truly totalitarian maleficence.

Saint-Exupéry did not send his letter to Breton. The link with Drieu would not have been apparent. Perhaps it was Breton's ultimate revenge that Saint-Exupéry's wife, Consuelo, who was given to throwing dishes at him during their numerous spats, was best described by the author's friend and translator Lewis Galantière as "Surrealism made flesh."[11] It was Galantière, moreover, who was the recipient of a second long letter, this one sent in November 1941, on the subject of the author's politics. In the course of an evening's argument at a restaurant in Chinatown, Saint-Exupéry found himself voicing all his reservations about the "democracy" responsible for the fiasco of the French Third Republic. By evening's end, Galantière, beside himself, told his friend that he was "clearly a fascist" (369).

The following day, Galantière found a pained seventeen-page letter under his door, the author's fullest elucidation of his reservations concerning parliamentary democracy, defined as the regime that had resulted in the "decadence" of his airborne monastery, Aéropostale. What, after all, was liberty in the mid-twentieth century? "My freedom today rests solely on a mass production that castrates us of our dissident desires; it's the freedom of a horse harnessed to a single road." The dispiriting examples are on the whole taken from American life: freedom to follow Babbitt in his choice among ready-made options, to go to the movies, "where Mr. Zanuck crushes one beneath his dictatorial foolishness," to select one of four models of General Motors cars. The freedom offered by our contemporary democracies is negative, and far removed from true freedom, which is indistinguishable from creative endeavor. As for equality, it is ultimately no more than the "obliteration of the individual by the mass."[12] There follows a

11. Schiff, *Saint-Exupéry,* 374.
12. Saint-Exupéry, "Lettre à Lewis Galantière," 152.

development that is vintage Tocqueville: "Your equality is fundamentally at odds with your liberty," the two being reconcilable only within the "termitarium." But it is fraternity that offers the most "inextricable problems." The squadron leader had nothing but contempt for the "benevolent indifference" among neighbors that passed for fraternity in contemporary democracies. His experience as a virtuoso of fraternity had shown him that it existed genuinely only where men were subject to something greater than themselves, interdependent in a hierarchical structure. "Men can be brothers only within what transcends them" (153). But that condition made short shrift of equality. Whereby the famous triad of the French Revolution appeared to buckle. Democracy, as it obtained even in the United States, simply will not do. The joys of baseball, life as an endless rush to relieve tedium, are thin gruel indeed compared to the constraints of a vibrant hierarchy. The letter ends with a warning. American youth seems, alas, ripe for the plucking: "Nazism could catch on in your youth like fire in an old barn. It's ready for it" (155). And this was the pilot who had risked his life in many a reconnaissance flight to fight Nazism.

Beyond the opposition between democracy and fascism, there remained the question of the specific situation of France and the Vichy regime. Saint-Exupéry addressed the question in rather spectacular terms at the turning point of the war in "An Open Letter to Frenchmen Everywhere." The text was written shortly after the Allied invasion of North Africa, but before General Mark Wayne Clark's surprise accord of November 22, 1942, placing French forces in North Africa under the command of Admiral Darlan, much reviled in New York as Pétain's putative heir. That temporal disjunction would considerably affect the reception of Saint-Exupéry's piece. Coming from the most celebrated Frenchman in New York, his letter would be much commented on throughout the exile community.

It began by acknowledging the complete German occupation of metropolitan France in the wake of the Allied invasion. France was now "nothing but a silence; she [was] lost somewhere in the night with all lights out, like a ship, her mind and spirit . . . absorbed into her physical being." The metaphorics of absorption, the concomitant passivity and loss of the transcendence that remains the constitutive dimension of human consciousness, had served Sartre in *La nausée*.

The protoexistentialist in Saint-Exupéry here implies that until one fathoms the strange passivity to which forty million French "hostages" had been reduced, the starvation compounded by the metaphysical nausea that they suffered, one can have little sense of the specificity of the French situation. "There is no common measure between the métier of the soldier and the métier of the hostage," no common measure "between freedom to fight and bearing the crushing weight of the darkness." Indeed, there is something almost sacred about the suffering and the martyrdom of the French under Nazi occupation: "They are the only true saints."

It would take France another quarter of a century to rediscover the rhetoric isolating, in almost religious terms, a group subject to nearly unfathomable suffering amid the general suffering of the war. For it was not until after de Gaulle's retirement from the political scene in 1968 that the "Vichy syndrome" saw fit to delineate the specificity of the "Holocaust," the genocide of the Jews in the Nazi camps. The travails of the Resistance seemed more ordinary in comparison. The Vichy syndrome, in the words of Henry Rousso and Eric Conan, had gone "Judeocentric."[13] Which is why Saint-Exupéry's offhand effort to quantify the demographic threat facing France under German occupation is of particular interest: "The rot of German prison camps yields only corpses. My country was thus threatened, purely and simply, with utter extermination, under legal and administrative pretense, of 6,000,000 men. France was armed only with sticks to resist this slave hunt." It is an astonishing passage. The Nazi camps, the unfathomable passivity and dehumanization, the "extermination," and the unthinkable figure of six million—the principal elements of the Holocaust complex—are all present, but the victims here are not the Jews, but the French. In light of the Vichy syndrome's obsession with French responsibility for the genocide of the Jews, Saint-Exupéry's "open letter" on a virtual holocaust of the French stands as the most paradoxical of sources for an entire strand of modern discourse.

In the face of that virtual holocaust, the sole proper response is humility, reverence, and reconciliation. First, humility. Of the French

13. Henry Rousso and Eric Conan, *Vichy, un passé qui ne passe pas* (Paris: Fayard, 1994), 75.

emigration, the author writes: "We do not represent France; all we can do is serve her." As for reconciliation, all that is needed is a proper understanding of the apparent divisions between the French: "We have never been divided except on the question as to the weight to be attributed to the Nazi blackmail. On the one hand, some said, 'If the Germans are determined to wipe out the people of France, they will wipe them out, whatever the French do. This blackmail ought to be despised.'" Thus presumably ran the Gaullist argument. "On the other hand, other people thought: 'It is not merely a case of blackmail but of blackmail unique for cruelty in the history of the world. Let France, refusing all capital concessions, employ every sort of ruse to delay the menace from day to day. The tone of the official utterances shows that when a Ulysses or Talleyrand is disarmed, there remain to him only words with which to deceive the enemy." Thus ran a generous reading of Pétain's *attentisme*. Gaullists and Pétainists, properly understood, would be not opposed, but part of a continuum. In Louis Rougier's parallel formulation, "every activist is the *attentiste* of a greater activist than himself." Both sections of the spectrum, moreover, were essential. "Of what use is the spiritual heritage if there be no heir?" ran what might be construed as Saint-Exupéry's defense of Pétain. It was counterbalanced by an implied defense of de Gaulle (or his American-backed rival, General Henri Giraud): "What good is the heir if the spirit is dead?"

If, as Rougier originally thought, Gaullists and Pétainists were part of a common and infinitely precarious effort, the hostilities dividing the principal factions of French émigrés were groundless. The German occupation of the whole of metropolitan France, Saint-Exupéry concluded a bit precipitously, meant that there was no more Vichy regime. What was needed was to seek union in voluntary combat against the occupiers. The diversion of gathering signatures on pro-Gaullist petitions that so preoccupied the Fifth Avenue *résistants* could now be relegated to the past. The "Open Letter," in conclusion, calls on all Frenchmen between the ages of eighteen and forty-eight in the United States to send telegrams to Secretary of State Cordell Hull volunteering military service in any way deemed useful. The *Times* was swept up by the novelist's rhetoric. On the day of publication it simultaneously editorialized: "Mr. Hull would be astonished if any but the merest negligible fraction of the French in America took their stand for disunity."[14]

There remained, to be sure, the tricky question of the political organization of France during the new military crusade against the occupiers. Saint-Exupéry opted merely to defer it. "The provisional organization of France is an affair of state. Let us leave it to Britain and to the United States to do the best they can." For those made uncomfortable by Saint-Exupéry's argument, including those whose bluff would now be called by the writer's invitation to put one's body on the line in actual combat, that passage offered a remarkably vulnerable target. Written before the American decision to throw its lot in with Darlan (but published in the midst of the uproar that choice had occasioned), Saint-Exupéry's text appeared in circumstances that glaringly invalidated its argument: it was clear to all that leaving the "provisional organization of France" to the Americans and the British might issue in some rather unsavory surprises. Not even Roosevelt's quip, defending the choice of Darlan by quoting the proverb to the effect that it was "permissible, in times of grave danger, to accompany the devil to the far side of the bridge," could assuage the outrage surrounding the nomination of Darlan.[15]

Reaction to the "Open Letter" was swift. Lindbergh told his wife that Saint-Exupéry's was the attitude of a saint.[16] E. K. Rand wrote to the Times that the Allies now had a triumvirate of stunning eloquence: "In this talented Frenchman we may greet a peer of our President and his self-styled 'lieutenant,' Churchill."[17] The Times also published a long letter of dissent from Henry Bernstein, the noted playwright whose recent frustrations on Broadway—his play Rose Buck closed after a few days—had resulted in his Gaullism, regarded as "fanatical" in some quarters, becoming even more aggressive.[18] Rumor in New York had it that shortly before the collapse of France, Bernstein, hosting a Parisian dinner party, had invited his guests to the balcony, placed a pistol to his head, and announced that he would blow his brains out

14. "To Frenchmen Everywhere," New York Times, November 29, 1942.
15. Aglion, Roosevelt and de Gaulle, 146.
16. Saint-Exupéry, Écrits de guerre, 219.
17. Letters, New York Times, December 2, 1942.
18. New York Times, December 6, 1942.

at the sight of the first *feldgrau* uniform.[19] The Germans came; he left for New York and installed himself as a fixture in the Waldorf-Astoria. His response to Saint-Exupéry may have given added currency to the malicious rumor. Bernstein suggested there was no need for the French to cable Cordell Hull, volunteering to serve, because they were all subject to the draft in any event. Better to send a letter to the secretary of state saying "that we love America; that we have not chosen it as a haven because of its plumbing but because the American way of life appeals to French minds, French hearts." Exit Henry Bernstein.

A second, more extended letter of dissent was published by Jacques Maritain in the weekly *Pour la victoire*. Maritain had arrived in New York on an academic mission early in 1940. His prewar critique of anti-Semitism (for which he was taken to task by Gide in the *Nouvelle Revue Française*), his subsequent efforts on behalf of such refugees as Jean Wahl and Marc Chagall, and his general eminence among American academics made him a spiritual guide of sorts for the exile community.[20] His early volume on the fall of France, *A travers le désastre*, saluted even by the surrealist journal *VVV* (in an article by René Etiemble quite critical of the "amoral weakness" of Saint-Exupéry), was one of the first monuments of Resistance literature.[21] The apartment at 30 Fifth Avenue he shared with his wife Raïssa was widely regarded as a center of the exile community.

In addition, Maritain was being actively courted by de Gaulle (in a series of letters beginning "Cher Maître") to serve in some administrative or advisory capacity with the Free French.[22] Significantly, he begged off, pleading first academic obligations in the United States, then issues of disagreement with tendencies within the Gaullist movement. In *A travers le désastre*, written in late 1940, his position was at bottom not far removed from that of Rougier—or Saint-Exupéry. Concerning the break between London and Vichy, he wrote: "I think that most Frenchmen, in private, would prefer to replace the notion of *break* here with that of a division of labor."[23] His attitude would evolve

19. Fritsch-Estrangin, *New York entre de Gaulle et Pétain*, 155.

20. Barré, *Jacques et Raïssa Maritain*, 479.

21. René Etiemble, "Review of French Books," *VVV* 1 (June 1942): 64–66.

22. See *Cahiers Jacques Maritain* 16–17 (April 1988): *Le philosophe dans la guerre*. For the Maritain–de Gaulle letters, see 59–90.

23. Quoted in Barré, *Jacques et Raïssa Maritain*, 485.

with time, but his reservations about the Gaullist "government in exile" would remain constant. As late as August 9, 1942, he was writing to his friend Yves Simon that the political horizon of Gaullism might well be, alas, no more than "Vichy without the Nazis" (500). To de Gaulle, he wrote of the error one would make in confusing the "political inspiration" requisite to the military mission the "Fighting French" had heroically taken on with any actual "political power" of a putative government in exile.[24] That last point, we shall see, survives even in the response to Saint-Exupéry.

Maritain's statement appeared on December 12, 1942. The central point of his argument, marked by expressions of "esteem" for the writer-aviator and acknowledgment of the "generosity" of his appeal, was that Saint-Exupéry's call for a united military front against the Germans in 1942 had been valid from September 1939 on—and that it was less than helpful to ignore that a portion of the French people had betrayed that obligation with the signing of the armistice in June 1940: "There are men who renounced that duty and broke that union: those who abandoned the fight on June 17, 1940, denounced our alliance with England, and cast the French people into the trap of the armistice. Saint-Exupéry should not have forgotten that."[25] The trap of the armistice: it was preeminently seen from the perspective of a noncombatant. Earlier in the year, Saint-Exupéry had published his version of the French defeat, *Pilote de guerre*. It was in certain respects a charter text of French existentialism. (Maurice Merleau-Ponty would end his masterwork, *La phénoménologie de la perception*, with a passage from Saint-Exupéry's book: "You dwell in your very deed [*ton acte même*]. Your deed is who you are.")[26] Now one of the more presciently existential observations in *Pilote de guerre* concerns the author's extension of the term "phony war" (*drôle de guerre*) to the actual period of combat that theoretically marked the end of the "phony war."[27] For the superiority of the German military machine was such that the true spuriousness of the war did not become patent until "combat" actually began. Because none of the customary strategic conditions obtained in the

24. *Cahiers Jacques Maritain* 16–17 (April 1988): 74.

25. Jacques Maritain, "Il faut parfois juger," in Saint-Exupéry, *Ecrits de guerre*, 222.

26. Maurice Merleau-Ponty, *Phénoménologie de la perception* (Paris: Gallimard, 1945), 520.

27. Saint Exupéry, *Pilote de guerre* (Paris: Gallimard, 1942), 128.

face of the German blitzkrieg, all the French could do was pretend to fight in the hope of saving appearances. "The drama of this particular rout is its way of stripping acts of all meaning. Whoever blows up a bridge can do so only with disgust. Such a soldier does not delay the enemy: he manufactures a ruined bridge. He destroys his country in order to extract from it a fine caricature of war!" (84). So runs Saint-Exupéry's version of what would emerge in Sartre as the category of the gesture (*geste*) or pseudoact. Sartre may have been right to say that one was never more free than under the German occupation because one's words had the weight of genuine deeds. Saint-Exupéry was of the opinion that one's acts never counted for less than during France's "caricature war" of 1940. The armistice, which was a betrayal for Maritain, was an existential necessity for Saint-Exupéry.

Rougier's position had been that the armistice, far from being a case of French betrayal, was one of strategic error on Hitler's part. And it is with that understanding that Saint-Exupéry's argument makes sense. To delay (the resumption of) combat until the Americans entered the war was to pursue the war on more favorable terms. Maritain argued in his response to Saint-Exupéry that there had been no reason to wait until Saint-Exupéry's call to resume combat because there "were men who, since the armistice, had endured the worst ordeals in order to continue the war alongside the Allies," by which he meant the Fighting French. But this gave short shrift to the military marginality of the Gaullist forces, who were pointedly excluded from the Allied invasion of North Africa.

Where Saint-Exupéry was more vulnerable was in his failure to acknowledge the extent to which the conditions imposed by the Germans were secretly welcomed in Vichy as instruments of the new regime's "national revolution." Saint-Exupéry (at his most deluded): "Our divergences of opinion do not touch our hatred of the invader, while at the same time we are all indignant, as are all the people of France, at the surrender of the foreign refugees, a violation of the right of asylum." Maritain (at his most astute): "Saint-Exupéry also forgets that many things were agreed to quite eagerly and even desired by the men of Vichy when they contributed to furthering their own priorities in internal politics."[28]

28. Maritain, "Il faut parfois juger," 224.

An emblematic event: the scuttling of the French fleet in Toulon in November 1942 before the Germans could seize it. For Rougier the act was the honorable fulfillment of a principal clause of the "gentlemen's agreement" he had hammered out with Churchill (on Pétain's behalf) in the fall of 1940. *Newsweek*'s cover story read "Honor and Country: The French Fleet Went Down Gloriously." "As the vessels slid to the bottom and the water closed over the motto *Honneur et Patrie* emblazoned on many of them, both honor and country were satisfied."[29] By the end of the article, de Gaulle's call to victory was described as an "echo" of Darlan. For Maritain as well, the scuttling of the French fleet took on emblematic value. In an admission that things could no doubt have been worse, he writes of the men of Vichy: "They could have surrendered the fleet. They didn't do so; they only prevented it from fighting for the liberation of France and the world, and drove it to a heroic suicide, the terrible symbol of the kind of heroism that nationalist defeatism and a policy of 'la France seule' might leave as the country's sole recourse."[30] For Maritain the best that Vichy could have in store would be a bout of suicidal heroics whose emblem would be the fate of the fleet at Toulon on the cold morning of November 27, 1942.

If all of France's ills stemmed from a treacherous armistice, only a resolute act of will could redeem the catastrophe. So many suppositions had been raised in defense of the armistice: imagine what would have been the fate of France if it had not signed. . . . "But it is not with *ifs* [*des si*] that such questions are resolved, but with a *no* when what is at stake for a man is the honor of his country and faith in her people" (226). Enter de Gaulle, who "has restored the honor of France" (228). The Fighting French "represent France morally, even if [and one recognizes a motif from Maritain's correspondence with de Gaulle] they don't represent her politically."

Saint-Exupéry was devastated. His call for unity had issued in a new polemic. Worse yet: however similar Maritain's impatience with the aviator's allergy to politics may have been to Breton's, Maritain was no Breton. Saint-Exupéry's admiration for the Catholic philosopher was total. He penned a page for *Pour la victoire*, claiming (unconvinc-

29. "Tragedy in Toulon," *Newsweek*, December 7, 1942, 22.
30. Maritain, "Il faut parfois juger," 225.

ingly) that Maritain's differences with him were a result of minor errors in translation from the French.

Then he wrote a remarkable letter to the philosopher, dominated by Saint-Exupéry's sense of utter admiration for the man he was saddened to think might now become his adversary: "I've read all your books with a kind of love. . . . I leave you to judge yourself this spiritual conflict between you and me."[31] To the extent that he was the Frenchman in the United States who counted for him more than any other, as Saint-Exupéry wrote, Maritain was a kind of anti-Breton. How could he be seen as a Vichy sympathizer, he asked the philosopher. The sole passage of *Pilote de guerre*, a volume already coming under attack in French New York, that might be misinterpreted in that sense was the quip that if a husband discovers that his wife is a whore (*gourgandine*), the way to restore honor to his household is not to denounce her to the neighbors. If such be a defense of Vichy, surely, he claimed, he was more Machiavellian than anyone had previously suspected. Or was it, as some suggested, that he had accepted the armistice? But unlike the others, his response ran, he had been at the heart of the French rout— "awash in the bloody collapse" (232). To have participated in combat under conditions in which France lost an unprecedented 150,000 men in two weeks prevented him from sharing in the notion of the surrender of an essentially intact French army. But perhaps his protestations were of no use. Maritain had suggested to him on the telephone that given what he, Maritain, was about to publish, there might be only limited grounds for further discussion between them; the evasiveness of this suggestion was devastating. The letter ended on a melancholy note: "Rest assured of my esteem, which nothing will ever diminish, but which is for me, this evening, the source of a good deal of suffering."

In the course of his letter to Maritain, Saint-Exupéry dismissed one issue that was wracking French New York at the time: the rivalry between Giraud (backed by the Americans) and de Gaulle (more or less backed by the British) to assume a principal role in newly liberated North Africa. In the writer-aviator's words, "the Giraud–de Gaulle problem is ridiculous," by which he meant that he would rally to the cause of whomever the Allies chose. That choice would soon become

31. Antoine de Saint-Exupéry, "Lettre à Jacques Maritain," in *Ecrits de guerre*, 230.

the subject of extensive controversy in both Washington and New York. In preparation for the Casablanca conference of January 1943 (shortly after the assassination of Darlan the previous Christmas), Roosevelt sent Churchill a telegram in which he jested that de Gaulle was the "bride" he was planning to pawn off on Giraud, the "bridegroom," at Anfa, the town adjacent to Casablanca at which the conference was actually held.[32] A staged handshake between the two French leaders was arranged for photographers, but the Giraud–de Gaulle duo was slated to give way in short order to de Gaulle's solitary leadership. The grounds for the eventual undoing of Giraud were invoked in tones of exasperation by Roosevelt in a letter of May 8 to Churchill:

I am sorry, but the conduct of the BRIDE continues to be more and more aggravated. His course of action is well nigh intolerable. . . . The war in North Africa has terminated successfully without any material aid from de Gaulle, and the civil situation with all its dangers seems to be working out well. . . . However de Gaulle is without question taking his vicious propaganda staff down to Algiers to stir up strife between the various elements including Arabs and Jews. He is expanding his present group of agitators who are working up counter-demonstrations and even riots. (153)

The episode referred to by Roosevelt—to which we shall turn presently—would soon become a focus of comment in New York, and of an essay by the young Hannah Arendt, recently arrived from France, in the *Contemporary Jewish Record*.[33] In 1871, a providential year in occupied France, the defeated French government issued a decree (in Tours, to which it had retreated) granting full French citizenship to the Jews of Algeria. The Crémieux decree, as it was called, was rooted in the French sentiment, according to Arendt, that the Jews were "the only trustworthy part of the population" and could be depended on to advance European interests in North Africa (117). For Arabs to achieve French citizenship, they would have to renounce polygamy and legally enforced female subservience, and few were prepared to do so. Anti-Semitic riots, quite common in Algeria—which sent Edouard Drumont, author of the anti-Semitic "classic," *La France juive,* to Parliament—were frequently attributed to the inequality established by the

32. Aglion, *Roosevelt and de Gaulle,* 149.

33. Hannah Arendt, "Why the Crémieux Decree Was Abrogated," *Contemporary Jewish Record* 6, no. 2 (April 1943): 115–24.

162   Crémieux decree. During the Vichy years, that decree was suspended. But the surprise for many came when General Giraud, become French High Commissioner in newly liberated Algeria, announced the abrogation of the law—in the name of eliminating "racial discrimination" (115).[34] Jews, deprived of their citizenship, would revert to the status of "natives," thus losing a right they had had since the Franco-Prussian War.

It was a bizarre outcome for a significant Allied victory against Hitler. In short order, Giraud (whose abrogation of the Crémieux decree had, according to Arendt, the principal result of bringing the Jews under the domination of the old-style reactionary colonials) found himself the object of vehement attacks in the New York press. The Gaullist *France-Amérique* went so far as to suggest that he was at bottom a fascist. The Crémieux scandal, which Roosevelt viewed as a Gaullist concoction, was sufficient to dampen enthusiasm for Giraud in many quarters of New York (despite the ringing "defense" of General Giraud published by Boris Souvarine in the *American Mercury*).[35] A lackluster visit to Washington later in the summer of 1943 did the rest. On November 9, 1943, Giraud was evicted from the national leadership. What Saint-Exupéry had described as the "ridiculous" Giraud–de Gaulle problem had been resolved. The dismissal itself would no doubt be counted by Saint-Exupéry's adversaries against him.[36]

These were anguishing years for Saint-Exupéry: the fights with Consuelo, a wife whom he thought he had shed in coming to America; an only partially successful operation, performed in California, to re-

34. In *Crusade in Europe,* 129, Eisenhower claimed that Darlan brought him a letter, apparently from the rabbi of Constantine, pleading with him to go "very slowly" in restoring rights to Jews in Algeria lest the Arabs stage a pogrom.

35. Boris Souvarine, "In Defense of General Giraud," *American Mercury* 56 (April 1943): 421–27.

36. Vindication of a sort would come posthumously. In 1982, Raymond Aron, the thinker whose legacy lay in quite simply and unspectacularly having been right over so many years, agreed to write a preface for a volume of Saint-Exupéry's war writings. If he did so, he wrote, it was because as a non-Gaullist in London, he had experienced the same doubts as Saint-Exupéry during the same years. "Gaullist propaganda," wrote Aron, "lashed out at the Vichy government with such violence that it seemed at times like a form of anti-French propaganda" (Saint-Exupéry, *Ecrits de guerre,* 8).

lieve recurrent bouts of fever whose origin—an infected shard from one of his crashes?—had never been fully diagnosed; and above all, the dogged reputation of being a Vichy sympathizer. That last burden makes particularly striking one feature of the works he published out of New York—their relation to the Jewish question. We have already heard of the antipathy of Gaullist New York—what Saint-Exupéry, in a moment of disparagement, would call "the fake-French mob [*la pègre des faux Français*] of New York"—for *Pilote de guerre* (193). The Americans might praise it. For Edward Weeks, writing in the *Atlantic Monthly*, it might well be the best response (with Churchill's speeches) that the Allies had found to *Mein Kampf* (195). It might be a "miracle" for the *Times* and "the most important book yet written about the war" for *Time*.[37] But for the French, the book's more enigmatic passages were all chalked up to "defeatism." Consider then the book's fate in Vichy France. Gerhard Heller, the Francophile head of the review section of the *Propagandastaffel*, gave the go-ahead for publication. The book sold out in a week—until it was discovered that it contained an encomium to the heroics of an emphatically Jewish pilot named Jean Israël. The repeated references to Israël's bright-red Jewish nose served as a red flag. The book was withdrawn from shops, Heller was disciplined for his oversight, and a campaign was launched in the collaborationist press against a book vilified as an exercise in "Judeo-bellicosity."[38]

And consider Saint-Exupéry's eloquent "Lettre à un otage," dedicated (like *Le petit prince*) to the author's friend Léon Werth and the simple but irreplaceable pleasures, now threatened with extinction, that they had shared: "You who are so French, I feel you to be imperiled twice over, as a Frenchman and as a Jew. I sense the full value of a community that no longer authorizes conflict. We are all of France as we might be of a tree, and I will serve your truth as you would serve mine. For us, Frenchmen of the exterior, it is a question, during this war, of freeing up the provision of seeds frozen by the snow of the German presence. It is a matter of bringing you succor, to you over there. A matter of making you free in the land where you have the

37. John Chamberlain, "Books of the Times," *New York Times*, February 20, 1942; "If It Die," *Time*, February 23, 1942.
38. Schiff, *Saint-Exupéry*, 365–66.

fundamental right to develop your roots."[39] It is not because his best friends were Jewish that Saint-Exupéry was in any way an anti-Semite.

The publisher of *Pour la victoire* once remarked of Saint-Exupéry: "With the exception of Simone Weil, who virtually starved herself to death in her desire to share the fate of her compatriots . . . , I never encountered anyone with a deeper physical sympathy for man and his suffering."[40] It is a curious parallel. Simone Weil, who died in the Resistance, was, as we saw, an anti-Semitic Gaullist. If Saint-Exupéry was a Vichy sympathizer, as his compatriots in New York never stopped suggesting, but he adamantly denied, he was preeminently a philo-Semitic Pétainist.

Only in New York.

39. Antoine de Saint-Exupéry, *Lettre à un otage* (New York: Brentano's, 1943), 71.
40. Saint-Exupéry, *Ecrits de guerre*, 204.

NINE

Saint-John Perse

Discontinuities

On the occasion of the awarding of the Nobel Prize in literature to Saint-John Perse in 1960, his old friend Henri Hoppenot waxed nostalgic on the joint passion for the poetry of Claudel ("the greatest French writer") that early on served as a bond in their friendship.[1] One nods in agreement; surely the expansive poetic line of Perse is as distinguished an heir to the Claudelian *verset* as French poetry has produced. Yet in order to grasp the wartime experience of the poet in his American exile, it is paradoxically the case of Claudel's monumental *other,* Paul Valéry—standard-bearer of French neoclassicism and a poet whose crystalline achievement seems utterly at odds, to use Perse's terms, with that of the "rhe-ist" author of *Anabase*—that offers the most instructive parallel.[2]

Valéry: the poet was the brilliant habitué of Mallarmé's salon, the most promising of the young Symbolists, who in 1892 forswore poetry (as ultimately deleterious to "Intelligence") in the name of an appar-

1. Henri Hoppenot, "D'Alexis Leger à Saint-John Perse," reprinted in *Honneur à Saint-John Perse* (Paris: Gallimard, 1965), 804. On Hoppenot's checkered career—as Darius Milhaud's librettist in the 1920s, Vichy's emissary to Uruguay during the early years of the war, then de Gaulle's envoy to Washington in 1943—see Nettlebeck, *Forever French*, 33.

2. In 1922, Leger considered presenting Valéry with a gift of fantastic appropriateness: the crystal skull found in the Aztec room of the British Museum (*Honneur à Saint-John Perse,* 464). Years later, he would claim in a letter to Caillois (January 26, 1953) that it was an error to view his poetry in terms of "crystallization" since his work—attuned to the "rhe-ism" of the pre-Socratics—was to be understood in terms of movement (Roger Caillois, *Poétique de St-John Perse* [Paris: Gallimard, 1954], 181).

ently more serious calling: the cultivation of Mind at its most un-poetically acute. It was not until André Gide, in 1913, proposed a collected edition of Valéry's early verse, capped by a new poem, that he found himself captivated again by his poetic vocation. "La Jeune Parque" awakens on a beach and refuses to relinquish her creator until he has not only written one of the great French poems of the century, but finds himself won over anew to his abandoned calling. Now, Perse: Saint-John Perse invents the enigmatic pen name of his poetic maturity in 1924 to accompany the equally enigmatically named volume *Anabase*. It will prove one of the most admired volumes of poetry of European modernity: T. S. Eliot, Giuseppe Ungaretti, and Walter Benjamin all line up to translate it. (Rilke too was tempted by the poem, and would have undertaken a translation were his "admiration" for the German version of Benjamin and Groethuysen not so emphatic.) No sooner has Saint-John Perse appeared on the European scene, however, than he goes into eclipse. An apparently more serious calling beckons. Under the tutelage of Aristide Briand, under the name of Alexis Leger, he becomes first that minister's cabinet chief, then, from 1933 until the fall of France, general secretary of the Ministry of Foreign Affairs, the effective head of French diplomacy during the years culminating in the outbreak of World War II. It is not until he is abruptly dismissed from his post in May 1940 and forced to flee Nazi-occupied France for England, and then America, that the poetic persona of Saint-Jean Perse resurfaces, on a beach once again ("sur toutes grèves de ce monde"), and lays claim to a poetic vocation he will never again relinquish. Perse: "Je vous connais, ô monstre! Nous voici de nouveau face à face. Nous reprenons ce long débat où nous l'avions laissé."[3] A telling difference: whereas Valéry's beach is on a mythical Mediterranean, Perse's—in a poem called "Exil"—is on Long Beach Island, New Jersey, where he had been received at Harvey Cedars, the home of his friend Francis Biddle, soon to be named attorney general of the United States by Franklin Roosevelt.[4]

3. Saint-John Perse, "Exil," in *Eloges* (Paris: Gallimard, 1960), 148; see also the English-language translation by Denis Devlin, *Exile and Other Poems* (New York: Pantheon, 1949), 17: "I know you, monster-head! Once more face to face. We take up the long debate where we left off."
4. On the circumstances in which "Exil" was composed, see Roger Little's edition (London: Athlone, 1973).

Archibald MacLeish was Saint-John Perse's Gide.[5] MacLeish's role in securing the poet wartime employment as a consultant at the Library of Congress has long been familiar. Less familiar are the details of his role in reawakening Perse's poetic vocation. At the first meeting between the two, MacLeish, for whom *Anabase* was the major poetic achievement of his generation, offered a position to Perse and went on sheepishly to suggest that he hoped his new circumstances would allow him to resume his "true life" as a poet. The suggestion, according to MacLeish, was disastrous. "He stiffened up, went to the door, turned around, and said: 'I shall never write again.' "[6] Nonetheless, MacLeish's thought appears to have borne fruit. In a delightful letter, recovered too late to make its way into the Pléiade edition, the Frenchman, signing himself Alexis Leger, already well ensconced in his Washington job, wrote to his administrative superior at the Library of Congress on June 26, 1941: "I have indeed run into Perse, one evening, amidst the astonishing nocturnal fauna of this Georgetown 'before the advent of sin.' "[7] The diplomat Leger's alter ego, moreover, appeared as surprised by the implications of the encounter as Leger himself: "No one struck me as more surprised to learn that a French poem might be published in America." Whereupon the writer informs his interlocutor that he is taking off for a few days at the seashore with his friends the Biddles. Shortly after Labor Day, Leger writes anew to MacLeish, enclosing his "poem on exile," which he dedicates to his addressee (8).

Thus was reborn, of a Georgetown night, the poet Saint-John Perse. What is most striking in the development is the will to keep the two identities—Saint-John Perse and Alexis Leger—discrete. It was something of an obsession. During the war, Perse graciously contributed his "Lettre à l'étrangère"—the epigraph read "Alien Registration Act"— to *Hémisphères,* the poetry journal that Yvan Goll was founding in Brooklyn. He insisted only that his "absolute pseudonymy" be re-

5. Gide, of course, was also "Saint-John Perse's Gide." The Pléiade edition of Perse's *Oeuvres complètes* (Paris: Gallimard, 1972) includes some twenty-eight letters written to Gide. Saint-John Perse was throughout his life as broadly well connected a figure as twentieth-century letters has produced—surely the only author to have been accorded both a cameo appearance in Proust's *Recherche* and a place of honor on the guest list for John F. Kennedy's inauguration.

6. Perse, *Oeuvres complètes,* 125.

7. Arthur Knodel, "Archibald MacLeish: Ami du prince taciturne," in *Espaces de Saint-John Perse* (Aix: Université de Provence, 1981), 3:9.

spected.[8] Shortly thereafter, *Time* magazine questioned Goll on the subject of the identity of "Mr. Perse" (112). When the poet revealed the identity of Alexis Saint-Leger Leger, and *Time* published it, Goll received a "furious letter" from Perse. Years later Max-Pol Fouchet was informed (in a letter of 1948) that "any link established between Saint-John Perse and Alexis Leger would irresistibly falsify the reader's vision and fundamentally vitiate his interpretation of the poetry."[9] That same year, after the appearance of a series of essays in *Critique* by Maurice Saillet attempting to demonstrate that there might be some significant connection between the exile of Alexis Leger and (the poem) "Exil" of Saint-John Perse, the poet wrote a long letter to Saillet's dedicatee, Perse's old friend Adrienne Monnier, ridiculing Saillet: "Still more absurd, infinitely, is this systematic search for a political personality, along with the arbitrary intrusion of contemporary history, with all its moral, patriotic, or social implications, in poems that cannot be pigeonholed in any temporal framework—poems bound to no special time or place, and that are always conceived, on their ideal or absolute plane, as a violent reaction against any notion (even of the most indirect sort) of 'committed' literature."[10] In the face of such insistence, one is intrigued less by the articulation between the careers of Leger and Perse than by the motivation behind the insistence on the untenability of any such articulation.

The discontinuity between Leger and Perse, moreover, is further complicated by a second discontinuity—that of the distance Leger seemed so adamant on maintaining between himself and de Gaulle. Leger, after all, had come to New York from London in 1940, and New York was intrigued about what failed to transpire between Leger and de Gaulle. Raoul Aglion, de Gaulle's representative in the United States, who spent long hours with Leger, does not hesitate to speak of the diplomat's "consuming hatred" of de Gaulle, claims to have been subjected to "tirades" against him, and assumes that Leger was responsible for Roosevelt's animosity toward the leader of the Fighting French.[11] The point of view was shared even by the *New York Post*

8. Roger Little, ed., "Saint-John Perse à Yvan Goll: Huit lettres inédites," in *Cahiers Saint-John Perse* (Paris: Gallimard, 1979), 2:118.

9. *Honneur à Saint-John Perse,* 654.

10. Perse, *Oeuvres complètes,* 553.

11. Aglion, *Roosevelt and de Gaulle,* 184.

gossip columnist Elsa Maxwell, who reported as late as June 20, 1944, that she feared that Leger's influence had been "detrimental to the Free French cause. He does not like de Gaulle who to him, I imagine, has been something of an upstart. . . . I am absolutely certain that it is the quiet persevering hand of Monsieur Leger that has advised against recognition of the French National Committee of Liberation as the Provisional French Government" (187). While fundamentally opposed to the Vichy regime, which had stripped him of his citizenship as early as October 1940, Leger, then, was as intent on keeping his distance from de Gaulle as he was from . . . Saint-John Perse. It was a perception indirectly registered by Jean Rollin, in a discussion of his meeting with Leger in New York (where he was to spend six months before moving to Washington) in 1940. It was Leger's refusal to stay with de Gaulle in London that created the possibility for the reemergence of the poetic persona of Saint-John Perse. And between de Gaulle (whom Leger held at bay) and Saint-John Perse (with whom he refused to be confused), Rollin posited a striking parallel: "By a move as assured and resolute as the one that led Charles de Gaulle to enter utterly into resistance, the man who inspired and executed the foreign policy of France from 1932 to 1939 entered into poetry."[12] The remark appears in a piece entitled "A New York en 1940." Rollin was perhaps not alone. Roger Caillois, from Buenos Aires, published an essay, "The Art of Saint-John Perse," in the first issue of Goll's *Hémisphères* that so exudes a sense of unprecedented achievement on the poet's part ("there are few works, in point of fact, as unsettling to the reader") that the rhetoric is faintly evocative of that surrounding de Gaulle during the same years.[13] To understand the poet during the years of the war is to come to terms with a curious triad: Saint-John Perse, Charles de Gaulle, and the man, Alexis Leger, obsessed with keeping his distance from them both.

But who—or what—was "Saint-John Perse"? The author, specifying that no reference to the Latin poet Persius was intended, ended up speaking of the newly minted name of the author of *Anabase* as though it were itself a miniature poem: the name "was freely welcomed as it imposed itself enigmatically on the mind of the poet, for

12. *Honneur à Saint-John Perse*, 786.
13. Roger Caillois, "Sur l'art de Saint-John Perse," *Hémisphères* 1 (summer 1943): 9.

reasons unknown to him, as in some ancient onomastic: with its longs and shorts, its strong or silent syllables, its hard or whistling consonants, in conformity with the secret laws of all poetic creation."[14] As such, the enigmatically fascinating pseudonym bears a curious relation to the odd title that so intrigued the poet. In 1912, long before composing the poem, he wrote to Paul Claudel: "I should merely like that it be granted me one day to conduct a 'work' like an *anabasis* under the guidance of its chieftains. (And the very word seems so beautiful to me that I should like to encounter the work that might assume such a title. It haunts me)" (724). Moreover, just as "Perse" was not to mislead the reader into positing a hypothetical relation with the Latin poet, so "Anabase," the poet noted, contained no allusion at all to Xenophon's *Anabasis* (1108). *Anabase* should rather be understood in the etymological sense of an expedition toward an interior that was no doubt simultaneously geographical, psychological, and linguistic. It was Albert Thibaudet who noted that between the two invented names—"Saint-John Perse" and "Anabase"—a common Asian, indeed Persian, thread seemed to run. How nice if it had been published on Rue de Téhéran.[15] Jean-Pierre Richard suggests that Perse on more than one occasion seems intent on inventing the bizarre genre of the "name-title," as though whatever "Saint-John Perse" might signify, it could do so solely as a function of its administration of the "Anabase" over which it presides.[16]

"Saint-John Perse" is preeminently the author of *Anabase*. Richard, in his intricate reading of the "name-title," attaches special importance to a note on the Greek word *basis* that the poet, significantly, appended to his projected translation of Pindar as a young man in 1908. The Greek *basis*, it was claimed, signified a cadenced "deployment" or march prior to the "execution" of the triumphal ode upon "the return of the conqueror [*vainqueur*] to his homeland [*patrie*]."[17] Richard (and I am inclined to agree with him) hears the cadence of the Greek *basis* in Perse's "ana-basis," which would mark

14. Perse, *Oeuvres complètes*, 1094.
15. *Honneur à Saint-John Perse*, 422.
16. Jean-Pierre Richard, "Petite remontée dans un nom-titre," in *Microlectures* (Paris: Seuil, 1979), 199.
17. Perse, *Oeuvres complètes*, 732.

the rhythm of the "conqueror," the "poet-traveler," consecrating his return.[18]

Consider the terms of that "conquest." *Anabase* is a poem of violent subjugation. A "stranger" appears, and around his strangeness a campaign of violence issues in the foundation of the city: "Un grand principe de violence commandait à nos moeurs."[19] The "stranger" is, as it were, a Nietzschean *Ubermensch:* "Il n'y a plus en lui substance d'homme" (101).[20] He represents "un chant de force pour les hommes, comme un frémissement du large."[21] His genius, which is never entirely distinguishable from the genius of the poem, lies in a capacity to elicit and provoke such unrest at the borders that invasive expansion seems a logical, indeed inevitable, course: "Pour nous qui étions là, nous produisîmes aux frontières des accidents extraordinaires, et nous portant dans nos actions à la limite de nos forces, notre joie parmi vous fut une très grande joie" (102).[22] As for the effete nations allergic to "our habits of violence," they stand forewarned: "Aux pays épuisés où les coutumes sont à reprendre . . . , vous nous verrez, dans nos façons d'agir, assembleurs de nations sous de vastes hangars, lecteurs de bulles à voix haute, et vingt peuples sous nos lois parlant toutes les langues" (103).[23] The future celebrated, in sum, is of peoples displaced, temporarily lodged beneath vast hangars, what the world still thought of as concentration camps. But perhaps such is the proper destiny of soft countries "infested with comfort." Meanwhile, should anyone resist the new "gay wisdom" and take solace in melancholy, "mon avis est qu'on le tue, sinon / il y aura une sédition" (96).[24] Whereupon new festivities are announced: "Des acclamations violentes, sous les murs,

18. Richard, "Petite remontée dans un nom-titre," 197.
19. Perse, *Oeuvres complètes,* 108. T. S. Eliot's translation: "A great principle of violence dictated our fashions." See Saint-John Perse, *Anabasis,* translated by T. S. Eliot (New York: Harcourt, Brace, 1938).
20. "There is no more substance of man in him."
21. "A song of strength for men, like a shudder of space."
22. "For us who were there, we caused at the frontiers exceptional accidents, and pushing ourselves in our actions to the end of our strength, our joy amongst you was a very great joy."
23. "In the exhausted countries where the ways of life are to be remade . . . , you shall see us, the way we do, gatherers of nations under vast shelters, readers aloud of decrees, and twenty peoples under our laws speaking all tongues."
24. "I say, let him be slain, otherwise there will be an uprising."

pour des mutilations d'adultes au soleil" (111).[25] And the poem comes to an end.

Here, then, in 1924, is a brilliant French epic of violent conquest, a poem replete with concentration camps ("sous de vastes hangars"), torture ("mutilations d'adultes"), and a will to the Gallic equivalent of Lebensraum. It was not for nothing that Perse's preferred interpreter, Roger Caillois (about whose political leanings Meyer Shapiro had chosen to warn readers of the *Kenyon Review*), began his discussion of the poet's "inspiration" by referring to the "innocent cruelty," "naïve iniquity," and "taste for violence" shamelessly indulged by Persian man.[26] If *Anabasis,* as Richard suggested, was in important ways the poem of the conqueror returning home, the conquest celebrated in the poem, however metaphorical, was not without resonances with a conquest much of Europe would suffer in relatively short order.

And Europe was dazzled by it. T. S. Eliot thought it "a piece of writing of the same importance as the later work of James Joyce, as valuable as *Anna Livia Plurabelle.*"[27] Ungaretti discovered in it "new sources of stupefaction" at every turn.[28] For Hugo von Hofmannsthal, the poem recalled the paintings of Poussin while remaining a work of modern times—"in the heroic and tender spirit of the France that engenders new saints and founds a colonial empire before its southern gates" (1108). MacLeish thought it one of the three or four books in the life of an author that change his vision of things (1106). Might Europe, in the words of its most distinguished poets lining up to do homage, have let the wildest of cats out of its proverbial bag? One has, in any event, little difficulty seeing why the architect of France's foreign policy would want to keep the author of *Anabase,* self-invented—per se—for the occasion, as far from Alexis Leger as might humanly be possible.

To this may be added the crowning irony that "Saint-John Perse," who came into existence sustaining a rich fantasy of the "conqueror returning to his homeland," had now reemerged when its author was negotiating the humiliations of one of the conquered *ejected* from his homeland. The chiasmus, the space within which the newly emergent

---

25. "Loud acclamations under the walls for the mutilation of adults in the sun."
26. Caillois, *Poétique de St-John Perse,* 129.
27. T. S. Eliot, preface to Perse, *Anabasis,* 12.
28. Perse, *Oeuvres complètes,* 1105.

Saint-John Perse ("J'habiterai mon nom") was writing his poetry, was excruciating (135).

What, then, of the opposition between Leger and his *other* other, de Gaulle? Some have attributed the incompatibility to a difference of views between a Leger fundamentally "Atlantist" in his sense of France and a de Gaulle sufficiently "continentalist" to eye "dear powerful Russia" as a principal focus of French diplomacy immediately after the war.[29] Raoul Aglion attributes Leger's misgivings to Paul Reynaud, France's perfidious prime minister when war broke out, promoting de Gaulle to the position of undersecretary of state even as he was maneuvering to remove Leger from his position as secretary general of the Foreign Ministry.[30] Leger was convinced that the bond between Reynaud and de Gaulle persisted, and that the leader of the Fighting French was not to be trusted.

The circumstances surrounding "the disgrace of Alexis Leger" form the heart of an important chapter of a widely read book published in New York by Pertinax in 1943 under the title *Les fossoyeurs*. In Pertinax's telling, Leger—in whose "vast verbal undulations" the reader may recognize the poet about to (re)become Saint-John Perse— was a strong defender of the British alliance and above all a man whose dialectical skills were so plainly superior to those of his adversaries that they could only hope to be rid of him through stealth.[31] At the center of the opposition were Reynaud's notorious mistress, Mme de Portes, and Paul Baudouin, an advocate of a reversal of alliances, who would eventually replace Daladier as minister of foreign relations. Reynaud, in the midst of the French military collapse, succumbed. A "private camarilla," as Leger would call it in a letter to Edouard Herriot, succeeded in removing him without any official having to assume full responsibility for a decision never openly explained to him.[32] Leger learned of the decision from the *Journal officiel*. He was then told by Reynaud that the important ambassador-

29. Julian Hurstfield, "Alexis Leger, les émigrés français, et la politique américaine envers la France, 1940–1944," in *Cahiers Saint-John Perse*, 3:199.

30. Aglion, *Roosevelt and de Gaulle*, 186.

31. Pertinax, *Les fossoyeurs* (New York: Editions de la Maison Française, 1943), 1:295.

32. Perse, *Oeuvres complètes*, 601.

ship to the United States was his for the asking, and he would be sent to Washington shortly to make the case for immediate American entry into the war. Leger suspected a ruse and immediately resigned from the Foreign Ministry, refusing to indulge the charade whereby a Frenchman from (almost) defeated France, having been freshly fired from his post, would then pretend to have the authority to work the "miracle" of bringing Roosevelt into the war. His memorable comment upon resigning: "I am entitled to reap the full dividend of injustice."[33] From Pertinax's point of view, Leger's removal was a key juncture in the war: "The disgrace of Alexis Leger perhaps marks the fatal turning point in the political evolution of France in the war. Had he been in his post ten days later, Weygand would have had a worthy adversary when he dared advocate a separate armistice before the Battle of the Somme had even begun. When one stops to think of the vacillations of various ministers in Tours and Bordeaux, of the small number of votes tipping the scales toward surrender in the cabinet, it becomes clear retrospectively that the dismissal of this particular functionary marked a fatal bifurcation" (303).

Les fossoyeurs thus tells, through the anecdote of Leger's professional "disgrace," a story of French honor in (personal) defeat that is virtually inseparable from the defeat of France. As though it might well have befallen Leger to rally the honor of France from England, for which he left on June 16. As if in confirmation, Churchill wired him almost immediately: "I shall never forget all you have done for the common cause during these long years. We are not yet at the end of the story. You have certainly not missed much so far."[34] Leger, moreover, was uncompromisingly prescient on the subject of the Vichy regime. His comments in a letter to Churchill on January 4, 1942, sound like the conclusions of contemporary historiography: "The actual policy of the current leaders in Vichy is not one of resistance within the limits of the Armistice (the so-called 'neck-in-a-noose' policy), but of spontaneous collaboration with Germany, tendentiously pressed to the point of violating on her behalf various of its clauses." (Wherein the Paxton-Marrus argument about Vichy being a step ahead of the

33. Pertinax, *Les fossoyeurs*, 299.
34. *Honneur à Saint-John Perse*, 715.

Germans in certain aspects of anti-Semitic policy seems adumbrated.) "That policy seeks to hide itself, drawing on the most exalted judicial authorities, behind an abusive interpretation of France's contractual obligations."[35] There could not, in sum, be a more forcefully articulated critique of the hypocrisy of Vichy.

And yet Leger chose to leave London (and de Gaulle) for the United States (and "Saint-John Perse"). Throughout the war, there were pressures for him to make common cause with de Gaulle. The general himself wrote in May 1942, inviting him to London. Leger responded, much as Maritain would, in the negative. The key issue was de Gaulle's pretension to constitute a provisional French government. For a diplomat such as he to become affiliated with Free France would mean to bolster its claims to legal existence as a political (rather than a military) entity: "It would be contrary to the conception I have of its role."[36] In June a cable from Churchill arrived: "I wish you could see your way to accept General de Gaulle's invitation to join the Free French National Committee over here." Leger responded—through the British Embassy in Washington—with regrets. On March 4, 1943, after the liberation of Africa (and amid the morass occasioned first by the appointment, then by the assassination, of Darlan), the embassy in Washington relayed a "secret" telegram from Churchill: "It would be most agreeable to me if you could visit Algiers as desired by your various English and American friends." Lord Halifax, the foreign secretary, even appended a postscript (729). To no avail.

Finally, after receiving a letter from Roosevelt requesting with some urgency that he come to Algiers and assume governmental responsibilities in a formation independent of the London committee, Leger responded—negatively—and ultimately set down his thoughts at some length on the question of the constitutional issues entailed in establishing, under the current extraordinary circumstances, a French government. Once again, it is the precedent of the Franco-Prussian War that holds sway. Leger submits to Roosevelt the text of a French law of February 1872, also known as the "Tréveneuc Law," and argues that it is, in French republican doctrine, the sole basis on which to constitute

35. Perse, *Oeuvres complètes*, 604.
36. *Honneur à Saint-John Perse*, 727.

a French government and that it is being flagrantly violated by the Gaullists at every turn. The law, passed when France was still partially occupied in the wake of the Franco-Prussian War, was intended to deal with the twin dangers of a governmental vacuum (should the National Assembly be illegally dissolved or prevented from convening) and abusive seizure of power by an adventurer. A mechanism, whereby local councils would send delegates to a provisional assembly and run the nation's affairs until the National Assembly could again convene, was promulgated.

For Leger, this was the sole basis for reconstituting a legitimate authority in France. For de Gaulle, who distrusted the local councils, a provisional government needed to be set up from above—and, worse yet from Leger's point of view, from without. For Leger, this amounted to a revolution hypocritically claiming to respect the sacrosanct "laws of the Republic." The idea of democratic representation on the basis of clandestine groups outside the country was ludicrous. "The fundamental idea behind all the projects elaborated in Algiers concerning the arrival in France is precisely the immediate seizure of an illegal power or the immediate exercise of a de facto administration clearing the way for such a seizure of power."[37] Spurious claims of "legitimacy" could not be invoked against the letter of the law. France's only hope, against the usurpations of Pétain, but also against the "repudiation" of the legal order by de Gaulle, "sole president" of the Algiers committee, was the text of the law of February 1872: "The guarantee assured by the Tréveneuc Law would thus apply immediately against the prefects of the usurpatory government of Vichy *as well as against all others*" (622, 626; emphasis added). A strong statement indeed.

Leger, in sum, refused to make common cause with de Gaulle, for fear of the violence to the law he embodied. But was not that climate of violence—"un grand principe de violence commandait à nos moeurs"—the very air breathed by the *anabasis* of Saint-John Perse, the very mood in which the poet-conqueror too "founds" his city? De Gaulle, Perse: two individuals Leger seemed equally, but differently, intent to keep at a distance. Reading *Les fossoyeurs,* reading Jean Rollin's memoir, one recalls how emphatically Leger, incarnating French

37. Perse, *Oeuvres complètes,* 626.

honor in defeat, leaving France for London, seemed destined to be (with?) de Gaulle. Instead he opted to (re)become Saint-John Perse. De Gaulle and Perse: the twin glories of the French spirit during the war.

But "Saint-John Perse," the poet as conqueror returning home (in Richard's formula drawing on *Anabasis*), was now in the cruelly parodic situation of the poet as one of the conquered ejected from his homeland, indeed officially stripped of his citizenship. It was in that devastating circumstance that he was invited to New York to deliver a memorial lecture on his mentor Aristide Briand at New York University on March 28, 1942. It was by all accounts a memorable occasion. Rougemont, who was present, observed that he doubted there was anyone who spoke a "French more in command of its nuances, more naturally memorable."[38]

Leger had been Briand's faithful collaborator from the time they had first met in Washington some twenty years earlier. Legend had it that the senior diplomat was so impressed with his junior that when Leger came to his ship to pay his respects on the occasion of Briand's departure, he all but abducted him: Leger traveled back to France—without luggage—with Briand. It was a bond that appears to have violated even the sacrosanct distinction between diplomacy and literature. Years later, he would reminisce about the unforgettable character of Briant, the governor of a colony of the shipwrecked, in Jules Verne's *Deux années de vacances*. The character had been inspired by Verne's young friend Aristide Briand, with whom he had spent many an afternoon singing opera.[39] Briand, then: the medium within which the discontinuity between diplomacy and literature might be unsettled.

The New York lecture evokes Briand in a nutshell: "All the landed aristocracy of a being of high frondescence [*un être de haute frondaison*] nourished at the vigorous roots of the people's tree [*aux fortes racines de l'arbre populaire*]."[40] For anyone who knew the birthplace islet of Alexis Leger, Saint-Leger-les-Feuilles, the vegetal image suggested something of an identification. At a key juncture of his talk, Leger pricked the ears of his audience with an obviously provocative

---

38. *Honneur à Saint-John Perse*, 614.
39. Tomás Eloy Martínez, *Lugar común la muerte* (Buenos Aires: Planeta, 1998), 58.
40. Perse, *Oeuvres complètes*, 606.

statement: "The attempted Franco-German rapprochement was the most courageous part of his labors" (610). It was one of the ironies of history that Briand's dream of 1930 had now turned into a nightmare. The elements of Briand's vision—a new European union, centered on Franco-German collaboration, resting on an ideological bed of pacifism—had become the elements of Pétain's France. Whence the horrendous chiasmus of recent French history: "Those in France who fought with greatest violence against the offer of collaboration tendered, in peacetime, in full agreement with the European community, by a strong and victorious France to a disarmed and republican Germany are the same who were one day to deem acceptable the offer of collaboration, tendered in wartime, in the interest of a Germanic order by a totalitarian, imperialist, and racist Germany to an enslaved, oppressed and isolated France" (611). The difference could not have been more acute. Yet it was the repetition mediated by that difference that appeared to hold Leger's attention. The discussion of Briand's policies comes to a climax in the following passage: "And do we not already detect an involuntary tribute to his thought in the German travesty that offers France, under the name of 'Ordre Nouveau,' and in one of those reversals of values conforming to Nietzschean doctrine at its purest, the transposition into Germanic style of the old project inscribed in the French memorandum of 1 May 1930?" (613). The contemporary political order was a viciously involuntary tribute to (and reversal of) the order envisaged in Briand's memorandum. That memorandum, we now know, was written entirely by Leger.[41]

There is, then, a devastating historical crisscross at the heart of Leger's political reading of Briand in 1942, even as there was a devastating crisscross at the heart of Saint-John Perse's return to poetry: the *vainqueur* had become the exiled *vaincu*. The resonances between the two reverse returns, one out of the diplomacy, the other out of the poetry, elicits as fundamental a harmonic as any in the *oeuvre* per se. Moreover, the fact that a superb meditation on the Gallic equivalent of Lebensraum, a motif out of 1930s diplomacy at its most catastrophic, figures at the inception of Perse's *oeuvre* offers further motivation to

41. The memorandum was "written entirely in his [Leger's] hand" (*Honneur à Saint-John Perse*, 698).

keep the careers of Leger and Perse as implausibly discrete as he (or they) never tired of doing.

In the winter of 1944, from the window of a New York street-corner hotel, Perse witnessed the first snowstorm of his exile. He would turn the experience into one of his major poetic achievements, the third poem of the series "Exil," "Neiges." The piece is preeminently a poem of New York. The lit skyscrapers are resplendently present as so many high cities: "Les hautes villes de pierre ponce forées d'insectes lumineux n'avaient cessé de croître et d'exceller, dans l'oubli de leur poids."[42] *Excelsior!* The boat sirens in the port ("meuglement de bêtes sourdes contre la cécité des hommes"), the chains on the tires ("grand bruit de chaînes par les rues"), the shovels of the black street workers ("comme gens de gabelle") all capture specific features of a snowstorm in 1940s New York.

Yet the poem—*Mallarmé oblige?*—has the quality of a whitening out. The specific violence of *Anabase,* the poem that gave us "Saint-John Perse," is there, but it has gone meteorological, as though it were an abstract property of space itself. The poem's most stunning image reads: "Il neigeait, et voici, nous en dirons merveilles: l'aube muette dans sa plume, comme une grande chouette fabuleuse en proie aux souffles de l'esprit, enflait son corps de dahlia blanc" (157).[43] The dawn-become-bird-become-flower, figure of inspiration, is racked from within—however much it serves as a figure for space or exteriority itself. The violence is no longer exercised against others. The conquering mystique of *Anabase,* before which Europe prostrated itself, has all but disappeared as the scene—of effacement—goes blank. The sand of the beach (of "Exil") has become snow, but the snow before long will take on the properties of an ocean. The street cleaners of New York work like *gens de gabelle,* but that salt tax and its servants, the poet once wrote, were from childhood the image par excellence through which he imagined France. Differences—between beach and

---

42. Perse, *Oeuvres complètes,* 157. Denis Devlin's translation: "Lofty pumice stone cities bored through by luminous insects had not ceased growing, transcendent, forgetful of their weight."

43. "It snowed, and behold, we shall tell the wonder of it: how dawn silent in its feathers, like a great fabulous owl under the breath of the spirit, swelled out in its white dahlia body."

ocean, New York and France—are effaced in the whiteness of "Neiges," a "plain-song" to efface the "traces of our steps." And what if that blankness were there above all to efface the epic of conquest and its sorry reversal, the devastating configuration within which the poetry of "Saint-John Perse," at its inception, was pursued? Such is the perspective opened up even as it is whitened out by the most glorious snowstorm in the history of French poetry.

TEN

Lévi-Strauss and the Birth of Structuralism

It was late June 1945, and the agent of the Office of Strategic Services filing his confidential report on the Ecole Libre may have been understandably perplexed. He had arranged to meet with the "cinema expert" Jean Benoit-Lévy, a prominent producer in France, only to be told that Benoit-Lévy was away for a couple of months and he was welcome to meet instead with Claude Lévi-Strauss. Was there no branch of French culture that was not in the hands of the Levites? Lévi-Strauss was "in charge of cultural matters" at the Ecole, and had just returned from a four-month trip to France. The agent was impressed. Lévi-Strauss, he wrote, "is most attractive, and has a very agreeable personality."[1]

There was no doubt in the agent's mind as to the loyalty of his interlocutor toward General de Gaulle, but that might mean different things to different agents. Lévi-Strauss's comment that "it might have been better to kill 50,000 collaborationists immediately," rather than go through the bureaucratic labors of juridical proceedings, for instance, might have reminded the agent of what Alexis Leger had been telling the Office of Strategic Services. In a report filed March 18, 1943, Leger claimed that de Gaulle "had linked himself irretrievably with Russia."[2] Surely, the rough justice of fifty thousand summary execu-

---

1. OSS Report FR-1052, "Visit with Mr. Lévi-Strauss of the New School, 66 Fifth Avenue, New York City," June 25, 1945, 1.

2. August Heckscher, OSS Interoffice Memo FR-557, "Interview with Alexis Leger," 3.

tions bespoke Russian (rather than Anglo-Saxon) habits. Lévi-Strauss was known to the Office of Strategic Services, moreover, as a practitioner of realpolitik at the Ecole. Against the more tender-minded advocates of uncompromising academic freedom, known as "the Maritain faction," Lévi-Strauss, prominent among the "de Gaullists," had maintained that members of the Ecole Libre faculty should make no secret of their political allegiances and register forthwith with the United States government under the Foreign Agents Registration Act. And if the Ecole as a result be regarded as "a veritable propaganda agency," as *Pour la victoire* suggested, so be it.[3] By the time the smoke cleared, Alexandre Koyré had been "ousted" as secretary general, according to the confidential Office of Strategic Services report of August 23, 1944. He was replaced by Lévi-Strauss.

It was by no means a given that the founder of "structural anthropology" would be a Gaullist. It was, after all, a principal tenet of Gaullist orthodoxy, prominently promulgated in the legendary radio address of June 18, 1940, that the French empire, undefeated, represented France's great hope for continuing the war. Empire was of the essence. But colonialism, as the anthropologist would later claim, was the "major sin of the West."[4] Simone Weil, whom Lévi-Strauss had known as a student at the Sorbonne, and with whom he would have discussions sitting on the steps of Columbia's Butler Library (or the Forty-second Street library), might have reminded him: the day of the fall of Paris, in her chilling formulation, was "a great day for Indochina." True, Simone Weil would go off to Gaullist London to serve— but in an oddly irrelevant way. And in any event, Lévi-Strauss was not about to be convinced by Simone Weil. Like many of the female intellectuals of his generation, she struck him as "excessive" (20). No, Lévi-Strauss's affinity, it turned out, would be with Simone's irascible brother, the mathematical topologist and then teacher at the Ecole Libre, André Weil, who would supply the anthropologist with an algebraic appendix to the first part of his major effort of the war years, *Structures élémentaires de la parenté.*

Lévi-Strauss's Gaullism, moreover, however vibrant in the eyes of the agent from the Office of Strategic Services in 1945, had its limits.

3. OSS Report FR-873, "Politics versus Academic Freedom," 10.
4. Lévi-Strauss and Eribon, *De près et de loin,* 213.

When Jacques Soustelle, the legendary anthropologist of Latin America, showed up in New York as de Gaulle's recruitment representative and invited Lévi-Strauss to London, he received a negative response. The student of kinship structures had little desire to leave the Forty-second Street library, where he did most of his research, to cavort with those he initially dismissed as the "Boulangistes of London." Moreover, there was a demystificatory brio about the man that marked the limits of his Gaullism, however apparently loyal he might appear. His insistence that France had "lost the war," and "the sooner that people realized this the better for all concerned," would have been anathema in Gaullist circles. And his gibe to the effect that Belgium, in its rush to cement relations with the United States, would now be in search of someone "to represent the spirit of Lafayette" (and would probably find him) seemed skeptical not merely of the Belgians but of the sacrosanct Franco-American figure of Lafayette himself.

Still, the agent was charmed to the point of repetition. He ended his report more or less as he began: the anthropologist's was "a most attractive personality." Lévi-Strauss's colleagues at the legendary Ecole, on the other hand, were not charmed. On December 3, 1945, Lévi-Strauss resigned his position as secretary general of the Ecole, and had opted not even to show up at the urgent faculty meeting of December 14. Henri Grégoire, the Belgian Byzantinist who presided over the meeting, vented his frustration. Personally, he was of the opinion that

the Ecole had proceeded generously with regard to M. Lévi-Strauss. Charged with defending the interests of the Ecole in Paris, and mandated by the Council on 23 December 1944, to submit to the competent authorities a unanimously adopted memorandum, M. Lévi-Strauss absented himself for a full five months during which he received his stipend without the slightest reduction. Yet neither during his absence, nor since his return can it be maintained that he loyally acquitted himself of the mission entrusted to him and which he had accepted . . . Not only did the Ecole pay M. Lévi-Strauss, *even though he was working against it,* but for five months it paid his replacement.[5]

The accusation was betrayal, and Grégoire was not alone in making it. A report was distributed at the meeting that summarized the letter the physicist Léon Brillouin had written as early as June 12, 1945, to com-

5. Minutes of Assemblée générale de l'Ecole Libre, December 14, 1945 (document in the Souvarine Archives at Houghton Library, Harvard University).

184 plain about Lévi-Strauss, deemed to be "unfaithful to his mission, since far from defending the interests of the Ecole and the text of the memorandum, he appeared to bring back with him a death sentence [*arrêt de mort*] for our institution."[6] Lévi-Strauss, it would appear, had gone off to Paris in late 1944—and stabbed his colleagues, or whoever remained of them, in the back.

His colleagues took two courses of action. The first consisted of awarding de Gaulle an honorary doctorate (with as fulsome a citation as might be conceived) while appealing to him for the future of the Ecole—that is, undoing the harm they feared Lévi-Strauss had already done. The second was to block Lévi-Strauss's salary as secretary general for the month of December 1945. The latter vote—by the faculty at the meeting of December 14—was unanimous against Lévi-Strauss. As for the appeal to de Gaulle, a measure of the desperation of the petitioners is detectable in the distortions of a key phrase in the minutes. According to Henri Grégoire's introduction to the Ecole's scholarly journal *Renaissance*, de Gaulle had twice said that "the Ecole was, during the dark years, the most consolatory success of the French cause."[7] According to the minutes of the Ecole's meeting of December 14, 1945, the "first University of La France Libre" was described by de Gaulle as "one of the most handsome successes of our cause during the dark years." According to the report distributed at the meeting, the general had characterized the Ecole as "the greatest or rather the sole success of La France Libre during the dark years." The crescendo plainly betrays a major anxiety. It was alleviated—in the eyes of those desperate for alleviation—in fairy-tale terms. When properly informed, the president of the provisional government, like a monarch, evinced "shock" at the Ecole's predicament: "The Ecole has nothing to fear from anyone; she is free and mistress of her fate. You did well in coming to me. I shall issue the necessary orders." In retrospect, de Gaulle's statement to the Ecole reads like a dress rehearsal for the legendary "Je vous ai compris" speech to French Algerians. In the spring of 1945, Lévi-Strauss returned to New York, we are informed by the historians of the New School, "with instructions to close the Ecole."[8]

6. Document in the Souvarine Archives at Houghton Library, Harvard University.
7. Grégoire, "Introduction," 11.
8. Peter Rutkoff and William Scott, *New School: A History of the New School for Social Research* (New York: Free Press, 1986), 170.

If Lévi-Strauss was a Gaullist, his behavior with regard to the Ecole in the spring of 1945, from the perspective of his colleagues at the December meeting, was of the sort that might confirm the worst putschist fantasies ("Pétainism without Pétain"?) attaching to de Gaulle's name. Had the anthropologist staged a coup behind the voting faculty's back, hijacked the eminent institution whose founding, in 1942, had evoked comparisons in a *Times* editorial with the flight of the scholars to Constantinople after the fall of Rome?[9] Lévi-Strauss has offered a somewhat different version of events. With the war coming to an end, the Ecole was divided into two groups. One consisted of French scholars eager to return to their eminent careers in France, convinced that the Ecole, a university in exile, had served its purpose, and should now be dissolved. The other group, for the most part consisting of recently naturalized French citizens, felt less sure of what might lie ahead for them in postwar French academia and preferred the "shelter" of the Ecole, an outpost of French culture on Fifth Avenue and Twelfth Street that every effort should be made to perpetuate.[10] On February 24, 1945, the *Times* ran an editorial chronicling the departure from the Ecole of twenty-five faculty members, including many of its most eminent figures: Maritain was about to take up duties as French ambassador to the Holy See; Gustave Cohen had resumed teaching at the Sorbonne; the great mathematician Jacques Hadamard, almost eighty, would head a scientific mission for the French government in London and Paris. The *Times,* as though in agreement with Lévi-Strauss's retrospective analysis, evoked the mythic glory of the Ecole as a reality now fading into the past.

From Lévi-Strauss's point of view, his trip to Paris was intended to resolve the conflict between the two groups—dissolutionist and anti-dissolutionist—at the Ecole. From the point of view of the faculty at the meeting of December 14, 1945, the trip of their (by then former) secretary general could only be as the representative of their wishes. A classic academic conflict. Lévi-Strauss, in the course of his trip to France, had apparently accepted a position as cultural counselor to the French Embassy in New York. (Whence, we may assume, the upbeat message about Franco-American collaboration that so pleased the

9. Editorial, *New York Times,* February 13, 1942.
10. Lévi-Strauss and Eribon, *De près et de loin,* 69.

interviewer at the Office of Strategic Services when they met at the New School.) On February 8, 1946, Lévi-Strauss, from his new offices at the Fifth Avenue mansion whose renovation he was overseeing, was able to send a letter to Henri Grégoire, the president of the Ecole Libre and the man who had led the fight to block Lévi-Strauss's salary two months earlier, officially granting what was left of the New School a reduced subvention from the French government of twenty-five thousand dollars, to be paid in four installments, for the academic year 1946.[11] Sweet revenge.

The conflict at the Ecole, then, was between a Franco-French group (the dissolutionists) and a tendentially Franco-American group (who were antidissolutionists). As his resignation from the Ecole's administration and the subsequent accusations of betrayal make clear, he was temperamentally part of the Franco-French constituency. (In *Paroles données*, he would describe with relish his declining of an unexpected offer from Harvard, brought in person by Talcott Parsons in 1953 to Paris.) Years later, in the face of the homogenizing tendencies of modernity, Lévi-Strauss would become a theorist of the imperative to keep cultures distinct—and of the willingness to pay the price of what might be misperceived in some quarters as "racism," a certain antipathy to what is culturally different, to do so.[12] Indeed, the author of *Mythologiques* went so far as to end his multiple-volume excursus on mythology with a veiled quotation from Gobineau's *Essai sur l'inégalité des races humaines* (223). It was a "signature" inspired, to be sure, not by racism, but by a "differentialist" passion that would soon be quoted by the French New Right under the banner of *le droit à la différence*.[13] (Gobineau was as much a "mixophobe," in P.-A. Taguieff's coinage, as Lévi-Strauss was.) The diacritical nature of language, that is, the central proposition of structuralism (according to which linguistic data exist *solely* by virtue of their opposition—or packets of oppositions—to other data), would find a destination of sorts in Lévi-Strauss's affirmation that every culture has a legitimate right "to be opposed to those surrounding it, to distinguish itself from them, in a

11. Letter from Claude Lévi-Strauss to Henri Grégoire, February 8, 1946, in the archives of the New School for Social Research.

12. Lévi-Strauss and Eribon, *De près et de loin*, 207.

13. Pierre-André Taguieff, *La force du préjugé* (Paris: Gallimard, 1987), 248.

word, to be itself."[14] In 1945, it became clear to Lévi-Strauss that it was time to resist the temptation to perpetuate the Ecole, to fall (entropically?) into the mold of Franco-Americanism. It was time to return to France—if only, newly credentialed, to make the return voyage to New York shortly thereafter as the official representative of the French government.

An assessment of the coup Lévi-Strauss was accused of having staged against the general assembly of the Ecole would, of course, depend on one's sense of the suitability of the norms of political democracy for the governance of an academic institution. Merit, after all, is rarely ascertained by majority vote. Significant light is shed, however, on Lévi-Strauss's views on political democracy at the time by a long review of Julien Benda's *La grande épreuve des démocraties*, published in New York in 1942, which the anthropologist wrote for the Ecole's journal *Renaissance*.

Benda was the antiromantic rationalist whose "clerkly" ideal had so influenced T. S. Eliot and his circle. A Jew, he had holed up in the walled city of Carcassonne in 1941 in order to write an uncompromising defense of liberal democracy and of the necessity to defend it with force against those totalitarian regimes whose cult of force had put peace-loving democracies at such risk. Lévi-Strauss describes Benda's book as the "most radiant image that liberal democracy can offer us of its own twilight."[15] All of the anthropologist's compliments, that is, are laced with a sense of the ultimate futility of Benda's admittedly courageous project. The image of the aged Jew in the medieval town arguing rationally against an adversary whose lowliest member could easily put an end to his life on racial grounds strikes Lévi-Strauss as being as absurd—and as "sovereignly unaware"—as it is "heroic."

The anthropologist's critique of the book is engaged on two fronts. On the one hand, the socialist that he was at the time engages in a predictable assault against liberal democracy on the ground that it is no more than a halfway point on the way to a classless society—a "first phase" at which Benda has carefully wanted to bring things to a stop. Democracy for Benda aspires to being a "restoration" of the principles

14. Lévi-Strauss and Eribon, *De près et de loin*, 248.

15. Claude Lévi-Strauss, review of *La grande épreuve des démocraties*, by Julien Benda, *Renaissance* 1, no. 2 (1943): 324.

of 1789. A call for the "possessing classes" to give up some of their privileges in the face of danger to the polity from without leaves the reviewer impatient for a relinquishing of all privileges. A reference to Tocqueville in praise of the British landed aristocracy and its very un-French loyalty to the social "inferiors" in its charge is cut short in disbelief. A surprising suggestion by Benda that there was no small measure of fanaticism in the Dreyfusard cause is milked by the reviewer for all it is worth.

A second front of Lévi-Strauss's critique is less conventional and may be tellingly articulated with the structuralism that the reviewer was even then inventing. For whereas democracy for Benda was famously the "reign of consciences" and its "a priori imperatives," structuralism was on its way toward affirming the centrality of an as yet unarticulated theory of the unconscious in any understanding of cultural practices. Lévi-Strauss is in the difficult position of having to affirm the diacritical *other* of consciousness even as he is constrained to admit that that *other* may well be, in Benda's terms, the *other* of liberal democracy as well. The anthropologist accepts the proposition that that *other* finds its most apt emblem in the domain of what the totalitarians call "race." But might there not be some interest in acknowledging—if not quite endorsing—that domain as well? The reviewer quotes Benda's critique of Action Française: "There exists an anti-democratic party, specifically in France, which maintains that by attempting to make men live in conformity with their historical past, and solely by such means, *it* is the party that respects reason. . . . We have compared that party to a doctor in a madhouse who, instead of curing his patients, would endeavor to have them live according to the conditions reason deemed appropriate to their madness, and who would declare that he was thus serving reason" (327). To which Lévi-Strauss retorts: "And yet such would be the case if the doctor in question were to observe that his patients' madness was incurable." And to the extent that one cannot be totally cured of the tissue of prejudices that is one's culture, Lévi-Strauss finds himself in the difficult position of affirming the mad (Maurrassian) doctor's position. Whereupon a quick retreat: to acknowledge the reality of "obscure and unconscious forces" is not to elevate them into "supreme values," but rather to integrate them into some larger synthesis. Years later, in his critique of the "myth" of revolution, Lévi-Strauss would not hesitate to embrace a position that was (timidly) already his in his critique of Benda: "True freedom can only have a concrete content: it is composed of balances among minor affiliations, small-scale solidarities— against which theoretical ideas proclaimed to be rational unleash their assault; when they have reached their goals, there is nothing left for them but to destroy each other. We can observe the results today."[16]

At this juncture in the wartime review, in the face of Benda's affirmation of the unreserved supremacy of reason and its dictates over nature and history, the anthropologist, fearful that in affirming reason's *other* he may be politically compromised, resorts to a pirouette. He reminds Benda of the Baconian precept that "one conquers nature only by obeying its laws."[17] But the paradox of an instance simultaneously beyond and within nature is that of the prohibition of incest, cornerstone of the unconscious, as it would be elaborated in *Structures élémentaires de la parenté.*

Finally, Lévi-Strauss calls Benda to task for his rallying to Renan's fusion of the notions of the nation and the social contract. Over the vexed question of Alsace-Lorraine, Renan had relinquished the critique of the Enlightenment he undertook in *La réforme intellectuelle et morale de la France,* and decided, against the Germans and their racialism, that a nation consisted of those who opted to be part of it. To this notion of the nation as implicit pact, Benda, citing Renan, rallied as well. Lévi-Strauss's critique again consists of acknowledging the indispensability of the obscure "material support" overlooked by the idealist project (328). In linguistics, the "material support" is, of course, the signifier (without which no ideal meaning can be articulated). In the case of the nation, the support is a "national territory." Lévi-Strauss sides with Père Ubu against Renan: "Without a Poland, there wouldn't be any Poles." Indeed, the model of a nationalism without territory, we are told, is Zionism, dismissed by the anthropologist as an "artificial" idealism.[18] To invoke the question of territory, though, is to raise the issue of an articulated surface, everything the linguists the reviewer was

16. Lévi-Strauss and Eribon, *De près et de loin,* 166.
17. Lévi-Strauss, review of *La grande épreuve des démocraties,* 327.
18. One shudders at the degree of assimilation Lévi-Strauss, an exiled Jew, would have to have assumed for Poland and Israel to be laughing matters for him in 1942.

learning to appreciate called *découpage*.[19] The critique of liberal democracy, in sum, was moving, in however gingerly a fashion, on tracks parallel to those that were leading Lévi-Strauss into structuralism.

The will to affirm the centrality of the "unconscious" at the expense of conscious intuition, a principal motif of French structuralism, was crucially fueled by two distinct strands during Lévi-Strauss's stay in wartime New York: the linguistics of Roman Jakobson and the aesthetics of the surrealists. The anthropologist was introduced to the linguist at the Ecole Libre by Alexandre Koyré. Jakobson recalls that his first impression was delight: "At last someone with whom I can drink the whole night through!"[20] It was a misjudgment; Lévi-Strauss detested alcohol, but it was the beginning of a lifelong association of uncommon fecundity. As for the surrealists, Lévi-Strauss had met André Breton at a stop in Morocco, made by the *Capitaine Paul Lemerle,* the lamentable ship that brought them both to America. They quickly struck up a friendship, eventually "dialoguing" together as readers on the radio station of the Office of War Information (50). Lévi-Strauss would contribute a moving text on Kaduvean Indian "cosmetics" to the New York surrealist review *VVV:* the erotic charge associated with dying cultural artifacts had long been a surrealist specialty.[21] But above all, the anthropologist would go antiquing with Breton and Max Ernst on Third Avenue. From surrealism, Lévi-Strauss absorbed a climate of "intellectual exaltation" and a fascination with the sparks generated by implausible juxtapositions. From Jakobson, he derived a sense of the benefits accruing from the elaboration of formal structures. Indeed, it would be possible to define French structuralism in terms of a uniquely New York configuration: Lévi-Strauss between Jakobson and Breton, the systemizing (*côté Jakobson*) of all that might be garnered from a technique or art of unexpected juxtaposition (*côté Breton*).

Years later, in separate articles in *Le regard éloigné,* Lévi-Strauss would pay homage to both Jakobson and the surrealists. A com-

19. In December 1938, Benda had sparred with the members of the Collège de Sociologie on the subject of democracy and national territory. For Georges Bataille, "territorial integrity" is the source of a (nationalist) mystique of the sort that the democracies needed, whereas for Lévi-Strauss it is a matter of "material support" without which the idealist project of liberal democracy would be inconceivable. See Hollier, *Le Collège de Sociologie,* 448–59.

20. Lévi-Strauss and Eribon, *De près et de loin,* 63.

21. Claude Lévi-Strauss, "Indian Cosmetics," *VVV* 1 (June 1942): 33–35.

parison of the key features of those texts will take us deeper into the configuration just evoked. The Jakobson article was, in fact, a preface to an edition of the lectures (on "sound and meaning") by which the anthropologist had been enthralled at the Ecole Libre in 1942–43. He went to the lectures in search of rudimentary guidance on the notation of languages he had encountered in his journeys to Brazil and emerged, "dazzled," with the principal intuitions of structuralism. The most important of these was an appreciation of the role of unconscious activity in cultural practices. Nicolai Troubetskoy had been right to affirm that "all reference to 'linguistic awareness' [*conscience linguistique*] must be eliminated in defining the phoneme."[22] Here then was that *other* of consciousness by which Lévi-Strauss seemed so attracted in his critique of Benda on liberal democracy, but an *other* apparently uncontaminated by issues of "race." Lévi-Strauss was captivated. The other key insight gleaned from Jakobson was an appreciation of the essentially diacritical nature of phonemic reality. "Distinctive features" derived their existence only from their opposition to others. Might the study of kinship structures (and specifically the prohibition of incest) be amenable to an "oppositional" analysis of the same sort as had proved so convincing in phonology? Such was the wager with which structural anthropology began.

Toward the end of his essay, Lévi-Strauss speculated on the existence of "mythemes," units of analysis that would be as shorn of a priori semantic value as phonemes are for the phonologist. A myth would throw up a grid (amenable to "mythemic" analysis) whose oppositions allow for the elaboration of a "matrix of intelligibility" within which elements of the world often at odds with each other might be implicitly integrated into a "coherent whole." Here then was a second side of structuralism, one concerned with the conditions of "mutual convertibility" of apparently disparate artifacts.[23] It is the perspective that would eventually see Lévi-Strauss, in *Le totémisme aujourd'hui,* imagining Bergson and Sioux mythology as transformations of each other. So long as the concern for mutual convertibility takes precedence over the principle of diacriticity, structuralism would tend toward universalism. Once diacriticity, however, is unleashed as

22. Claude Lévi-Strauss, "Les leçons de la linguistique," in *Le regard éloigné,* 197.
23. Lévi-Strauss and Eribon, *De près et de loin,* 180.

the politics of "differentialism," structuralism, as we have seen, will find no more congenial inspiration than Gobineau. . . .

Lévi-Strauss's essay on Jakobson's lectures of 1942–43 ends with an amusing riff in the spirit of structuralist "convertibility." Jakobson, in his concluding lecture, had adduced Mallarmé's celebrated observation about the apparent arbitrariness of the French words for *day* and *night: jour* sounds far darker than the apparently sparkling *nuit*. The linguist follows Mallarmé in proposing that poetry redeems the apparent arbitrariness of the signifier: "Poetry successfully eliminates this discordance by surrounding the word *nuit* with grave vowelled vocables; or alternately it highlights semantic contrasts which are in harmony with that of the grave and acute vowels, such as that between the heaviness of the day and the mildness of the night."[24] Lévi-Strauss draws his inspiration from Jakobson's (final) lecture of 1943 with a personal variant on the latter suggestion. Given the crisscross between the pair of signifiers and their signifieds, he confesses that he has always—almost unwittingly—effected a reverse crisscross of sorts that makes good the communication of signifiers and their signifieds. "For me, *le jour* is something that lasts, *la nuit* something that occurs or supervenes, as in the expression *la nuit tombe*, 'night falls.' One denotes a state, the other an event."[25] It seems entirely appropriate that the "durative aspect" of the day should correspond to the grave *jour,* and the "perfective" punctuality of night should be linked with *nuit.* Whereby Lévi-Strauss's reverse crisscross, the stuff of a personal myth, effects the communication or mutual convertibility of signifiers and signifieds. All this as a final observation on Jakobson's last lecture of 1943 at the Ecole Libre.

As for surrealism: "Une peinture méditative" presents Max Ernst, Lévi-Strauss's partner in antiquing in wartime New York, as an unacknowledged source of structuralist thought on the centrality of the unconscious. The fundamental passivity of the author was an Ernstian motif before it was Lévi-Straussian. Then there is the motif of the implausible juxtaposition. The "structural method," we are told, is in no way troubled to recognize its own inspiration in Max Ernst's for-

24. Roman Jakobson, *Six Lectures on Sound and Meaning* (Cambridge: MIT Press, 1978), 114.
25. Lévi-Strauss, "Les leçons de la linguistique," 200.

mula advocating "a linking or rapprochement of two (or several) elements of apparently opposite nature against a backdrop whose nature is opposed to theirs."[26] Whereupon Lévi-Strauss, in a spirit curiously akin to that informing the Mallarméan riff in the essay on Jakobson, undertakes to analyze the prototypal case of just such a disconcerting juxtaposition: Lautréamont's "fortuitous encounter on an operating table of a sewing machine and an umbrella." The anthropologist's riff this time takes off as a kind of Pongean duel between two "points": "Each of the two is endowed with a point, one which, in the case of the umbrella, is protective or surmounts, like an ornament, a gently curved dome that is soft and elastic to the touch; and which, in the case of the sewing machine, is a sharp, aggressive point placed at the lower extremity of an angular arm, just where it bends downward. A sewing machine presents itself as an ordered arrangement of solid parts whose hardest one, the needle, has the function of piercing a fabric; an umbrella, quite to the contrary, is graced with a fabric whose function is not to allow itself to be pierced by random liquid particles: rain" (329). By the end of the analysis, sewing machine and umbrella have become "inverted metaphors" of each other. The apparent arbitrariness of their "encounter" (as arbitrary as the encounter of a surrealist and a structuralist on an immigration line in Morocco?) has been as masterfully undermined as the arbitrariness of the signifiers *jour* and *nuit* in the "myth" on Mallarmé in the Jakobson essay. Indeed, what we have attempted in rudimentary manner in these comments has been nothing so much as to construct the "matrix of intelligibility" or "conditions of convertibility" of a passage on Ernst (via Lautréamont) and a passage on Jakobson (via Mallarmé). Call it French structuralism, but remember how rooted it is in its creator's experience of wartime New York.

They had been extraordinarily rich years for the author of *Tristes tropiques*. Years later, he would reminisce about his first impressions—after a harrowing trip by way of the Antilles—of New York. The weave of the urban fabric seemed astonishingly loose. As soon as one left the central axis of Fifth Avenue—and more and more as one moved either east or west—a kind of amorphousness crept into the structure of the city, a feeling of "anything goes" (chalet, brownstone, red-brick car-

---

26. Claude Lévi-Strauss, "Une peinture méditative," in *Le regard éloigné*, 328.

cass, or empty lot) for which the Frenchman could come up with no better word than *faubourien*—the opposite of our manicured *suburban*.[27] But if Manhattan was spatially heterogeneous, like some geological eruption of the urban surface, it was even more so temporally. Lévi-Strauss's Manhattan was an island that seemed to have inherited all the antiques in the world. He would spend many a day—with Ernst, with Breton—on Third Avenue purchasing artifacts dumped (as "doubles") by a local museum, some of which he would sell to his friend Jacques Lacan after he returned.

He would return to Paris in late 1944—amid the acrimony at the Ecole, by way of London and Dieppe—in relative triumph. The lessons of Jakobson and the surrealists were already bearing fruit. Lucien Febvre, the eminent historian, would soon comment in the pages of *Annales* on a scholarly paper he had published in *Renaissance*.[28] Its subject was "split representation" in the arts of Asia and America, and most spectacularly in the flamboyant "cosmetic" face painting— "more beautiful than beauty itself," in the words of one missionary— of the dying Caduvean tribe whose fate Lévi-Strauss evoked as well in the pages of *VVV*. Split representation: amid the "crosses, tendrils, fretwork, and spirals," it was as though a body had been split apart, "bisected" and "laid out flat," the two halves joined only at the tip.[29] The result, in the case of Caduvean face painting, was strikingly erotic, imbued with a "subtle element of sadism" (279). Ultimately, the split in the design figures the split between body—of nature—and the design that inscribes it into the superior realm of culture, or spirit.

Lévi-Strauss in New York thus served as spokesman for the Caduveo, a waning nation of virtuoso "cosmeticians," marked above all by the "split representation" that defined them. He would return to his waning nation famed for its cosmetics and suffering under the "split representation" of its role in a world still at war. Nature/culture? Body/spirit? Such was the drama racking France, as Saint-Exupéry wrote in his "Open Letter" in the *New York Times:* "France had to be

27. Lévi-Strauss, "New York post- et préfiguratif," 345.
28. Lucien Febvre, "Emprunts ou fonds commun d'humanité," *Annales* (1951): 379–81; see also Claude Lévi-Strauss, "Dédoublement de la représentation dans les arts de l'Asie et de l'Amérique," *Renaissance* 2–3 (1944–45): 168–86, which was reprinted in Lévi-Strauss, *Anthropologie structurale* (Paris: Plon, 1958).
29. Lévi-Strauss, *Anthropologie structurale*, 275.

saved both in flesh and in the spirit. Of what use is the spiritual heritage if there be no heir? What good is the heir if the spirit be dead?"[30] An intriguing but far-fetched analogy, it will be claimed. But the value of intriguing but far-fetched analogies, promoted to the beatific complexity of "homologies," would be a central intuition of structuralism, as the article on "split representation" was at pains to insist: even if the hypotheses born of such analogies should prove to be "unacceptable, they [were] destined to elicit, precisely because of their inadequacy, the criticism and research that [would] one day enable us to progress beyond them."[31]

Structuralism would know a delayed eminence in France. The country was in the throes of existentialist enthusiasm, and proof, if any be needed, might be offered by the commotion surrounding the visit of Jean-Paul Sartre to New York during the first weeks of January 1945. Things were clear to Sartre, and he reported on them in two articles cabled to *Le Figaro* on January 21 and 22. French émigrés to the United States, he wrote, were massively Pétainist, as one might well expect from the "timorous petits-bourgeois" that they for the most part were. Americans, moreover, were prepared to follow the lead of the French nationals in their midst. And yet there was a second image of France abroad, one linked to the French Revolution and associated with the name de Gaulle. It was a winning image, and gradually, according to Sartre, Americans such as Walter Lippmann could be heard saying that the French were following de Gaulle the way we followed Washington. The Pétainist backlash was not long in coming. Whereupon, without the slightest evidence, Sartre cavalierly accuses Henri de Kérillis, whom he does not name, of having been "bought" by high finance or the State Department, the sole explanation offered for his disillusionment with de Gaulle.

As for Anne Morgan, who organized the Coordination Council of French Charities, Sartre deemed that she may have loved France, "but she loved her poorly." Only full support for the blockade was commensurate with the tough love France now needed. Giraud was no more than a younger, less compromised version of Pétain, according

---

30. Antoine de Saint-Exupéry, "An Open Letter to Frenchmen Everywhere," *New York Times Magazine*, November 29, 1942.
31. Lévi-Strauss, *Anthropologie structurale*, 273.

to Sartre. Animosities in French New York were reaching a fever pitch. There was a "battle of New York" that some were already comparing to the Dreyfus affair. And in Sartre's Manichean version, the right side—de Gaulle and revolution—had won. New York in 1945 was deliriously celebrating the Resistance. Sartre, who was greeted effusively as a representative of the Resistance, was initially taken aback. It would not, after all, have been difficult to find a more worthy representative of the Resistance than the author of *Les mouches*. But the philosopher of *Being and Nothingness* decided to take a broader view of matters: "In point of fact, it would be according too much importance to our persons to entertain such nuances [*que d'avoir de ces délicatesses*]." Only a narcissist, that is, would spoil the good feeling by pointing out that the praise being extended him was altogether misdirected. "Our persons are not what matters here; through them, and simply because we are French, these demonstrations of friendship, as tactful and touching as they are, are addressed to the Résistants of France, that is, to a democracy in combat." Thus the hardheaded Marxist, with consummate bad faith, ushering in an age of resistentialism.[32]

It would be another fifteen years before the polemic between Lévi-Strauss and Sartre would erupt in the French intelligentsia. But émigré New York already offered—indeed, already was—a particularly powerful lens under which a number of the issues later promoted to such stunning prominence were already laid bare.

32. For a discussion of misleading versions of Sartre's wartime activities in the *Atlantic Monthly* (December 1944)—where he was characterized as "one of the military leaders of the [Resistance network] FFI"—and *Vogue* (July 1945), see Susan Suleiman, "Choosing Your Past: Jean-Paul Sartre and the Liberation," forthcoming in *Contemporary French Civilization*.

ELEVEN

#

Coda

Normandie's List

And what *was* France if not a certain way of turning on a faucet?
— RÉGIS DEBRAY

The Allied invasion of Normandy remains the crowning moment of the United States' participation in the war. More than two years earlier, however, the United States' seizure of the *Normandie,* queen of the Atlantic and two-time winner of the Blue Ribbon, at Forty-eighth Street on the Hudson River conjured up a precedent for the great day that was simultaneously so dismal in its consequences and so hyper-realistically gigantic in its manifestation that one is hard put to imagine that the allegory it appeared to visit on New Yorkers did not freeze plans for the D-day invasion in their tracks.

The *Normandie,* from the time of its inauguration in 1934, was a floating museum of French arts and techniques, an "87,000 ton gem" of French workmanship, as the *New York Times* called it. It was the world's first thousand-foot ship, the apotheosis of art deco sumptuousness, and, as such, quintessentially French. In notes prepared for his wife, Vita Sackville-West, Harold Nicolson observed that the "whole ship gives one exactly, but *exactly* the impression of an *exposition des arts décoratifs.*"[1] And as of September 3, 1939, when Britain's

---

1. Harvey Ardman, *Normandie: Her Life and Times* (New York: Watts, 1985), 153. I am indebted to Ardman's book for much of the background concerning the history of the *Normandie.*

Athenia was torpedoed two hundred miles west of the Hebrides Islands, the *Normandie,* the boat of Marlene Dietrich, Cole Porter, and Ernest Hemingway, the boat of the Abraham Lincoln Brigade, vacationing movie stars, and escaping Jews, was consigned to immobility in its berth at Pier 88 in New York (325).

It was hard not to read the stalled ship of dreams as an emblem of defeated France in its *attentiste* limbo. The *Times* commented that "the *Normandie*'s present condition is reminiscent of a summer resort hotel that has been closed down for the winter." The purser took Morris Markey, writing for the *New Yorker,* on a tour. In the great dining room, he paused to ask whether the visitor had ever read the books of Rider Haggard. For this was "like one of those queer rooms in his jungle palaces" (323). A skeletal crew was retained; most of the rest went off to join de Gaulle (by way of Canada), but it was the passivity of the *Normandie,* the kitsch immensity of this "sleeping beauty" at their doorstep, that haunted New Yorkers.

The *Normandie* had always aspired to embodying a myth of France, and now it could embody the essential nostalgia and otherworldliness of myth itself. Robert Wilder in the *New York Sun:*

The sight of the *Normandie,* stained and fettered, is all the more depressing if you can recall her in the days of her glory. Everything which France once represented—gaiety, color, and vitality—were embodied in this ship, and her sailings from New York, usually at noon, were unrivaled. They were events with scarlet-coated page boys flitting up and down her magnificent staircases or through the paneled corridors, the famous from a dozen walks of life crowding her lounges and cabins. She was France and the line's assertion that the passengers were in France when they crossed the gangplank was no mere playing with words. (263)

On December 12, 1941, four days after Pearl Harbor, the United States, deciding this particular myth was a luxury it could no longer afford, dispatched a Coast Guard detail to "seize" the ship. The *Normandie,* in the language of the *Times,* was "occupied" and would soon be put to military use. A formula was sought to establish proper compensation for France. The *Times* ran a telling short piece about reactions in Vichy. There was, to be sure, sadness that a ship that "symbolizes the very height of French art and industry" should now be flying another flag, but Vichy seemed intent on underscoring the difference between the United States, which at least paid money for what it took, and Great Britain, which never offered compensation for its seizure of boats. The *Times* article also noted that the ship was of particularly "tricky disposition," a point the *Normandie*'s captain had registered at a time, we read, when the "de Gaullists urged that she be turned over to them."[2] Here, then, was a scenario that would be played out time and again during the war: the United States government revealing that it had even less use for de Gaulle than it had for Pétain. We do not know what de Gaulle's reaction to the seizure of the *Normandie* was, but, given Gaullist designs on the ship, we may assume that the entire incident served as a dress rehearsal for, say, de Gaulle's reaction to the Allied invasion of North Africa, a military campaign from which he was pointedly excluded: "Well, I hope that Vichy will throw them back into the sea. One doesn't make one's way into France by breaking and entering."[3]

The particular myth embodied by the *Normandie*, even as the silt built up around its hull, was about to enter the age of advanced technology with a vengeance. It would become a troop carrier, with its name changed, inevitably, to the *Lafayette*. Perhaps the remainder of the allegory was sealed by that choice of a name. Sainte-Beuve once remarked that it was Lafayette, hero of democracies, who had transformed the "idol of honor into another idol: that of popularity."[4] For Roberto Calasso, with Lafayette, an alliance was established "between Good Causes and Stupidity" (21). Indeed, Calasso wrote an extraordinary genealogy of modernity around the opposition between Lafayette and his "true opposite," Talleyrand. Let the *Normandie*'s "tricky disposition," about which Captain Le Heure warned the Gaullists, stand for Talleyrand, and Lafayette's "alliance of Good Causes and Stupidity" stand for . . . the *Lafayette*. The allegory advances.

The *New York Times*, evincing a thoroughgoing pragmatism, was jubilant at the seizure and projected transformation of the *Normandie*. "The Normandie ought to be glad," it editorialized. "Now she is free again. Since late in August, 1939, she has been lying in a dock in midtown Manhattan, a great dispirited hulk of steel, looking seedier week by week, deserted by the handful of admirers that used to stare

2. *New York Times*, December 18, 1941.
3. Schiff, *Saint-Exupéry*, 390.
4. Quoted in Roberto Calasso, *The Ruin of Kasch* (Cambridge: Harvard University Press, 1994), 21.

up at her tall bows, bridge and funnels. But on Friday the United States took her over, probably for a transport or airplane carrier, and in due course one of the most brilliant liners in the world will be cutting salt water again."[5] For the pragmatist, the *Normandie* would be happy because it would be moving with its characteristic swiftness. Never mind where.

The transformation began. The legendary artwork of the mythic ship, all that had its admirers calling it a floating museum, was removed and stored for eventual restoration after the war. And then disaster struck. On the afternoon of February 9, 1942, just two months after Pearl Harbor, a thick plume of black smoke began making its way from the Hudson River across midtown Manhattan. There was fear in some quarters that a second Japanese attack had targeted New York. But no, the fire was coming from the upper decks of the *Normandie*. Despite fears of sabotage, despite a prominently publicized German claim of responsibility for the fire, it was quickly determined that the blaze was the result of an accident. During the removal of a stanchion in the grand salon, sparks from an acetylene torch had ignited a number of burlap-covered life-jacket bales. The flames spread rapidly. When a hose was located, it quickly became apparent that its French fitting would not match the newly Americanized fittings of the standpipes.[6] As the fire raged, some were of the opinion that the destruction caused by the blaze might merely serve to accelerate the transformation of the ship. But soon a second danger loomed. As various fireboats made their way to Pier 88 and began inundating the upper decks, the *Normandie,* some of whose upper cabins were now reservoirs, began to list. Here was a remedy that might well prove worse than the ill it was intended to cure. The more prescient among those directing operations wanted to halt the flooding of the upper cabins even if the fire were not yet completely extinguished, but Mayor La Guardia, who had cut short a radio address about subway fares to rush to the pier, decided that it was out of the question to allow a fire to rage unchallenged in midtown Manhattan.

The *Times* observer (February 10, 1942) seemed caught up in the spectacle of it all: "A stream of water under high pressure arched

5. Editorial, *New York Times,* December 17, 1941.
6. Ardman, *Normandie,* 303.

through the darkness, and within an hour the new blaze seemed quenched." The *Normandie*'s list became more and more pronounced, but it was not until about twelve hours after the blaze began that things came to a disastrous head. The *Times*'s description is remarkable: "There was nothing of the convulsion in the river that onlookers had predicted. It was rather a subsiding, the ultimate completion of the giant's appointed course." What is striking in this evocation of the capsizing of the *Normandie,* the result of an industrial accident, is the insistence that such an accident constituted in any way the "completion" of an "appointed course." One would be inclined to counter the *Times*'s report with the Mallarméan principle according to which a throw of the dice (or spark of a torch) would never abolish chance were the notion of a shipwreck on Forty-eighth Street not so ludicrous.

The aestheticization of the catastrophe has the feel of a stunningly cavalier writing off of France itself. One savors, with Gaullist urgency, the allegorical force of that completed "course." To perceive the sense of necessity, of aesthetic fulfillment, with which New York's newspaper of record accedes to the "subsiding" of the *Normandie,* the aggravation of a French tragedy through American incompetence or, to recall Calasso's phrase, Lafayette's alliance of "Stupidity and Good Causes," is to appreciate, among other things, the pertinence of de Gaulle's case against Roosevelt.

The *Times* continued to be moved by the pathos of it all. The following Sunday, February 15, "The Saga of a Ship" evoked the rescue of a suffering heroine, "lashed to a dock while the paint peeled from her sides and she grew gray and old," by a practical American hero: "And then Uncle Sam took her over and stripped her for grim duty, took away all her frills and furbelows." As for the final tragedy, it was chalked up to the elements—fire and water—that is, to fate itself. If the spectacle from Twelfth Avenue of the huge deactivated ship had undeniable pathos, the sight of the capsized hulk lying in the mud seemed grotesque in its immensity. John McClain wrote in the *Journal American* that "it was as though the Empire State Building had slowly teetered and fallen sideways into the street" (340). The *Normandie,* moreover, was no *Titanic.* The spectacle of the "stricken giant lying on her side in fifty to sixty feet of water and mud" seemed more farcical than tragic to some. At best, it had "the dignity of a leviathan which has threshed away its life in the shallows," as Robert Wilder put it (362).

Salvage efforts began. A small city of engineers and salvage divers—"Normandieville," as it was called—was erected on Pier 88. A "salvage school" for operations elsewhere was set up around the carcass of the floating palace. To the allegorist, a certain future of Europe already appears to be in the balance. When the ship was finally refloated, after some eighteen months, the hull damage was extensive. Worse yet, the months of submersion had ruined the propulsion machinery utterly. All Roosevelt's advisors recommended against the lengthy and expensive effort that would be needed to restore the ship to use. The president's death on April 12, 1945 removed the *Normandie*'s most faithful supporter from the scene.

What to do with what remained of the ship? The artwork that had been removed from the *Normandie* before transformation would now never be restored. Auctions were held at the United States Customs Seizure Rooms on Varick Street in lower Manhattan. In thousands of material ways, New York—indeed, America—became palpably more French. For the ship itself, become a kind of anti–Statue of Liberty in New York harbor, humiliating suggestions came pouring in. Showboat? Floating casino? Memorial to Franco-American friendship? The most sinister possibility appeared in the *Washington Times-Herald* of October 12, 1945. The *Normandie,* it was said, was being considered as a possible target for an atomic bomb. "Experts declared it would be highly important to determine the extent of destruction by an atom bomb on a floating target the *Normandie*'s size" (403). The plan, however rich with lessons, was scrapped.

So was the *Normandie.* The ship was purchased by Lipsett, the company that had already junked the Second Avenue El, and was dismantled after being towed to a dock in Port Newark, New Jersey. The hull, on which the name "Lafayette" never got to appear, was now emblazoned in white with the name LIPSETT. Destination: the very steel mills of Pennsylvania whose glory Saint-John Perse had sung in a memorable image of "Neiges": "De très grands lacs, où les chantiers illuminés toute la nuit tendent sur l'espalier du ciel une haute treille sidérale."[7] Meanwhile, Léon Blum, another relic of the glory days of

---

7. Perse, *Oeuvres complètes,* 158. Denis Devlin's translation: "Great lakes, where worksites lit up all night stretch a long sidereal vine across the espalier of the sky."

the *Normandie,* journeyed to America and negotiated a compensation package for France with Carl Vinson, then secretary of the treasury.

With its artwork auctioned off on Varick Street and its body smelted in the mills of the Midwest, the *Normandie,* France incarnate, had become part of the fabric of America. America would now turn it into myth. It would show up in popular fiction, to be sure. In a battle in a farmhouse in Irwin Shaw's *Young Lions,* a glass covered "French Line" poster of the ship is struck by a bullet. "The glass covering the *Normandie* shattered into a thousand pieces, the picture shivered on the wall, with a large hole at the waterline of the great ship, but it did not fall."[8] The resonances would not have been lost in New York City. There was a second, more urban myth of the ship that so artfully marries a certain essence of wartime France and a certain essence of 1940s Manhattan that one is tempted to draw this chronicle to a close by recounting it. Charles ("Lucky") Luciano, the notorious Mob leader, hatched a plan, in concert with Meyer Lansky and several other associates, to secure his release from Dannemora prison in upstate New York. Once Thomas Dewey, the prosecutor who had put Luciano in jail (and a man familiar with Luciano's scope of action), was elected governor, it might be possible for Luciano to offer a public service to the state of such magnitude that Dewey would grant him a pardon in exchange. In early 1942, according to Luciano's account, he was visited in Dannemora by Albert Anastasia, who had come with a plan. Anastasia claimed to have worked out an arrangement with his brother, who had influence with the International Longshoremen's Association. If his associates could implement a hair-raising act of sabotage in the port of New York, say, aboard the *Normandie,* the government might panic and ask for protection from the longshoremen, at which point Luciano would negotiate his release in exchange. The fire did break out; extensive investigation determined beyond all reasonable doubt that it was the result not of sabotage, but of carelessness; but Luciano, to his dying day, claimed that it was Anastasia's men who were responsible for the blaze.[9]

There is an intrinsic efficacy of myth. After the *Normandie* capsized on Forty-eighth Street, both the navy and the office of New York

8. Quoted in Ardman, *Normandie,* 400.

9. Details of the Luciano legend have been taken from his "memoir": M. Gosch and M. Hammer, *The Last Testament of Lucky Luciano* (Boston: Little Brown, 1975).

District Attorney Frank Hogan decided that all precautions should be taken to protect the security of the New York waterfront. Thus began "Operation Underworld." The Mob's services would be sought. Luciano was brought into the negotiation, and eventually transferred from Dannemora to the far less harsh setting of Great Meadow prison in Comstock, New York—before being freed and dispatched to Sicily at the end of the war.

The *Normandie*—France's dream ship, France *as* dream ship—had been interned, seized, set ablaze, flooded, capsized, disassembled, and sold for scrap in wartime New York. Its treasures had been auctioned off throughout—and far beyond—the city, its very frame recycled in a thousand automobiles. In the seedier recesses of the New York waterfront, though, there remained a legend in which the fates of the dream ship and the Mob leader were inextricably meshed. In its articulation of the sublime and the sinister, it is as bizarre a legacy of the French experience in wartime New York as we have been bequeathed.

INDEX

Index